MW01136231

"What does it mean to be God's 'holy' people, both individually and corporately? How might we speak of divine and human agency in sanctification, and navigate the complexities of the relationship between justification, faith and sanctification? These essays open up multiple conversations to help us with such questions and more—conversations between the authors, between historical figures and contemporary debates, and between theology, pastoral practice and ethical action. The result is a volume that both clarifies some of the issues at stake and advances the debates, and that speaks not only to scholars but also to the church."

Suzanne McDonald, Western Theological Seminary

"Kelly Kapic has drawn together some fine chapters from some of the very best of both established scholars and bright newcomers on a theme at the heart of the Christian life. This slim volume is a remarkable accomplishment."

Brian Brock, University of Aberdeen

SANCTIFICATION

EXPLORATIONS IN THEOLOGY AND PRACTICE

EDITED BY

KELLY M. KAPIC

IVP Academic

An imprint of InterVarsity Press
Downers Grove, Illinois

InterVarsity Press
P.O. Box 1400, Downers Grove, IL 60515-1426
World Wide Web: www.ivpress.com
Email: email@ivpress.com

InterVarsity Press® is the book-publishing division of InterVarsity Christian Fellowship/USA®, a movement of students and faculty active on campus at hundreds of universities, colleges and schools of nursing in the United States of America, and a member movement of the International Fellowship of Evangelical Students. For information about local and regional activities, write Public Relations Dept., InterVarsity Christian Fellowship/USA, 6400 Schroeder Rd., P.O. Box 7895, Madison, WI 53707-7895, or visit the IVCF website at www.intervarsity.org.

Scripture quotations, unless otherwise indicated, are from The Holy Bible, English Standard Version, copyright ©2011 by Crossway Bibles, a division of Good News Publishers. Used by permission. All rights reserved.

While all stories in this book are true, some names and identifying information in this book have been changed to protect the privacy of the individuals involved.

Cover design: David Fassett
Interior design: Beth McGill
Images: Holy Spirit (photo)/Godong/UIG/The Bridgeman Art Library
    ©Chris Schmidt/iStockphoto

ISBN 978-0-8308-4062-5 (print)
ISBN 978-0-8308-9693-6 (digital)

Printed in the United States of America ♾

Library of Congress Cataloging-in-Publication Data
Sanctification : explorations in theology and practice / edited by
Kelly M. Kapic.
    pages cm
  Includes index.
  ISBN 978-0-8308-4062-5 (pbk. : alk. paper)
1. Sanctification   Christianity. I. Kapic, Kelly M., 1972– editor.
  BT765.S26 2014
  234'.8—dc23

2014033347

P	23	22	21	20	19	18	17	16	15	14	13	12	11	10	9	8	7	6	5	4	3	2	1
Y	34	33	32	31	30	29	28	27	26	25	24	23	22	21	20	19	18	17	16	15	14		

To

Tabitha Kapic,

Susan Hardman Moore,

Elizabeth Patterson,

Dayle Seneff

and

Lynn Hall

Each of you has, in various ways, had a profound impact on my life,

especially through your own particular experiences of faith amid

diverse struggles. In both strong and subtle ways, each of

you has pointed me to the promises and call

of sanctification in Christ by his Spirit.

I remain deeply in your debt.

CONTENTS

PART THREE: THEOLOGICAL AND PASTORAL MEDITATIONS ON SANCTIFICATION

INTRODUCTION

While there is nothing new under the sun, different seasons do make us sensitive to changes in our environment. When winter dawns our attention turns to jackets, scarves and gloves; when spring arrives the renewed warmth of the sun beckons us outside. On cue, the seasons come and go and we would be foolish to treat them all the same. Each needs our attentiveness in due course, as each has a particular power over our lives and calls for us to respond accordingly.

Similarly, the church often lives through different doctrinal seasons. With the faith, we embrace the truth of God in all its varied theological realities, but inevitably there are periods when one truth requires our renewed consideration. At times we discover we have neglected or distorted a biblical truth, and the result is similar to realizing you are trying to live through winter in your shorts and T-shirt. Sure, it can be done, but it is certainly not a healthy way to exist.

In recent decades debates about justification have dominated the attention of many Protestants. While at times the cool winds of that season can still blow with great power, there are indications that a new season, with new challenges, is at hand. Evangelicals in particular demonstrate strong signs of a growing need to revisit the topic of sanctification. Fresh concern about this vital theological locus is surfacing, which is wonderful since this is where the church so often lives and breathes.

Set free from the dominion of sin, "saints" are set apart for kingdom purposes: as God is holy, so he has called his people holy and promises to renew them in the image of his Son. In a way this is a simple idea. Yet, as will become apparent in the essays that follow, the topic of sanctification is profoundly intertwined with all manner of other topics, beyond simply its contested relationship to justification. Although justification remains a key idea that can never be left behind, one must also learn to appreciate how sanctification relates to ethics, union with Christ, ecclesiology, adoption, eschatology and so on.

Evangelicalism appears to be in a season of struggling with how best to think about sanctification. What is the relationship between "faith" and human responsibility? How might human agency relate not only to questions of God's saving grace but also to the way he sustains and preserves us by his grace? Does effort undermine the role of faith? How does all of this relate to our creaturely existence as it is fundamentally empowered by the Spirit? How do we understand the promises of God as we live in the eschatological tension of the now and the not yet?

At the more popular level we see mistrust and misunderstanding perpetuated. For some, the temptation is to reduce the gospel to moral improvement, while for others, human effort appears irrelevant—if not downright antithetical—to the Christian life. On the one hand, a number of prominent voices have emphatically focused their message on the "gospel," by which some tend to mean narrowly "justification by faith alone." Such voices have at times appeared to provide balm to wounded souls; too many have labored under the suffocating weight of certain forms of rigid fundamentalism that reduced the gospel to a list of oppressive rules. To be told over and over of God's unflinching love and grace, of your secure position as declared righteous because of Christ's righteousness, can be both liberating and invigorating to such anguished listeners.

On the other hand, some raise the concern that such a perspective, if left undeveloped, might actually risk perverting grace rather than fully proclaiming it. They worry that if in the process of declaring the "good news" we end up belittling the significance of human will and agency, we are not ultimately liberating people; we might be undermining the fullness of gospel *life*. Not only is the believer set free *from* the condemning power of sin, but they are also set free *to* love and serve others, *to* grow and *to* flourish under God's care. A growing multitude echoes this renewed emphasis on personal piety, holiness and justice concerns even as it has welcomed renewed exploration on the topic of human agency.

While many of the representative voices on both sides of this come from the Reformed tradition, this conversation is being engaged in by a much larger audience, including many across the spectrum of evangelicalism.

Unfortunately, much of the current conversation is only taking place at the more popular level. In this book, we offer something a bit different. It is not intended as a direct engagement with those particular popular authors, but rather provides some "outside" perspective from theologians who are nevertheless also deeply concerned with the Protestant doctrine of sanctification (and justification!). Representing a good portion of the breadth of the Reformed tradition, these scholars gathered in Edinburgh a number of years ago to offer extended reflections on sanctification. Most of the essays in this book grew out of that Edinburgh Dogmatics Conference.

No attempt has been made to provide a unified perspective on sanctification here—we are not presenting some new school of thought or anything like that, as some of the subtle disagreements even within this volume indicate. Instead, this is an opportunity to explore the doctrine of sanctification; offer various proposals that might stimulate further thought and discussion; and also hopefully encourage pastoral reflection that is biblically, theologically and historically informed. It is our great hope that these essays by ecclesial-minded scholars might stimulate and foster this growing discussion.

Beginning and ending with ecclesial concerns, this volume opens with a homily and closes with theological and pastoral meditations: we aim to place this discussion squarely within the life of the church, even if at times it can appear somewhat technical or philosophical. The following brief reviews of the essays in this volume aim to give potential readers a survey of the work, hopefully orienting them to some of the directions in which the discussion will move.

Derek Tidball's homily on holiness as the restoration of God's image combines careful exegesis with pastoral wisdom. Using Colossians 3:5-17 as a lens for understanding what it means for a believer to be holy, he proposes that the meaning of holiness in this passage is threefold: to have a Christlike character, to have a Christ-renewed mind and to belong to a Christ-renewed community. Holiness is relational because the church is the place where a new *habitus* is cultivated, where the image of God is restored.

Richard Lints opens up the first section by addressing the relationship between sanctification and faith, and how this relationship is similar to and different from justification and faith. Eschewing any simple dichotomy between sanctification and justification, Lints suggests that faith is just as operative in sanctification as it is in justification: both are "exterior"; that is, sanctification is just as much dependent on divine grace as justification. In this way, the law in sanctification functions sapientially for the believer, rather than judicially. Sanctification is not primarily about moral progress but about the Spirit's restoration of human desires and worship.

Although Henri Blocher's essay has close affinities to Lints's, Blocher advances the discussion by providing nuanced definitions and a fresh discussion of law and obedience, as well as carefully navigating the relationship between faith and human agency. After providing a sound introduction to sanctification's key motifs and to the basic questions surrounding the relationship between justification, sanctification and faith, Blocher argues that sanctification is by faith because sanctification occurs in Christ and requires the renewed believer continually to adhere to a person outside of herself. But sanctification by faith is different from justification by faith in that sanctification is progressive and incremental, involving work and response. The works involved, however, are not "meritorious" in any sense, for Blocher maintains the monergistic givenness of holiness by the Spirit in sanctification, just as in justification.

Brannon Ellis hopes to enrich conversations between sanctification and justification by considering the place of union with Christ in sanctification, especially in terms of the communion of the saints. Ellis argues that to be made new by Christ is inextricably bound to being "in" Christ, which in turn is inextricably bound to belonging to the church. In doing this, he does not collapse soteriology and ecclesiology into one another, but emphasizes the inseparability of the new covenant membership with the mystical union. In this respect, rather than seeing union with Christ as holding a particular place on the *ordo salutis*, it spans the *ordo*'s outworking of redemption from beginning to end.

Bruce McCormack's essay is historically centered, comparing the theologies of John Wesley and Karl Barth and exploring their respective contributions to the doctrine of sanctification. At first glance this might look like an odd pairing, but McCormack insightfully shows how Barth's notion of sanctification, though it differs philosophically from Wesley's, is not far from Wesley in that they both affirm the possibility—indeed, the actuality—of Christian perfection now. For Barth, of course, this Christian perfection is different from Wesley's in that Barth argues that perfection is not possible within a person *herself*, but it is found in Jesus Christ. Sanctification on this conception highlights not so much personal, private piety but communal participation in the life-ministry of Jesus.

Michael Horton's essay, which begins part two, is a helpful prolegomenon to addressing the role of agency and ethics in sanctification. Specifically, he explains just how sanctification *works*, given the real activity of both God and humans. Rejecting both theological determinism and theological openness, Horton suggests that God sanctifies humans by acting on, with and within creaturely reality. This "cooperation" rests on the analogical assumption that God and humans act in a single event without disrupting the other's free action.

In "Sanctification and Ethics," Oliver O'Donovan offers a fresh framework for interpreting the practical meaning of sanctification. Arguing that the usual terms employed in the sanctification conversation are reductive and overly binary, O'Donovan challenges the reader to see sanctification as it unfolds from the threefold chord of faith, love and hope, in that order. Significantly, O'Donovan argues that sanctification is only incremental in that it involves the acquisition of practical wisdom. The wisdom of love and faith, though, is insufficient unless it is "led out" by hope into vocation and ethics, which clings to the promises of God and anticipates the resurrection life that is to come.

James Eglinton also considers sanctification as it relates to ethics, but with a historical bent toward Herman Bavinck's theology of sanctification. By exploring Bavinck's thought, Eglinton delves into a rich historical proposal that illumines a way forward for understanding the intricate relationship between dogmatics and ethics. With regard to sanctification, Eglinton musters Bavinck's insights to suggest that whereas justification consists of an objective declaration, sanctification consists of *both* an objective declaration of holiness and a subjective process of becoming more holy.

In order to liberate the Christian conception of holiness from misrepresentations that present it as stifling and life-denying on the one hand or over-realized on the other, Ivor Davidson ably starts off part three by providing a dogmatic account of how the theological foundations of this doctrine should inform our lives. This task leads him to reconsider the manifestation of Yahweh's holiness in the Bible, which culminates in Christ's life, and in contemporaneous Christian praxis. God, *in se*, is wholly other and, as such, is qualitatively unique and incomparably holy. This holiness, as exemplified in the life of Christ, often confounds us: it exhibits an intense jealousy for sinners and concomitant concern for sinful creatures. And because of the definitiveness of Christ's holiness, Davidson argues that believers are, in a very real sense, holy *now*. Christian participation in his holiness imitates the cruciformity of Jesus through enacting a life-activity of repentance and faith.

I, Kelly Kapic, offer some reflections on the relationship between physical suffering and sanctification. Employing the theological virtues of faith, hope and love, I argue for the importance of the community during times of suffering and struggle. Drawing on the likes of Kierkegaard and Luther, for example, I suggest that we should view our Christian life, especially during times of great difficulty, in much more communal ways. Put simply, when we are having trouble believing, our sisters and brothers in Christ believe for us—thus representing us to God; when we find it almost impossible to have hope, fellow saints bring us the fresh waters of promise in a way we can drink of them—thus representing God to us; finally, such faith and hope requires a context of love, otherwise the call to faith can become insensitive and the appeal to hope abusive. But in the context of love, the people of God grow in grace and truth as they sustain one another in faith and hope. In a brief conclusion, I raise three theological images as correspondents to these truths: cross, resurrection and feast—each of them provides the rich background for how we experience and understand faith, hope and love.

Like Ellis in his essay, Julie Canlis offers an incisive reflection on union with Christ and its connection to sanctification. Aiming to provide a creative and fertile discussion without getting bogged down by what she sees as recent unhelpful infighting about this doctrine, she argues that union with Christ was meant to ensure adoption and to unify the ecclesial community. Far from being a substantial infusion of grace or a purely legal transaction, adoptive union is made real by receiving the *person* of Jesus, not just his mere benefits, and this is always through the *person* of the Holy Spirit. In this thoroughly interpersonal affair, the Spirit is the one who makes us daughters and sons and empowers us to live out our sonship in meaningful action.

Peter Moore's essay, "Sanctification Through Preaching," looks to the pedagogical method of John Chrysostom to offer wisdom for contemporaries in pastoral leadership who are concerned with the sanctification of their people. Confronting traditional notions of education and transformation as merely the transfer of ideas, Moore shows how Chrysostom emphasized the sanctifying effect of encountering another disciple and being transformed by his *gnōmē* (γνώμη), that is, his "chosen life trajectory." Accordingly, he argues that sanctification often occurs as the believer lives with and inevitably starts to follow a Christian mentor, since that embodied guide points them to the good life of communion with God.

Many should be thanked for helping make this volume possible, but only a relatively few can be mentioned here. First and foremost, it is only by the generosity of Rutherford House and under the leadership of Andrew McGowan that this work exists. Second, I have been greatly assisted by two former students of mine: Grady Dickinson at the start of the editorial process, and even more by Jimmy Myers, who helped me in endless ways to see it to completion. Third, while the opinions expressed in this publication are those of the authors and do not necessarily reflect the views of the John Templeton Foundation or Biola's Center for Christian Thought, this publication benefited from a research fellowship at Biola University's Center for Christian Thought, which was made possible through the support of a generous grant from the John Templeton Foundation. I was able to complete this manuscript while beginning my time at CCT. While there, Dave Strobolakos carefully reviewed the manuscript for me, and Steve Porter, C. Stephen Evans, Thomas Crisp, David Horner, William Struthers, James Wilhoit, Christopher Kaczor, Rachel Dee, Evan Rosa and others provided a fantastic working environment. Fourth, Brannon Ellis, David Congdon and Andy Le Peau, all of whom represented IVP Academic very well, deserve thanks for their productive encouragement, feedback and help. Finally, volumes like this are only as good as the contributors, and I am thankful to those who were so receptive to editorial feedback and took the time to revise their essays with the hope that they might prove useful to a wider audience. Our great hope and prayer is that readers may find this volume in some ways helpful, drawing them back to consider afresh what it means to be united to Christ, sanctified by his Spirit and drawn into genuine communion with the living God and his people.

ABBREVIATIONS

CD   Karl Barth. *Church Dogmatics*. Edited by Geoffrey W. Bromiley and Thomas F. Torrance. 4 vols. in 13 parts. Edinburgh: T & T Clark, 1956–1975.

CO   *Ioannis Calvini Opera quae supersunt omnia*. Edited by Guilielmus Baum, Eduardus Cunitz and Eduardus Reuss. 59 vols. Corpus Reformatorum 29–87. Brunsvigae: Schwetschke, 1863–1900.

ET   English translation

KD   Karl Barth. *Die Kirchliche Dogmatik*. 4 vols. in 13 parts. Munich: Chr. Kaiser, 1932; Zürich: Theologischer Verlag Zürich, 1938–1965.

WA   *D. Martin Luthers Werke* [Weimarer Ausgabe]. Weimar: Böhlau, 1883–1993.

CONTRIBUTORS

Henri Blocher is professor of systematic theology at the Faculte Libre de Theologie Evangelique, Vaux-sur-Seine, France. His works include *Original Sin: Illuminating the Riddle* (InterVarsity Press, 2001), *Evil and the Cross: An Analytical Look at the Problem of Pain* (Kregel, 2005), *La Doctrine du Christ* (Edifac, 2002) and *La Bible au microscope* (Edifac, 2006).

Julie Canlis earned her PhD from the University of St Andrews, winning the 2007 John Templeton Award for Theological Promise for her work on John Calvin. Her book *Calvin's Ladder* (Eerdmans, 2010) won the *Christianity Today* Award of Merit for Theology in 2011.

Ivor J. Davidson is professor of systematic and historical theology at the University of St Andrews. He is author of *A Short History of Arianism* (Cambridge University Press, 2013), *The Birth of the Church* (Baker Books, 2004), *A Public Faith* (Baker Books, 2005), editor of the two-volume *Ambrose: De Officiis* (Oxford University Press, 2002) and coeditor with Murray A. Rae of *God of Salvation: Soteriology in Theological Perspective* (Ashgate, 2010).

James Eglinton is Meldrum Lecturer in Reformed Theology at New College, University of Edinburgh. His publications include *Trinity and Organism: Towards a New Reading of Herman Bavinck's Organic Motif* (T & T Clark, 2012) and articles such as "To Transcend and to Transform: The Neo-Calvinist Relationship of Church and Cultural Transformation" (*The Kuyper Center Review* 3 [2012]).

Brannon Ellis (PhD, University of Aberdeen) is acquisitions editor for Lexham Press. He is the author of various essays as well as *Calvin, Classical Trinitarianism, and the Aseity of the Son* (Oxford University Press, 2012).

Michael Horton is J. Gresham Machen Professor of Systematic Theology and Apologetics at Westminster Seminary, California, as well as the editor in chief of *Modern Reformation* magazine and host of White Horse Inn. Some of Horton's many books include *Covenant and Eschatology: The Divine Drama* (Westminster John Knox, 2002), *Lord and Servant: A Covenant Christology* (Westminster John Knox, 2005), *People and Place: A Covenant Ecclesiology* (Westminster John Knox, 2008) and *The Christian Faith: A Systematic Theology for Pilgrims on the Way* (Zondervan, 2011).

Kelly M. Kapic is professor of theological studies at Covenant College. Some of his publications include *Communion with God: The Divine and the Human in John Owen's Theology* (Baker Academic, 2007), *God So Loved, He Gave* (Zondervan, 2010), *A Little Book for New Theologians: Why and How to Study Theology* (IVP Academic, 2012), as well as serving as coeditor with Bruce McCormack of *Mapping Modern Theology* (Baker Academic, 2012) and coauthor with Wesley Vander Lugt of *Pocket Dictionary of the Reformed Tradition* (InterVarsity Press, 2013).

Richard Lints is Andrew Mutch Distinguished Professor of Theology and vice president for academic affairs at Gordon-Conwell Theological Seminary. His publications include *The Fabric of Theology* (Eerdmans, 1993), *Renewing the Evangelical Mission* (Eerdmans, 2011), *Progressive and Conservative Religious Ideologies: The Tumultuous Decade of the 1960s* (Ashgate, 2010) and *Personal Identity in Theological Perspective* (coedited with Michael Horton and Mark Talbot, Eerdmans, 2006).

Bruce L. McCormack is Charles Hodge Professor of Systematic Theology at Princeton Theological Seminary. He is author of *Karl Barth's Critically Realistic Dialectical Theology: Its Genesis and Development, 1909–1936* (Oxford University Press, 1995), *Orthodox and Modern: Studies in the Theology of Karl Barth* (Baker Academic, 2008), as well as serving as coeditor of such volumes as *Karl Barth and American Evangelicalism* (Eerdmans, 2011) and *Mapping Modern Theology* (Baker Academic, 2012). McCormack is also a member of the Karl Barth Stiftung in Basel, Switzerland, and the North American coeditor of the *Zeitschrift für Dialektische Theologie*.

Peter Moore (PhD, Macquarie University) is lecturer in theology with the Timothy Partnership in Sydney, Australia, and has served as a Presbyterian minister for twenty-three years. His work has included an extensive mentoring ministry supporting Presbyterian, Anglican and Baptist pastors. Moore's publications include "Gold Without Dross: Assessing the Debt of John Calvin to the Preaching of John Chrysostom" (*Reformed Theological Review* 68, no. 2 [2009], which is also his PhD title), "Plain Talk with a Gilt Edge: An Exploration of the Relation Between 'Plain' Biblical Exposition and Persuasion, in Chrysostom and Calvin" (*Westminster Theological Journal* 73, no. 1 [Spring 2011]) and a recent essay on Chrysostom in *Studia Patristica*, vol. LXVII (Leuven: Peeters, 2013).

Oliver O'Donovan is professor emeritus of Christian ethics and practical theology at the University of Edinburgh. His numerous publications include *The Problem of Self-Love in Saint Augustine* (Yale University Press, 1979), *Begotten or Made?* (Oxford University Press, 1984), *Resurrection and Moral Order* (Eerdmans, 1986), *Peace and Certainty* (Eerdmans, 1989), *The Desire of the Nations* (Cambridge University Press, 1996), *Common Objects of Love* (Eerdmans, 2002) and *The Ways of Judgment* (Eerdmans, 2005).

Derek Tidball is currently visiting scholar at Spurgeon's College, London, and he serves as editor of the widely used Bible Speaks Today Bible Themes series. Previously, he was principal of the London School of Theology. He is author of *Skillful Shepherds: An Introduction to Pastoral Theology* (Zondervan, 1986), *Who Are the Evangelicals? Tracing the Roots of Modern Movements* (Marshall Pickering, 1994) and *The Reality Is Christ: The Message of Colossians for Today* (Christian Focus, 1999).

An Opening Homily

1

HOLINESS

Restoring God's Image

Colossians 3:5-17

Derek Tidball

Put to death, therefore, whatever belongs to your earthly nature: sexual immorality, impurity, lust, evil desires and greed, which is idolatry. Because of these, the wrath of God is coming. You used to walk in these ways, in the life you once lived. But now you must rid yourselves of all such things as these: anger, rage, malice, slander, and filthy language from your lips. Do not lie to each other, since you have taken off your old self with its practices and have put on the new self, which is being renewed in knowledge in the image of its Creator. Here there is no Greek or Jew, circumcised or uncircumcised, barbarian, Scythian, slave or free, but Christ is all, and is in all.

Therefore, as God's chosen people, holy and dearly loved, clothe yourselves with compassion, kindness, humility, gentleness and patience. Bear with each other and forgive whatever grievances you may have against one another. Forgive as the Lord forgave you. And over all these virtues put on love, which binds them all together in perfect unity.

Let the peace of Christ rule in your hearts, since as members of one body you were called to peace. And be thankful. Let the word of Christ dwell in you richly as you teach and admonish one another with all

wisdom, and as you sing psalms, hymns and spiritual songs with grat-
itude in your hearts to God. And whatever you do, whether in word or
deed, do it all in the name of the Lord Jesus, giving thanks to God the
Father through him.

COLOSSIANS 3:5-17 NIV[1]

Michelangelo sculpted his exquisite *Pietà*, the statue of Mary nursing her
crucified yet serene son, when he was just twenty-four. It was the only
sculpture he ever signed. Installed in St. Peter's Basilica, Rome, in 1500, the
Pietà stood there mostly undisturbed[2] until Laszio Toth, a thirty-three-year-
old Hungarian-born Australian, attacked it with a hammer in 1972. Toth's
onslaught resulted in severe damage to the nose, left eye and veil of Mary as
well as leaving her left arm shattered. Onlookers reportedly took some of
these shattered pieces away as souvenirs. The masterpiece of Renaissance art
was now a damaged masterpiece in need of restoration. Over succeeding
months the sculpture was painstakingly repaired by taking a block of marble
from its back, where the hole left behind would not be seen, and restoring
the *Pietà* to its original image.

Holiness may be defined in many ways. The heart of holiness lies in the
restoration of God's image in us. As with the *Pietà*, an enemy has entered
our world and attacked human beings, who were made in the image of God
(Gen 1:27), leaving us damaged and lacking. We are spoiled masterpieces.
The enemy's attack is not the whole story explaining our fall from God's
gracious intention at creation. Like any statue, we pick up the grime of life,
and the pollution of our fallen world takes its toll. Unlike a lifeless statue, the
defacement of God's image in us is due not only to enemy attack or to the

---

[1] All scripture verses in this chapter are from the NIV 1984.
[2] It sustained minor damage when being moved in 1736 and was displayed briefly in New York
in 1964.

effect of a fallen environment but also to much self-harm, as we choose to live in disobedience to and alienation from God. The cumulative result of the onslaughts of the devil, the world and the flesh is that we are spoiled masterpieces in need of restoration.

Christ is the masterful craftsman who painstakingly sets about the work of restoring God's image in us through his Holy Spirit.

Colossians 3:5-17 does not say everything there is to be said about sanctification, but it takes us to the heart of Christ's work of restoration. The Christians in Colossae had a wrong understanding of how God's image could be restored in them. They believed that holiness would develop through the adoption of ascetic practices or through undergoing extraordinary spiritual experiences (Col 2:16-23). But their belief was mistaken because it was based on an insufficient grasp of the work of Christ's sufficiency.

In correcting them Paul explains the meaning of holiness in three dimensions.

Holiness Is to Have a Christlike Character

Paul provides the Colossians with two lists of characteristics that are incompatible with living a life in Christ. The first starts with actions and leads to attitudes: "sexual immorality, impurity, lust, evil desires and greed, which is idolatry" (Col 3:5). The second goes in the reverse direction, starting with attitudes and leading to actions: "anger, rage, malice, slander, and filthy language" (Col 3:8) and lying (Col 3:9). These attitudes and actions, he said, were to be "put to death" (Col 3:5) as surely as a crucified man was put to death, and got rid of (Col 3:8) as surely as last week's rubbish is removed by the trash collectors.

He gives several reasons why we take such decisive action, including the avoidance of the "wrath of God" that is coming (Col 3:6). But the deeper reason is not a pragmatic one—in order to avoid punishment—but a more worthy one. We divest ourselves of these qualities because they are incompatible with our identity as Christians. Using language that by common consent picks up the image of baptism, where candidates would disrobe to be baptized and clothe themselves in new garments after emerging from the water, Paul reminds them that in becoming followers of Christ, they have "taken off [the] old self with its practices and have put on the new self, *which is being renewed in knowledge in the image of its Creator*" (Col 3:9-10).

In perhaps more contemporary terms it is a question of whose uniform we are wearing. Uniforms display not only what we are called to do but also to whom we belong and whose management we are under. Are we wearing the old and shabby uniform of Adam or the renewed designer clothes of Christ? The context suggests that the "self" spoken of here refers not so much to the personal, inner, motivating power of sin as to our corporate identity. As Douglas Moo explains, "The contrast of the 'old self' and 'new self' alludes to one of Paul's most fundamental theological conceptions: the contrast between a realm in opposition to God, rooted in Adam's sin and characterized by sin and death, and the new realm, rooted in Christ's death and resurrection and characterized by righteousness of life."[3] The corporate dimension surfaces clearly in verse 11, and is a crucial, if neglected, dimension of the meaning of holiness.

The "putting off" of the old uniform in verses 5-9 is balanced by the "putting on" of verses 12-17. Holiness does not consist of stopping bad behavior and eschewing sinful attitudes alone but of replacing them with good behavior and pursuing Christlike attitudes. Years ago, Michael Griffiths warned that "there is a kind of Christian negative holiness which rejoices in discarding various forms of worldliness, but which leaves the individual stark naked."[4] Paul would have us clothed "with compassion, kindness, humility, gentleness and patience" (Col 3:12). Then he calls us to "put on love, which binds them all together in perfect unity" (Col 3:14). These are characteristics that describe Jesus Christ perfectly. We all know of Christians who believe themselves to be holy because they avoid certain things, but they are inhibited people, often pharisaical in disposition, who, as Mark Twain said, are "good in the worst sense of the word." Holiness is more than avoiding sin. It is cultivating the character of Christ in us.

Although the "self" spoken of here is corporate, the implications are personal and individual. We are each called to work out the reality of our transfer to the new realm of being under Christ. The difficulty we face is that the old realm still exists. Since it has not yet been destroyed it still has some attraction for us. So working out our new position is often a struggle, but in

---

[3]Douglas Moo, *The Letters to the Colossians and to Philemon*, Pillar New Testament Commentary (Grand Rapids: Eerdmans, 2008), p. 268.
[4]Michael Griffiths, *Cinderella with Amnesia* (London: Inter-Varsity Press, 1975), p. 78.

the gradual transformation of our characters into Christlikeness we see the new realm dawning and advancing toward its fullness.

To help us understand further, Paul focuses on the role that our minds play in this.

HOLINESS IS TO HAVE A CHRIST-RENEWED MIND

On this occasion Paul does not say that we are being renewed in the image of our Creator but that we are being "renewed *in knowledge* in the image of [our] Creator" (Col 3:10). Why does he insert the words "in knowledge," which seem to interrupt what might be the more natural flow of his words?

The account of the fall in Genesis 2:17 draws attention to the importance of the mind in causing humanity's downfall; consequently, it is vital that that which played such a crucial role in causing the problem should be addressed in the giving of the solution. Adam and Eve were told by God, "You must not eat from the tree of knowledge of good and evil" (Gen 2:17). While it is difficult to unpack the meaning of the tree's mysterious title in full, it is evident that this was a tree that would provide Adam and Eve with knowledge beyond what was good for them as human beings. Its fruit would lead them to know everything as God knows it and so to become independent from their Creator, dispensing with the need for him, and leading them to live autonomous and self-sufficient lives.

The mind in Hebrew thought was not so much about abstract intellectual or philosophical thought, as in the Greek world, but about practical wisdom. So we must be careful not to apply this life of the mind simply to the importance of correct theological discussion, much beloved in academia. That may miss the point. The way we think shapes the way we live and governs what we do. As Proverbs 4:23 puts it: "Be careful how you think; your life is shaped by your thoughts" (TEV). This is as true of young rioters as of aid workers, of middle-class materialists as of selfless monks, of school dropouts as of university professors. All need their minds renewed in Christ. It is about thinking correctly, as God would have us think, so that we might live correctly. As Paul expressed it in the parallel text in Ephesians 4:22-24, "You were taught . . . to be made new in the attitude of your minds; and to put on the new self, created to be like God in true righteousness and holiness."

Paul tells us that such a renewal is going to be a *progressive work of God.*

He uses the passive continuous tense: "which *is being* renewed." Paul is not intent here on encouraging passivity, which leaves the work of transformation wholly up to God and treats the believer as if he or she were an anaesthetized body, undergoing an operation by a divine surgeon. There are plenty of active commands in the context to prevent us from falling into that error (although we may want to debate exactly how the divine and human interact). His point is rather that the renewal of the mind, and so of God's image in us, is a process: it does not take place in an instant, nor has it taken place fully yet. When the allied forces withdrew from Iraq and returned the country to the new regime in Baghdad, they wrote what was called "a script for reconstruction." Believers, having withdrawn from being under Adam's regime and now serving under Christ's lordship, are engaged by the grace of God and in the power of his Spirit in enacting a script for reconstruction throughout their lives. Peter O'Brien speaks of it as "the believers' progressive ability to recognize God's will and command" and to live in accordance with it.[5]

If it is progressive and we have an active part in it, it means we must work out our new identity daily, learning new habits, adopting new disciplines, practicing the steps that will enable us to become the persons God intended us to be, manifesting his image in the world. The transformation of character does not just happen. It happens, as Tom Wright has recently pointed out, partly in the same way we learn anything, by adopting those steps that help us get to our goal and practicing them until they "become habitual, a matter of second nature."[6]

If holiness is progressive, it is also *purposeful.* The goal is not that we should just become better people, nicer neighbors (although that should be a byproduct) and certainly not necessarily more astute or pedantic theologians, but that we should be renewed "in the image of the Creator."

In Colossians, such a phrase drives us back to the "hymn" in Colossians 1:15, which celebrates the Son as "the image of the invisible God" and the one in whom, through whom and for whom all things were created. So the goal is to become Christlike. In the words of C. F. D. Moule, re-creation "is *in the*

---

[5]Peter T. O'Brien, *Colossians, Philemon,* Word Biblical Commentary 44 (Waco: Word, 1982), p. 192.
[6]Tom Wright, *Virtue Reborn* (London: SPCK, 2010), p. 27.

pattern of Christ, who is God's Likeness absolutely."[7] This is none other than the ancient call to "be holy because I, the LORD your God, am holy" (Lev 19:2), updated by the new covenant, which gives us the advantage of seeing what it means to be perfectly holy, what the unblemished image of God looks like in a human being, and so what it means to be truly human, modeled by the person of Christ.

To be holy is to have the image of God, given to us at creation, restored in us. It is, therefore, to be truly human and truly Christlike.

HOLINESS IS TO BELONG TO A CHRIST-TRANSFORMED COMMUNITY

The whole thrust of Paul's writing in Colossians 3 prevents us from taking holiness as limited to personal ethics or individual character. It is about living in the new community. Again this is the new covenant outworking of God's unchanging desire to have people of his own, evident first in the Garden of Eden, but then advanced through the call of Abraham and in the calling of Israel. So holiness is relational, and no one can claim to be holy if they are isolated or insulated from others who name Christ as Lord. Isolationist Christians are a contradiction to what it means to be in Christ. Holiness is about belonging to a holy people (Ex 19:5; 1 Pet 2:9).

In Colossians 3:11-17 Paul expresses the nature of a Christ-transformed community, first negatively and then positively.

Negatively it is clear that the old identity markers that discriminated between people in the conventional world—that is, the world of Adam, of the old self—no longer have currency. They are like an ancient, defunct currency that no longer has any trading value. Four such boundaries are mentioned. They are ethnic ("no Greek or Jew"), ritual ("circumcised or uncircumcised"), cultural ("barbarian, Scythian") and social ("slave or free").[8] A church where such distinctions matter has not understood holiness. An individual who is racist, who judges people by their religious rituals, or is a social snob, or for that matter, one who is sexist, has not begun to understand the meaning of holiness.

---

[7]C. F. D. Moule, *The Epistle of Paul the Apostle to the Colossians and Philemon*, Cambridge Greek Testament Commentary (Cambridge: Cambridge University Press, 1968), p. 120.

[8]On the choice of these boundary markers and the difference between this list and that in Gal 3:28, see Derek Tidball, *In Christ, in Colosse: Sociological Perspectives on Colossians* (Milton Keynes: Paternoster, 2011), pp. 58-60.

By contrast, *positively*, the only thing that matters is that "Christ is all and is in all." Consequently, if holiness is living in his image, we relate to one another as he related to others. That means

- the character of Christ will shape us (Col 3:12-14): "compassion, kindness, humility, gentleness and patience," bearing with one another and forgiving as he forgave us;

- the peace of Christ will rule between us (Col 3:15): causing us to settle disputes and arguments and working for unity;

- the word of Christ will dwell in us (Col 3:16): so that all we do will seek to be consistent with his message; and

- the honor of the name of Christ will determine our behavior (Col 3:17) in every dimension of our lives.

For many Christians this corporate dimension is the missing dimension of holiness. I know many who would never dream of getting drunk or committing adultery, and rightly so, yet have no conscience about having a row in church or speaking in a racist way or espousing other socially divisive attitudes.

Holiness is wider than we think! Holiness is about

- our separation from sin;

- our devotion to Christ;

- our adoption of godly habits; and

- our identification with Christ in practice.

But holiness is also about

- the individual and relational dimensions of our lives;

- the detailed and specific as well as the general and comprehensive aspects of our living;

- our doing and our being;

- our thinking and our acting; and

- our being passively transformed and actively obedient.

Holiness is the painstaking restoration, by the most skilled craftsman of all, of ruined masterpieces in the image of their creator.

PART ONE

Sanctified *by* Grace *Through* Faith *in* Union with Christ

2

LIVING BY FAITH—ALONE?

Reformed Responses to Antinomianism

Richard Lints

The just shall live by faith.

HABAKKUK 2:4 (NKJV), CITED IN ROMANS 1:17,
GALATIANS 3:11 AND HEBREWS 10:38

When the prophet says, "The just shall live by faith," the statement does not apply to impious and profane persons, whom the Lord by turning them to faith may justify, but the utterance is directed to believers and to them life is promised by faith. We must have this blessedness not just once (in justification) but must hold to it throughout life. To the very end of life believers have no other righteousness than that which is described as the free reconciliation with God by faith.

JOHN CALVIN[1]

---

[1]John Calvin, *Institutes of the Christian Religion*, ed. John T. McNeill, trans. Ford Lewis Battles, Library of Christian Classics (Philadelphia: Westminster Press, 1977), 3.14.11. All quotations from Calvin's *Institutes* are from this edition.

The gospel is the story of God creating, redeeming, sustaining and consummating a people for his own possession. In that narrative is embedded the entire Christian life. There is no other story that narrates our reconciliation with God past, present or future. As a gift from God, the gospel is received by faith alone. The gospel is also continually embraced by faith throughout the entirety of the Christian life. Protestant traditions have generally affirmed that faith in the triune God of this gospel is the sole instrumental ground of justification. They have spoken with less than a ringing consensus about faith as the instrumental ground of sanctification. If the gospel is God's redeeming actions past, present and future, and faith is the instrument by which believers embrace it, consistency would suggest that there is essential continuity to the role of faith in justification and sanctification. That is not the case for many Protestants, and many Protestants in the Reformed tradition specifically. This essay attempts to get at the underlying reasons why this is so.

The argument unfolds in several stages. It begins by tracing the erroneous assumption that good works (in contrast to faith) are necessary to sanctification in order to avoid the problem of antinomianism. It is erroneous because sanctified believers remain always sinners and there is no partial righteousness sufficient to satisfy the critics of antinomianism. In effect, there are two types of antinomianism; only one is to be avoided, and *sola fide* is not susceptible to the dangerous type. Faith is the orientation of persons outside of themselves. As such it is the instrument by which believers embrace divine holiness, and it restrains them from notions of achieving holiness themselves. Divine holiness is nothing less than the ongoing presence of the Holy Spirit to believers. Because of that presence, the law ceases to function forensically (i.e., acting as judge) and instead operates sapientially in the life of believers. The final section of the argument suggests that the conceptual resources of imaging and idolatry underwrite a reorientation of the doctrine of sanctification that does not depend on notions of good works or moral progress.

If the gospel is the narrative of God's creating, redeeming and consummating work in Christ, there is no progress beyond the gospel in the Christian life. There is no story beyond the story. The Christian life is about growing deeper into the gospel, which therefore implies living by faith, not beyond faith. The significance of *sola fide* in this context is, quite simply, immense.[2] Faith alone constitutes the means by which sinners are reconciled to the living God, and by virtue of which they continue to cling to reconciliation to God as their only hope. It is vital not to refer to this faith as the good work of the sinner, which would wrongly connote that sinners engage God by being good enough. Their relationship with God is and always is based on grace. It is God who graciously reconciles sinners with himself as an act of his divine compassion.

Being reconciled is not only initiated by God but continues by virtue of his grace. We may refer to Christian holiness as that ongoing work of divine grace by which reconciliation with God is sustained in the life of the believer. Holiness attaches to the divine declaration that his people are set apart in Christ. The creaturely counterpart to this divine declaration is faith. Yet in many Protestant traditions, the believer's actions (i.e., their good works) in sanctification come perilously close to being precisely another instrumental ground of one's ongoing reconciliation before God.[3] The logic of this tendency is simply that the alternative appears to be some form of antinomianism, wherein the actions of believers are inconsequential to the covenant relationship to God. If one downplays the necessity of "good works" in sanctification, then one appears dangerously close to answering Paul's rhetorical question of Romans 6:1, "Are we to continue in sin that grace may abound?" in the affirmative. Yet, as I shall argue, by emphasizing the necessity of good works in sanctification, the risk is that one's continued reconciliation with their covenant Lord will be based on a "boast" before God, which Paul expressly denies in Romans 4. The danger of boasting is mitigated only by keeping faith as central to sanctification as it is to justification. As Calvin reminds, "Let us not consider works to be so commended after free justification that they afterward take over the function of justifying man or share this office with faith."[4]

---

[2]John Webster, *Holiness* (Grand Rapids: Eerdmans, 2002), p. 87.
[3]See George Hunsinger on the later traditional Protestant tendency to see sanctification as the "completion" of justification and eventually as its virtual replacement. "What Karl Barth Learned from Martin Luther," in *Disruptive Grace: Studies in the Theology of Karl Barth* (Grand Rapids: Eerdmans, 2002), p. 298.
[4]Calvin, *Institutes* 3.17.9.

TWO COURTROOMS?

Protestants have often interpreted Paul's rhetorical question in Romans 6:1 as implying the necessity of good works in sanctification.[5] There can be no antinomian license to sin in the face of divine grace, so the argument goes. Charles Hodge offers a representative exposition of the Protestant framework of sanctification in the light of this fear of antinomianism. "Justification," he writes, "is a forensic act, God acting as judge, declaring justice satisfied so far as the believing sinner is concerned, whereas sanctification is an effect due to the divine efficiency."[6] On this rendering justification is the declaration of God toward sinners based solely on the finished work of Christ. Sanctification, by contrast, is the inward renewal of character that results from the infusion of the Holy Spirit as the gracious gift of God to those who are justified. Faith is the means by which believers embrace the full penal satisfaction of Christ's death on the cross on their behalf. After that and by means of the impartation of divine grace, "sinful acts become more infrequent and holy acts more and more habitual and controlling."[7] The Holy Spirit provides the "occasion for the exercise of . . . submission, confidence, self-denial, patience and meekness as well as faith, hope and love."[8] Real moral progress appears to be the hallmark of sanctification. Hodge goes so far as to say, "The best Christians are in general those who not merely from restless activity of natural disposition, but from love to Christ and zeal for his glory, labor most and suffer most in his service."[9]

But what does "best" amount to in this instance? It appears from Hodge's exposition that "best" is a qualitative term applied to believers who are more cooperative with the Holy Spirit's inward renewal of their character. The language of "best" implies a scale defined by the amount of "holy acts" performed by the believer and the infrequency of "sinful acts" performed. That scale determines the "happiness or blessedness of believers in a future life in proportion to the devotion to the service of Christ in this life."[10]

---

[5]Louis Berkhof, *Systematic Theology* (Grand Rapids: Eerdmans, 1939), p. 532. Charles Hodge, *Systematic Theology* (repr., Grand Rapids: Eerdmans, 1982), 3:238-44.

[6]Hodge, *Systematic Theology*, 3:213.

[7]Ibid., 3:226.

[8]Ibid., 3:230.

[9]Ibid., 3:230.

[10]Ibid., 3:243.

The scales of divine justice operate according to two different and conflicting principles for Hodge. From one angle, the justice of God is satisfied by Christ's death as the federal representative of his people and the imputation of Christ's righteousness to them. In this divine courtroom, the innocent one (Jesus) has been declared guilty in the place of the guilty ones (believers), and in turn the guilty ones have been declared innocent in place of the innocent one. But evidently in another divine courtroom nearby with those very same believers, as Hodge says, "a man shall reap what he sows, and God will reward everyone according to his works."[11]

The reason Hodge backs himself into this corner is straightforward. To avoid any hint of Roman Catholic moralism on the one hand, Hodge affirms double imputation with respect to justification. To avoid any hint of antinomianism on the other hand, he affirms the necessity of good works in sanctification. He cites Luther's denunciation of Agricola as the confirming historical evidence that Protestants are committed to the necessity of good works.[12] Good works are not meritorious in justification, but they are "rewarded" and appear to have a judicial function in sanctification according to Hodge.

Hodge attempted to suppress the overtly meritorious consequences in his doctrine of sanctification by arguing that the Holy Spirit is the efficient cause of these good works, and therefore they accrue no merit on behalf of the believer: they are rewarded but not because of any merit. This curious reality is made more perplexing by the odd asymmetry of justice in this second courtroom of sanctification. Good works are rewarded, while bad works receive no condemnation. Justice, or some form of it, appears to work in only one direction. Hodge appears to think that good works function as instrumental, nonmeritorious grounds in sanctification analogous to the manner in which faith functions as the instrumental, nonmeritorious ground in justification.

The problem is twofold. First, in Hodge's portrayal justification is grounded in faith precisely because good works are in sufficiently short supply as to warrant condemnation rather than reward. But in sanctification, there appear to be a sufficient supply of good works to warrant blessing. Second and more importantly, Christ's redeeming work is entirely sufficient

---

[11]Ibid., 3:244.
[12]Ibid., 3:238.

for the reconciliation of sinners, but in the courtroom of sanctification the verdict is based on the good works of believers as well.[13] There appear to be works worthy of a reward without being meritorious. At the very least this is confusing.

The tacit assumption in Hodge is that good works as well as faith are actions of the human will, whose meritorious standing is avoided by the causal precedents of the Holy Spirit. However, faith must be distinguished from good works at the very point where Hodge wants to make them analogous. Faith has no "boast" (i.e., merit) before God not only because of its causal ancestry in the Holy Spirit but also primarily because its reference point lies outside of itself. The causal conditions of faith appear irrelevant to its meritorious standing (or lack thereof) in Romans 3 and 4. There is no reference to the work of the Holy Spirit's producing faith at the critical juncture in Paul's argument against moralism ("having a boast") nor against antinomianism ("a license to sin"). Rather, Paul depicts faith in contrast to works, as hoping and trusting in something (Christ) outside of one's self (Rom 4:3-5, 21-25). It has a fundamental exteriority about it in this respect. By contrast, works have no such fundamental exteriority about them. They belong to the one who does them. When works are conceptually contrasted to faith, it is the contrast between an action without an external reference and an action with an external reference. In this regard, Hodge responded to the antinomian criticism only by implicitly affirming self-referencing action, or self-righteousness in theological terms.

What is required is a reframing of the issues. There is a danger of antinomianism but not of the sort portrayed by Hodge. Let me suggest that there are two different (and contrasting) forms of antinomianism, only one of which is theologically dangerous. Antinomianism type 1 affirms that obedience to law cannot serve as the basis of a relationship to God. Antinomianism type 2 affirms that there is no normative moral center within the triune community. Both forms of antinomianism work against the intuition that moral norms are intrinsically connected to God by means of obedience

---

[13]Berkhof concurs with Hodge at this point: "All humans will appear before the final judgment. The sins of believers will be manifest as pardoned in Christ. There will nonetheless be different degrees of heaven enjoyed by those who are pardoned. These degrees will be determined by what is done in the flesh." See *Systematic Theology*, p. 732.

to the law. Type 2 repudiates the connection between the divine being and fixed moral norms. "Freedom in Christ" according to antinomianism type 2 entails a freedom from all fixed moral norms.[14] One upshot of type 2 antinomianism is the embrace of the self as the determiner of all moral standards. By contrast, antinomianism type 1 affirms that there are fixed moral norms in the divine being but that obedience to them does not serve as the basis of the relationship to God. That relationship, after the fall, is grounded in divine grace.[15]

Type 1 antinomianism should actually be embraced if faith is the sole instrument by which believers lay hold of Christ. Type 2 antinomianism should be rejected because divine holiness requires a normative moral center. Arguing for the former notion of antinomianism and against the latter requires that the difference between faith and works in sanctification is accentuated and any hint of intrinsic righteousness in sinners is avoided.[16] Calvin pungently reminds: "God does not as many stupidly believe once for all reckon to us as righteousness that forgiveness of sins concerning which we have spoken in order that having obtained pardon for our past life, we may afterward seek righteousness in the law. This would be only to lead us into false hope, to laugh at us and mock us."[17]

SIMUL SANCTUS ET PECCATOR

"There is no greater sinner than the Christian Church," said Luther in his Easter Day sermon in 1531.[18] Calvin's rhetorical flourish may be less startling, but his conviction is remarkably similar in this regard.

---

[14]Reinhard Hütter argues that Protestant liberalism manifests the Protestant pathology to be free from all moral norms. See *Bound to Be Free* (Grand Rapids: Eerdmans, 2004). This is what I have called antinomianism type 2.

[15]Calvinists who are self-consciously not Lutheran often accuse Lutherans of embracing antinomianism. And many Lutherans often criticize the Reformed tradition of legalism. See Scott Murray, *Law, Life and the Living God: The Third Use of the Law in American Lutheranism* (St. Louis: Concordia, 2002), pp. 90-95; and G. C. Berkouwer, *Faith and Sanctification* (Grand Rapids: Eerdmans, 1952), pp. 163-93, for representative tendencies of Lutherans and Reformed respectively.

[16]I am here siding with Calvin against Osiander (Calvin, *Institutes* 3.6.5-12) on the matter of intrinsic righteousness but against the tendency following Calvin to attribute significant moral renewal in believers at the heart of the Spirit's work of sanctification.

[17]Calvin, *Institutes* 3.14.10.

[18]Martin Luther, *Werke*, Weimarer Ausgabe 34:1.267. As quoted in Webster, *Holiness*, 73.

The best work that can be brought forward from them is still always spotted and corrupted with some impurity of the flesh and some dregs mixed with it. Let a holy servant of God choose from the whole course of his life what an especially noteworthy character he thinks he has done. Let him well turn over in his mind its several parts. He will somewhere perceive that it savors of the rottenness of the flesh. We have not a single work going forth from the saints that if it be judged in itself deserves not shame as its just reward.[19]

Whatever else may be said about works performed by believers, it is clear that essential goodness is not one of their primary attributes. Sin and grace are never mere "quanta" in process, grace increasing and sin decreasing.[20] The situation in which believers find themselves is always one in which their works are tinged with sin. Their obedience is always filled with mixed motives. Their actions are never devoid of self-centeredness. So it is that there is no such thing as a gradual purification by which their need for the forgiveness of sins would diminish. They remain sinners through and through. They are also, surprisingly, declared holy and sanctified by God.

Both Luther and Calvin affirm that believers are simultaneously sanctified and sinful, but how so?[21] At the very least sanctification must not be equated with intrinsic righteousness, nor with a notion of inward renewal that implies the (increasing) absence of sin. The simultaneity of sin and sanctification prohibits the interpretation of sanctification as ethical self-improvement, nor can sanctification signal the emergence of self-sufficiency in any form.[22]

When Paul declares the saints at Corinth to be sanctified (1 Cor 1:2) it is not grounded in their good works. It is by virtue of belonging to Christ that they are declared sanctified. There is also a surprising reversal of this claim later in the very same chapter, namely, that Christ is the sanctification of the saints (1 Cor 1:30). Paul was making the claim that belonging to Christ was the meaning of their sanctification. The saints are sanctified "in Christ," not "in themselves."

There is no stage in the life of the sanctified believer that the forgiveness

---

[19]Calvin, *Institutes* 3.14.9.
[20]Berkouwer, *Faith and Sanctification*, 75.
[21]See contrasting accounts of this in Berkouwer, *Faith and Sanctification* (chap. 4, "The Origins of Sanctification," pp. 71-97); and George Hunsinger, "A Tale of Two Simultaneities: Justification and Sanctification in Calvin and Barth," in *Conversing With Barth*, ed. John McDowell and Mike Higton (London: Ashgate, 2004), pp. 68-89.
[22]Webster, *Holiness*, 81.

of sins is not absolutely central to their relationship to God. G. C. Berkouwer refers to this as the "constant commerce with the forgiveness of sins" in the life of the believer.[23] There is no point, in other words, when Christ ceases to be the representative mediator between them and God. This also is to resist the notion of an infused principle into believers by which they become Christlike and thereby are less in need of divine forgiveness. Grace is not like an antibiotic given to the sick patient to ward off the infection of sin and enabling them to take on a less sinful posture.

If dependence on divine grace is a hallmark of sanctification then faith is the primary expression of this orientation precisely because faith orients the believers outside of themselves.[24] In this regard repentance rather than moral exertion is the appropriate response that flows from this faith. Repentance manifests the ongoing necessity of divine forgiveness. And insofar as divine forgiveness is in view in every act of repentance, it is grounded in the gospel declaration of reconciliation through the death and resurrection of the Son. Salvation is not grounded in the believer's being like Christ, but rather being forgiven "in Christ."[25] It is not grounded in any notion of a partial righteousness or holiness in the believer.[26]

Calvin goes so far as to suggest that the works of believers are acceptable to God only because Christ's righteousness has been imputed to these works.

> After forgiveness of sins is set forth, the good works that now follow are appraised otherwise than on their own merit. For everything imperfect in them is covered by Christ's perfection, every blemish or spot is cleansed away by his purity in order not to be brought in question at the divine judgment. Therefore after the guilt of all transgressions that hinder man from bringing forth anything pleasing to God has been blotted out, and after the fault of imperfection, which habitually defiles even good works is buried, the good works done by believers are accounted righteous, or what is the same thing, are reckoned as righteous [Rom 4:22].[27]

---

[23]Berkouwer, *Faith and Sanctification*, p. 84.

[24]This follows Berkouwer's comment, "Faith is not a point of departure for a fresh emission of power or a human function or potency producing other effects, but of faith as true orientation toward the grace of God and as the life which flourishes on this divine grace, on the forgiveness of sins." *Faith and Sanctification*, p. 27.

[25]See Hunsinger, "What Karl Barth Learned from Martin Luther," p. 285.

[26]See Calvin, *Institutes* 3.14.13.

[27]Ibid., 3.17.8.

SANCTIFYING FAITH

Faith is the instrument by which we lay hold of Christ, because faith has a reference point outside of itself. Protestant affirmations of *sola fide* with regard to justification have thus seemed logically connected to the *solus Christus* claims of the gospel. The exteriority of faith draws the attention of believers outside of themselves to Christ. As the instrument through which believers look outside themselves, faith is the "true orientation toward the grace of God."[28] As articulated in the gospel this grace is the source of the church's well-being. By faith, the church embraces "the life which flourishes on this divine grace, on the forgiveness of sin."[29] *Sola fide* communicates the notion that there is no other hope of forgiveness outside the divine grace of the gospel. *Sola fide* also communicates that divine grace stands in contrast to any and all internal reference points in the sinner.[30] As Calvin says, "Faith is something merely passive, bringing nothing of ours to the recovering of God's favor but receiving from Christ that which we lack."[31]

The gospel is received rather than achieved by believers, and thus all the benefits given in the gospel are received by faith.[32] The gift of the Holy Spirit is one of those "benefits" and no less than other gifts given in the gospel, so the Holy Spirit is received by faith. The presence of the Spirit is not contingent on the merit of anything in the church or the believer, but comes strictly as a result of the mercy of the Father at the behest of the Son. It is in this regard that sanctification does not require a different act of faith than justification.[33] It is the same faith through which the gift of the Holy Spirit is appropriated as the faith through which Christ is embraced. More properly it is by the gift of the Holy Spirit that the full gift of Christ is given to the church. And therefore sanctifying faith is not different in its orientation than justifying faith.[34]

---

[28]Berkouwer, *Faith and Sanctification*, p. 28.

[29]Ibid., p. 29.

[30]Berkouwer: "Faith, though not creative, preserves us from autonomous self-sanctification and moralism." Ibid., p. 93.

[31]Calvin, *Institutes* 3.13.5.

[32]George Hunsinger writes, "Salvation as Luther understood it was not essentially a process but a person . . . not a work but a gift." "What Karl Barth Learned from Martin Luther," p. 295.

[33]Michael Horton writes, "In both [justification and sanctification] Christ is the object, the gospel is the means of its communication from God and faith is the means of our receiving it from him." *The Christian Faith* (Grand Rapids: Zondervan, 2011), p. 650.

[34]As Herman Bavinck writes, "In sanctification, it is exclusively faith that saves us." *Reformed Dogmatics,* vol. 4, ed. John Bolt, trans. Jan Friend (Grand Rapids: Baker Books, reprint 1979), p. 243.

It is God who sanctifies (1 Thess 5:23) in sustaining the church in fellowship and relationship. He sanctifies by saving his people "in Christ" and pronouncing the verdict of their innocence as both a fully accomplished reality and a future, yet-to-be-fully-experienced reality. Between the already dimension and the not-yet dimension, the Holy Spirit is the down payment on the promised full, face-to-face presence of the living God and the fully experienced face-to-face relationship with the living God in the new heavens and new earth (Eph 1:13-14).

The "already" external reference point of faith is the completed mission of Christ (life/death/resurrection/ascension). Different but not in conflict, the not-yet, external reference point of faith is the work of Spirit by whom all of history will reach its consummation in the new heavens and the new earth. Faith is no less oriented outside of itself in the not-yet dimension than in its already dimension. Works is contrasted with faith in the already dimension since there is no other "work" than the work of Christ on which the sinner depends for the forgiveness of their sins and their reconciliation to the triune God (Rom 4:3-5; Gal 3:10-14). In the not-yet dimension, faith is contrasted with sight since what can be seen is a less reliable indicator of the end of history than is faith in the providential presence of the Holy Spirit (2 Cor 5:7; Heb 11:1-3).

THE OBJECTIVITY OF HOLINESS

John Webster writes of the church's "alien holiness" in ways that are strikingly analogous to Luther's convictions about the believer's "alien righteousness."[35] The reason is straightforward. Holiness is a property of God, and it is God's presence in the church that renders the church holy as such. Christ's finished work is the basis of the divine presence in the church extended as a gift to the church by the promised Holy Spirit. When Christ declared to the disciples in the farewell discourse of John 14 that it is better that he go away, it is precisely better because he would send the Holy Spirit after his departure. God's actual presence in and with the church is made manifest in the enduring presence of the Spirit from Pentecost forward. It is the presence of the Holy Spirit that sanctifies the church in the period between the ascension and the consummation.

---

[35]Webster, *Holiness*, p. 62.

As it would be wrong to suppose that the imputation of Christ's right-eousness entails the exchange of some property between Christ and the be-liever, so the Pentecost gift of the Holy Spirit is not in the first instance about an exchange of properties between the Spirit and the believer.[36] The Holy Spirit's holiness is proper to himself rather than merely a means by which the church takes on this divine property gradually over time. Holiness is not about the changes that the Spirit effects in the life of the church, but about the presence of the Holy Spirit himself.[37] The primary benefit of the Spirit's presence is the Spirit. In this regard sanctification is about the ongoing res-toration of the relationship with God by the person of the Holy Spirit.[38]

As a person of the divine triune community, the Holy Spirit enters into a living relationship with the church that Protestant evangelicals have often (rightly) referred to as a personal relationship, signaling the reality that there are persons in relationship with each other. Granted that three of the persons are divine in nature, the relationship between God and his people is none-theless aptly described as personal. As with the Son, so with the Spirit, the relationship with the church is always personal, which entails that the Spirit always remains a "thou" to the church's "we." The gift of the Spirit is the im-partation of the Spirit as a person in a vital and living relation to believers.[39]

Holiness in the church is predicated not on the basis of the church's work and worship, but rather on the sanctifying work of the Holy Spirit in making Christ manifest through the work and worship of the church. In this sense, the church's holiness is always "in Christ" (1 Cor 1:2; Eph 5:26; Heb 2:11). It is the presence of the Holy Spirit that mediates the ascended (and enthroned) Christ in and to the church. It is not the work of the church that completes the work of Christ and by which then the church becomes holy. The work of Christ is that by which those who were "far off have been

---

[36]See Berkouwer, *Faith and Sanctification*, p. 79.

[37]Berkouwer cites Bavinck approvingly when he writes, "The regenerate person is no whit differ-ent in substance from what they were before their regeneration." *Faith and Sanctification*, p. 87.

[38]Space prohibits the longer argument that the presence of the Spirit is never absent the presence of the Son and the Father. The trinitarian nature of the argument is in the background precisely to bring to the fore the oft-forgotten personhood of the Spirit in the discussion of divine holiness.

[39]Kelly Kapic writes, "Real spirituality is not fundamentally about self-improvement but about an intimacy and communion with the triune God that transforms the believer's life." "Evangelical Holiness: Assumptions in John Owen's Theology of Christian Spirituality," in *Life in the Spirit: Spiritual Formation in Theological Perspective*, ed. Jeffrey P. Greenman and George Kalantzis (Downers Grove, IL: IVP Academic, 2010), p. 101.

brought near" to God (Eph 2:13). Our proximity to the triune God restores the church to its status as "living" rather than "dead," a proximity entirely dependent on the reconciling work of Christ redemptively present to the church by the Holy Spirit.

WHOSE LAW? WHICH ANTINOMIANISM?

Paul's claim that justification accrues by faith alone (Rom 4) leads him to ask the question, "Are we to continue in sin that grace may abound?" (Rom 6:1). This question arises at the end of Paul's argument in Romans 5, where he has made the case that human disobedience brings death and Jesus' obedience has brought life. There is no mention in Romans 5 of an instrumental role given to a believer's obedience in the matter of salvation. In Romans 4 Paul made it clear there is no "boast" to be made by Israelites (nor Gentiles) before God. As Romans 2 proves, it is not merely that there is to be no boast in Israel's privileged status as possessors of Torah, but there is no boast because of their inability to obey Torah. In contrast to earlier midrash traditions that understood Abraham to have been justified on the basis of obedience to God and thereby to have a "boast" before God, Paul argued instead that Abraham believed (in contrast to working) and he was reckoned as righteous.[40] Faith lays no claim to a boast for the one who exercises it because its hope and trust is in another. Neither Abraham nor his natural descendants, the Israelites, were to be counted as righteous on the basis of their obedience, not because obedience was not requisite to righteousness, but because they were in actual fact disobedient sinners, as were the Gentiles.

Having made the case in this fashion, Paul confronts the next natural question: If obedience cannot bring salvation, should we disobey and thereby have more of God's grace of forgiveness to enjoy? This so-called antinomian accusation of Romans 6:1 (repeated in Rom 6:15; 7:7; 9:14) addresses the consequences of their union with Christ. Nowhere in Romans 6 does Paul broach the possibility that the believer's obedience sustains his or her union with Christ. Christ sustains that relationship. His work (the entire messianic mission) and his continued mediating presence through the Spirit is the sole ground of their assurance of salvation (Rom 5:5).

---

[40]Simon Gathercole makes this argument at length in *Where Is Boasting? Early Jewish Soteriology and Paul's Response in Romans 1–5* (Grand Rapids: Eerdmans, 2002), pp. 232-47.

The rhetorical question of Romans 6:1 and Romans 6:15 points at the reality that Christ is the answer to the antinomian accusation. Being united to Christ means being united to his rule as covenant Lord. The church's relationship to Christ is such that his presence continues to fulfill the terms of the covenant in her life. The paradox of sin and grace in the covenant becomes clear as Paul writes in the imperative, "Let not sin therefore reign in your mortal body, to make you obey its passions" (Rom 6:12).[41] Remembering that "sin" is not an external force, but simply another way of speaking of the self, Paul is saying, "Be free from the rule of yourself."[42] But wherein is the "rule of self" broken? In none other than the presence of Christ as mediated by the Holy Spirit, whose temple is now the gathered believers. It is the temple of the Holy Spirit not as a function of the causal cooperation of the human will, but because in fact the Holy Spirit is dwelling with his people.[43]

The antinomian accusation is answered by appeal to the ongoing presence of the Holy Spirit, for which there is a "natural" reaction of delight in the believer. The accusation is not answered by an appeal to greater moral responsibility on the part of the believer. The anti-antinomian is the one who confesses that Christ lives and those who were formerly dead now live because they are near him. "The death he died he died to sin, once for all, but the life he lives he lives to God" (Rom 6:10). This exchange (death and life) is made present by the Holy Spirit and has become the sum and substance of sanctification.

Accordingly the law no longer exercises its judicial function over the believer. It no longer accuses or rewards. As Paul affirms in 1 Timothy 1:9, "The law is not laid down for the just but for the lawless and disobedient." The law

---

[41]Hunsinger comments, "Despite the sin which clings to us so closely," wrote Luther, "yet grace is sufficient to enable us to be counted entirely and completely righteous in God's sight because his grace does not come in portions and pieces, separately, like so many gifts; rather it takes us up completely into its embrace for the sake of Christ our mediator and intercessor, and in order that the gifts may take root in us." "What Karl Barth Learned from Martin Luther," p. 297.

[42]John Webster writes, "The polarization of freedom and obedience that is endemic in modern anthropology is part of the pathology of the modern spiritual history of the self. In the freedom given to me in Christ, I am bound to God's grace." *Holiness*, p. 94.

[43]Michael Horton remarks, "In causal and metaphysical grammars justification and sanctification becomes a debate over the mechanics of the inner life. In communicative and covenantal grammars justification has to do with the Covenant Lord pronouncing a courtroom verdict upon the servant [Jesus] that issues in a completely new ontological ethic and eschatological orientation including the inner life in its sweep." *Covenant and Salvation: Union with Christ* (Louisville, KY: Westminster John Knox, 2007).

loses its power in Christ. Justification has removed the weight of the law on believers. There can be no return to the forensic character of the law in sanctification, lest the completed work of Christ be undermined. Antinomianism type 1 simply affirms this reality. The law is no longer the basis by which our place in the covenant with God is based. Accordingly the law does not return to its judicial function in sustaining that place in the covenant with God. In sanctification the law functions in a nonforensic fashion. It no longer has an accusatory or a rewarding function. As Paul says to believers, "You also have died to the law through the body of Christ, so that you may belong to another" (Rom 7:4). Believers belong forensically to Christ (in justification) by virtue of which they now stand in a different (i.e., nonlegal) relationship to the law.

What is the nonlegal relationship to the law in which believers now stand? It is a sapiential relationship. The law is now the source of wisdom in the life of believers.[44] It is pedagogical rather than judicial in its function.[45] Wisdom is no less normative than forensically oriented law, but its "force" is surely different. Wisdom celebrates that which is good, and thereby draws its adherents to how (theological) reality works rather than uniquely how one is punished or rewarded.[46] The consequence of disobeying or obeying wisdom is not punishment or reward, but rather dissatisfaction or satisfaction.

Antinomianism type 2 denies that there is any wisdom in the ongoing functions of the law. "Freedom from the law" in this case denies that there is a moral center that holds. All moral norms are negotiable and liable to cultural reinterpretations. In contrast with antinomianism type 2, Paul continues to appeal to the normative character of moral commands, not in

---

[44]This is not to claim that the authors of the New Testament depicted the law as equivalent to wisdom. The "law" with some exceptions in the New Testament refers to the Mosaic law and is most often a reference to the Sinai covenant. Wisdom on the other hand is much less historically tied down in the hands of the New Testament writers. Its referent is also far more ambiguous, though not thereby any less consequential. For two different treatments of law and wisdom in the hands of the New Testament writers, see Eckhard J. Schnabel, *Law and Wisdom from Ben Sira to Paul* (Tübingen: Mohr Siebeck, 1985); and C. Marvin Pate, *The Reverse of the Curse: Paul, Wisdom and the Law* (Tübingen: Mohr Siebeck, 2000).

[45]This is Bernhard Lohse's term in depicting Luther's view of the law in the life of the Christian. See his *Martin Luther's Theology: Its Historical and Systematic Development*, trans. Roy A. Harrisville (Minneapolis: Fortress, 1999).

[46]See Roland Murphy, "The Personification of Wisdom" in *Wisdom in Ancient Israel*, ed. John Day, Robert P. Gordon and H. G. M. Williamson (Cambridge: Cambridge University Press, 1995), pp. 222-33.

virtue of their judicial function, but rather in terms of their source in the character of God (e.g., Rom 6:13-14).

James goes so far as to call the law in the life of the Christian the "law of liberty" (Jas 1:25; 2:12). Accordingly it is the law in its penalty phase that no longer functions forensically. Its "judgment" is now found in the delight it brings as one follows its wisdom. James writes of the "blessing in his doing" of the law (Jas 1:25). Like wisdom, the law of liberty is its own good. Its blessing is intrinsic because, in fact, as we know from the larger witness of the canon, the law of liberty is Christ as mediated by the Spirit.

The history of the antinomian controversy has often focused theologically on the third use of the law famously enunciated in the Formula of Concord, section 6.[47] One of Luther's close associates at Wittenberg, Johann Agricola, appears to have started the controversy by dismissing the usefulness of the Sinai covenant for Christians. Philipp Melanchthon sought to persuade Luther that Agricola's influence should be stopped lest Protestants be susceptible to Roman Catholic criticisms of promoting a license to sin.[48] Luther did finally succeed in securing Agricola's recantation of his views, though it is not clear from the historical record whether Luther himself ever felt comfortable with embedding the third use of the law into Christian confession.[49] There is little doubt, however, that he saw benefit for believers in paying attention devotionally to the Ten Commandments as the summation of the law. His Small Catechism urges on believers that God "promises grace and blessing to all that keep these commandments."[50]

In the language of the Formula of Concord, the third use of the law is "a fixed rule according to which they [believers] are to regulate and direct their whole life." While careful to exempt believers from the curse of the law, the formula nonetheless affirms that because believers are still sinners, they are

---

[47]The formula was written largely by Martin Chemnitz and David Chytraeus in 1577. It can be found in any of the standard collections of the Book of Concord such as *The Book of Concord: The Confessions of the Evangelical Lutheran Church*, ed. Robert Kolb and Timothy J. Wengert, trans. Charles Arand (Minneapolis: Fortress, 2000).

[48]See Scott R. Murray, *Law, Life and the Living God* (St. Louis: Concordia, 2002) for a helpful historical introduction to the controversy.

[49]On Luther's relation to the "third use" controversy, see James A. Nestingen, "Changing Definitions: The Law in Formula VI," *Concordia Theological Quarterly* 69 (2005): pp. 259-70.

[50]*Triglot Concordia: The Symbolical Books of the Evangelical Lutheran Church* (St. Louis: Concordia, 1921), p. 678.

still in need of judicial restraints on the desires of the flesh. However, the formula also distinguishes the works of the law from the fruits of the Spirit in such a fashion that the judicial function of the law ceases to operate normatively in the life of believers. "Works, which are done according to the Law, are and are called works of the Law as long as they are only extorted from man by urging the punishment and threatening of God's wrath. Fruits of the Spirit, however, are the works which the Spirit of God who dwells in believers works through the regenerate, and which are done by believers so far as they are regenerate [spontaneously and freely], as though they knew of no command, threat, or reward" (6.4–5). Sinners relate to the law as that which condemns and threatens. Believers relate to the Spirit as the one in whom there is divine life and according to whom they walk with neither threat nor reward before them. The law remains an ethical standard in its third use, but it has lost its forensic bite. It can no longer condemn or punish. The formula is clear that the law cannot justify or contribute anything to a person's righteousness, but it can point the way toward peace and justice in the life of the believing community. It does this when the Holy Spirit works on the human heart through the gospel and drives the believer to the repentance that arises from faith.[51]

It is fair to say that many later Protestant traditions reasserted a forensic bite in the use of the law in the church.[52] Alarmed by the moral laxity of the believing community, the church increasingly wielded the law as a stern taskmaster, with the hope that moral rigor could be recovered among those who too often appeared to them as lapsed Christians. Moral progress often became the primary evidence of a believer's sanctification, a progress that could be measured by appeal to some observable command of the law. Questionable and odious evangelical practices arose identifying objective standards and practices to verify moral progress.[53] In the twentieth century

---

[51]Nestingen, "Changing Definitions," p. 260.

[52]It is ironic that though Calvin uses the specific language of the three uses of the law (*Institutes* 2.7.12), it is nowhere picked up in any of the historic Reformed confessions. See Merwyn S. Johnson, "Calvin's Handling of the Third Use of the Law and Its Problems," in *Calviniana: Ideas and Influence of Jean Calvin*, ed. Robert Schnucker (Kirksville, MO: Sixteenth Century Journal Publishers, 1988), pp. 33-51.

[53]Berkouwer writes disapprovingly of this general evangelical approach: "Sanctification is not a process, certainly not a moral process, but it is being holy in Christ and having part, through faith, in his righteousness." *Faith and Sanctification*, p. 104.

a variety of strands of evangelicalism gave the law an increasing stature in doctrines of sanctification as a reaction to the perception of "cheap grace" in American Christianity.[54] Cheap grace was simply another name for the spiritual accommodation to a consumer and therapeutic culture of American evangelicalism. As a version of antinomianism, cheap grace may appear at a distance from the moral antinomianism in Protestant liberalism. In actual fact, cheap-grace evangelicals and moral-antinomian Protestant liberals share a common antinomian heritage, though they situate it on vastly different theological paradigms. They are both versions of antinomianism type 2 insofar as they implicitly reject a moral center in God, though they do it for different reasons. Protestant liberalism has been driven by the concern for ideological relevancy, and sought a revisionist Christian ethic that more nearly matched the ethos of their times.[55] Cheap-grace evangelicalism was never a coherent movement but more precisely a set of evangelical tendencies enamored of cultural relevance and attached to a doctrinally conservative confession.[56] The rejection of cheap-grace evangelicalism or of moral-antinomian liberalism, however, does not warrant a forensic understanding of sanctification. What each aberration requires is an affirmation of the enduring relevance of law but not in a forensic manner. The response to both tendencies lies in affirming a sapiential "use" of the law in the life of the Christian community and not the forensic use of the law.

A brief word should be said about the moral imperatives of Scripture. An extended account of the law in the life of the Christian community must wrestle with the covenantal context of moral imperatives in their concrete historical situations. There may be universal moral principles, but the moral imperatives found in Scripture always apply to parties in a covenant. Casting an eye across the canon, it is important to distinguish those dimensions of the covenant(s) that have been fulfilled in Christ from those dimensions that are ongoing parts of the covenant, as well as those dimensions of the covenant that will be part of the consummated eternal relationship with the triune God.

---

[54]This is Dietrich Bonhoeffer's memorable phrase in *The Cost of Discipleship*, trans. R. H. Fuller (New York: Macmillan, 1955).

[55]Classic examples might include Joseph Fletcher, *Situation Ethics: The New Morality* (Philadelphia: Westminster Press, 1962); and John A. T. Robinson, *Honest to God* (London: SCM Press, 1963).

[56]See Eldin Villafane, *Beyond Cheap Grace: A Call to Radical Discipleship, Incarnation, and Justice* (Grand Rapids: Eerdmans, 2006).

Careful and hard exegetical work is required to properly differentiate the moral dimensions of covenants as they are enacted across the entire breath of Scripture. And surely an adequate hermeneutical framework is required to situate the exegetical conclusions in their appropriate canonical context. Though it is not the purpose of this essay to accomplish those tasks, it is imperative that any discussion of the law in the life of the believing community must be adequately supple and nuanced to account for the diverse historical contexts of law in their redemptive place in the canon.[57]

SANCTIFICATION, IDOLATRY AND THE RESTORATION OF THE SENSES

An important conceptual bridge linking moral imperatives (law) and wisdom (i.e., forensic and sapiential uses of the law) in the canon is the conceptual framework of worship and idolatry. God creates humans in such a fashion that their greatest delight is to be found in the worship of their Creator. By contrast idolatry is the corrupted worship of an alternative object of honor and respect and thereby leads to endless dissatisfaction.[58] Idolatry and worship are deeply personal and relational and thus often closely related in the canon to marital metaphors for (in)fidelity.[59]

Humans are constituted to reflect that which they worship.[60] In this sense they are created to image God. Worshiping an idol not only subverts the relationship between the creature and the Creator but also corrupts the creature insofar as they begin to reflect the "dead" idols. Worship of an idol is an offense against the created order of things and thereby becomes a moral offense in the covenant between the Creator and the creature. Death is the "natural" consequence of idolatry and becomes the penal consequence of it as well.

---

[57]These concerns are manifestly important, for example, when considering the ongoing force of the fifth commandment: "Honor your father and your mother, that your days may be long in the land the LORD your God is giving you" (Ex 20:12). How is "land" to be interpreted as applicable to the new covenant? However one answers this question, the historical context of the Sinai covenant must be taken into account.

[58]Moshe Halbertal, *Idolatry* (Cambridge, MA: Harvard University Press, 1992). See especially chap. 1, "Idolatry and Betrayal," pp. 9-36.

[59]See Raymond C. Ortlund Jr., *Whoredom: God's Unfaithful Wife in Biblical Theology* (Grand Rapids: Eerdmans, 1996).

[60]G. K. Beale, *We Become What We Worship: A Biblical Theology of Idolatry* (Downers Grove, IL: IVP Academic, 2008).

It is appropriate to speak of worship as wisdom (Ps 111:10) and also to speak of worship as commanded (Deut 6:4). The worship of the living God gives rise to a natural delight of the creature in his or her Creator. Humans are made in such a fashion to find their delight in the One who made them.[61] In the language of the psalmist, the "splendor of holiness" is the sufficient ground for drawing the human agents into the worship of their Creator and covenant Lord. Worship is also a moral command in the covenant that regulates the relationship of the Creator and creature. So the command to love the Lord your God with all your heart, soul and strength is at the center of the covenant between YHWH and Israel, even as Jesus' summary of the whole law begins with the same command (Mk 12:28-34).

As a kind of wisdom, worship celebrates that which is good, and thereby draws its adherents to how (theological) reality works rather than uniquely how one is punished or rewarded. The central consequence of worship is not reward but satisfaction. Though there is a moral character to worship, moral imperatives do not function in our union with Christ as laws that punish or reward, but rather as principles of worship.

As an act of corrupted worship, idolatry depicts sin along a spectrum of freedom and slavery.[62] Idolatry asserts independence from God and enslavement to the idols. Worship that arises out of the gospel, by contrast, frees one from the idols and makes one a servant of the living God. The drama of redemption plays out in part as a drama of competing objects of worship in the "eyes" of human persons.[63] "Eyes" function not only as organs by which one perceives the material world but also as windows into the human heart through which objects of worship are appraised.[64]

"Having eyes but not seeing" is scriptural shorthand for worshiping as ultimate something other than YHWH (Is 6). Sensory-malfunction language connotes that sense in which persons relate in analogous ways to objects of

---

[61]Leora Batnitzky, reflecting on Franz Rosenzweig's work on idolatry, writes, "The root of idolatry is a misunderstanding about the ways in which meaning is created and human identity is constituted," in *Idolatry and Representation* (Princeton, NJ: Princeton University Press, 2000), p. 6.

[62]Timothy J. Keller, *Counterfeit Gods: The Empty Promises of Money, Sex, and Power, and the Only Hope That Matters* (New York: Dutton, 2009).

[63]See Richard Lints, "Imaging and Idolatry: The Sociality of Personhood and the Ironic Reversals of the Canon," in *Personal Identity in Theological Perspective*, ed. Richard Lints, Michael Horton and Mark Talbot (Grand Rapids: Eerdmans, 2006), pp. 204-25.

[64]Eph 1:18 uses the phrase "the eyes of your heart" in just this fashion.

worship as they do the material objects.[65] Hearing sounds is a function both of having the appropriate sensory organs in working order as well as the presence of "sounds." Having "ears to hear" is a manner of speaking in the canon that points at having the appropriate worship organs in working order in the presence of the divine Word (e.g., Deut 29:4; Ps 115:6; 135:17).

The "worship organ" that Scripture speaks of most is the human heart. It is the place where one's treasures are stored (Mt 6:21). It is that from which flows every kind of evil (Mt 15:18). Being given a new heart is to be given a properly functioning disposition to worship YHWH rather than idols (Ezek 11:19). This promise of a new heart is the promise of the new creation in which God will re-create his people (Deut 30:6). As an act of the new creation, the gift of a new heart is nothing other than a properly functioning organ to worship God. As God redeems humans, the human heart begins to find delight in that which delights God.

Faith is the theological category that depicts this orientation of delight in the God who redeems. It is not a faith once and done, but rather an ongoing faith that looks to God in Christ as its proper object of worship. It is sometimes weak, sometimes strong, but in its inner direction, its hope lies outside of itself in the God who redeems. By the presence of the Holy Spirit, the doxological nerve endings have been brought back to life, by means of which they begin to find satisfaction in the covenantal relation to God, and in whom they begin to sense the delight of that which is genuinely good.

Conclusion

In sanctification it is not a believer's moral progress in view, but rather the (relative) restoration of their worship organs. In the Christian life, the moral imperatives of Scripture guide the understanding of worship and many of its attendant consequences.[66] Obedience is motivated not by reward but by delight. Obedience motivated by reward is more nearly a sign of corrupted worship. And so no Protestant doctrine of sanctification ought to affirm the "rewards of obedience," as Hodge has done. This promotes both the very

---

[65]See Beale, *We Become What We Worship*, pp. 71-84.

[66]One of the chief consequences of worship is the love of neighbor. The summary of the law in Matthew 22 connects love of God with love of neighbor on the grounds that the latter is *like* the former.

"boasting" that the New Testament authors reject and the enslavement to self-interest at the heart of most idolatry. By contrast faith as the enduring orientation, which shuns any "boast" before God, resists rewards as its motivation. It continues to cling to the God who redeems because God alone satisfies hearts.[67]

While this account has not exhaustively depicted the nature of sanctifying faith, it has argued for the exteriority of faith as central to any Protestant doctrine of sanctification. If the law can no longer condemn or reward, then obedience must arise in believers from the orientation of faith, which looks to God as the one alone who will ultimately satisfy their longings. This has suggested that moral imperatives apply to believers as a form of wisdom. Obedience that flows from the gospel in the Christian life arises from a delight in God. The danger of immorality, like the danger of idolatry, is restrained in the life of the believer not by appeal to penal consequences (nor rewards for obedience) but rather by a continued proclamation of the gospel in all its glorious richness. Christians are to live by faith because Christians no longer live under the threat of the law, but in the promise of the gospel.

---

[67]A necessary reminder is that the disobedience of believers results not in condemnation but in dissatisfaction, itself a sign that God's redeeming work is not yet finished in believers. That dissatisfaction is also a reminder of the present condition of the human heart wherein believers sometimes "do not do the good I want, but the evil I do not want," even as they "see in my members another law waging war against the law of my mind" (Rom 7:19, 23).

3

SANCTIFICATION BY FAITH?

Henri Blocher

En hagiasmō pneumatos kai pistei alētheias.

2 Thessalonians 2:13

Why put the question mark in my title? Is it warranted when such passages as 2 Thessalonians 2:13 and Acts 26:18 link faith and sanctification so closely? Indeed, I would not deny what John Calvin preached: "By faith we are obedient to God, by faith we are sanctified in his service,"[1] and I confess with Herman Bavinck that "faith . . . is the means of sanctification par excellence."[2] But one must admit that the way faith operates in sanctification—the exact relationship between the two—has been variously construed and remains somewhat obscure. "Being completely holy by faith alone" just as one is "righteous by faith alone"—the slogan of Robert Pearsall Smith—is upheld by a specific strain of evangelical spirituality, and deserves scrutiny.[3]

The present contribution aims at reaffirming, with some nuances, the cardinal role of faith in sanctification, including the relevance of the *sola fide*

---

[1] Second sermon on Ephesians (on Eph 1:3-4), *CO* 51:264. The preceding words are, "Faith is supreme: through faith we receive the Holy Spirit, through faith we endure our hardships" (my translation).

[2] Herman Bavinck, *Reformed Dogmatics*, vol. 3, *Sin and Salvation in Christ*, trans. John Vriend, ed. John Bolt (Grand Rapids: Baker Academic, 2006), p. 257 (§482).

[3] Ibid., p. 246, on Pearsall Smith. There appear to be contemporary evangelical expressions of this as well.

principle; then it looks at comparing this role with the role of faith in justification, especially in view of the teaching—in the Wesleyan tradition—of a distinct exercise of faith necessary for sanctification (implying a "second blessing" of some sort); finally, certain issues involved are explored in order to make some rather uncommon suggestions. To properly begin, however, I will summarize the view of sanctification that this inquiry presupposes.

SANCTIFICATION: DEFINITIONS, AGENCY AND FAITH

Sanctificare means making *sanctus*, "holy." "Sanctification," translating *hagiasmos* in New Testament Greek,[4] is the name for that operation that makes God's people "holy" for him. Part of what makes the idea of sanctification difficult to handle, however, is that it involves different (though related) polarities.

One polarity is that of *consecration* and *moral change*. Undoubtedly, the background of the notion, in the Old Testament, is the panreligious sense of the "sacred," the mystery that both terrifies and fascinates (*tremendum et fascinans*). It defines itself by separation from what is "profane" (*profanum*, "before the temple") and what is common (*to koinon*, which takes on the sense of unclean, unholy, Acts 10:14). In other words, things and people are "sanctified" when they are consecrated for and dedicated to exclusive divine use; they are set apart in order to belong to God as his special property (*sĕgullâ* for Israel as a holy nation in Ex 19:5-6). Yet the character of Yahweh entails that the requirements of holiness be expounded in terms of righteousness, truthfulness and solidarity; thus sanctification also denotes moral change, a fact that becomes more and more prominent in the Old Testament, and dominates in the New. We shall come back later to this combination of religious and ethical dimensions, but it may be said that classical evangelical thought has been mostly preoccupied with moral transformation. The locus of the change has been identified as the "subjective disposition and *habitus* . . . , the whole man in heart, disposition, inclination, desire, motive, interest, ambition and purpose."[5]

---

[4]On *hagiasmos* see the fine synthesis offered by David Peterson, *Possessed by God: A New Testament Theology of Sanctification and Holiness* (Leicester: Apollos, 1995), pp. 139-42.

[5]John Murray (in his chapter on regeneration, but the wording suits what theologians have held of sanctification), *Collected Writings*, vol. 2, *Select Lectures in Systematic Theology* (Edinburgh: Banner of Truth, 1977), p. 170.

A second polarity is that of the *initial and decisive moment* in a person's temporal existence and the *process* that follows to the end of earthly life. The New Testament uses *hagiasmos* for the foundational event of in-breaking grace and the beginning of new life, the life of the coming age. This event breaks with former allegiances and modes of behavior "once for all" (Heb 10:10)[6] and coincides with conversion/regeneration:[7] hence the designation "the saints" for all church members. But the New Testament also speaks of sanctification as a task still to be completed, as a work in progress (1 Thess 5:23; the present participles in Heb 2:11; Rev 22:11). The question then arises concerning possible discontinuities in the process. The language of evangelical theology has tended to select "regeneration" for the initial work and "sanctification" for the process: "It [sanctification] is distinguished from regeneration as growth from birth, or as the strengthening of a holy disposition from the original impartation of it."[8] As a reaction against the one-sidedness of the classical concentration on process, mainly moral process—sin itself, with which those being sanctified are to wrestle, being understood in moral terms—recent scholarship has emphasized the "definitive" event at the beginning and "making sacred" (not virtuous) as the root meaning.[9] What should stimulate thought is the very presence of the bipolarities, their inner necessity and the problems that are attached.

VOCABULARY

The relevant evidence from Scripture is not confined to uses of the lexical families of *qdš* and *hagios*. "The exegete's temptation," says Graham Cole, "is not to see ideas of sanctification in biblical texts because certain specific words [of those families] are not used."[10] Indeed, the same topic is dealt with in other terms, and these illuminate other facets. When sanctification is spoken of, it

---

[6]All biblical translations are mine, unless otherwise noted.

[7]The refinements urged by John Murray fail to convince me. He argues in *Select Lectures*, p. 285 n. 2 that "definitive sanctification" should not be subsumed "under the topic 'regeneration.'"

[8]Augustus H. Strong, *Systematic Theology* (1907; repr., Philadelphia: Judson, 1958), p. 871.

[9]I feel that such a reaction is not totally absent from Peterson's fine monograph. See *Possessed by God*, pp. 35-36, 43-44, and 81, where he tends to minimize the moral dimension; on p. 75 the injunction in Heb 12:14 is interpreted: "The readers were to seek holiness as a practical expression of their sanctification in Christ."

[10]Graham Cole, "Sanctification," in *Dictionary for Theological Interpretation of the Bible*, ed. Kevin J. Vanhoozer (Grand Rapids: Baker Academic, 2005), p. 721b.

is very often commingled with the idea of cleansing: perfecting holiness means purifying oneself from what defiles flesh or spirit (2 Cor 7:1).[11] This is not far from healing, for sickness often produces uncleanness and therefore is not far from renewal. Renewal, the gift of resurrection life, is a work of the new creation; it enables Christ's disciple to walk in newness of life, to "grow in grace" and into the likeness of Jesus Christ himself (see 1 Jn 3:3), who is being "formed" in the believer's life (Gal 4:19). It is already glorification, as Peterson argues,[12] a transformation "from glory to glory" (2 Cor 3:18).

Van Ruler, says G. C. Berkouwer, "offered a collection of terms he found in Kuyper: infusion of new life, a new capacity, irradiation, to plant a germ of life, new habits of will, the descent of imperishable seed in the soil of our heart, to implant in our innermost a new attitude, to change the innermost core of our being. And the verbs are: to infuse, to irradiate, to increate, to inculcate, to implant, to enter into, to descend into, to cultivate."[13] Apart from the predominance—quite typical in Kuyper—of metaphors drawn from biology, the most disputed notion in Kuyper's understanding is the infusion of grace. For many critics (especially on the Barthian side), it smacks of Roman Catholicism. Berkouwer shows that it does belong to the Reformed heritage[14] and is warranted by the language of Scripture, provided one avoids the *donum superadditum* scheme and a "substantialist view of grace."[15] "Infusion" is indeed acceptable if we remember that it is a metaphor and that grace is a personal attitude and activity on God's part, changing the human *habitus* in a covenantal context (interchange and dialogue). The term guards against a view of grace of the *as if* kind, or against a merely dialectical association: *simul iustus et peccator*. I would still prefer "imparted," as it is less metaphorical and less liable to misunderstanding.

---

[11]*Hagnos* in Greek is a further cognate of *hagios*.

[12]Peterson, *Possessed by God*, pp. 120-26.

[13]G. C. Berkouwer, *Faith and Sanctification*, trans. John Vriend (Grand Rapids: Eerdmans, 1952), p. 79.

[14]Ibid., pp. 79-84. On p. 82 he quotes Herman Bavinck's *Gereformeerde Dogmatiek* (Kampen: J. H. Bos, 1901), 4:234: "The error is that Rome made this infused righteousness the ground for forgiveness and hence built religion on the foundation of morality. Believers do, however, become partakers of the righteousness of Christ through infusion."

[15]Berkouwer, *Faith and Sanctification*, pp. 79-81, 85, and 87. *Donum superadditum*, a gift superadded, is the phrase Roman Catholic theology used for righteousness added by grace to nature (itself weakened by sinfulness but not spiritually dead); the same theology tends to speak of grace as a substance, a thing.

The Agent

The agent of sanctification is *God* (e.g., 1 Thess 5:23). Here also, however, an interesting duality surfaces in Scripture: those addressed by God's Word are commanded to sanctify *themselves* (e.g., Lev 11:44; 2 Cor 7:1, *epitelountes*, meaning normally "bringing about, achieving"). The form "seek [or 'pursue,' *diōkete*] . . . sanctification" (Heb 12:14) suggests how the two (God's act and ours) can come together, as does the reference to the Holy Spirit, inasmuch as he is God within us, God penetrating and moving our innermost self (indeed, taking our side in prayer, praying with us, Rom 8:26-27; Rev 22:17). Sanctification is specifically assigned to the Spirit by weighty pronouncements (e.g., 2 Thess 2:13; 1 Pet 1:2)—remembering that the Spirit is the Spirit of Christ, and that his mission consists in taking what is Christ's and communicating it to us through the Word (Jn 16:14-15), thus making us partakers of Christ.

Faith

The Spirit's "masterpiece" (*chef d'oeuvre*) is *faith*, as Calvin said, through which he makes us one with our head, the Lord Christ, who through his death and resurrection becomes the fountain of all spiritual benefits.[16] Here I simply adopt the traditional analysis of saving faith (*fides*) as involving *notitia*, *assensus* and *fiducia*,[17] insisting, however, on the way the three components are intimately interwoven. Certainly there can be no *responsible* trusting without a minimal amount of information and a positive evaluation of its quality, but can there be *true* assent in matters of life and death without a measure of prior trust? Such a schizophrenic inconsistency is ultimately unthinkable: if trust is missing, somewhere assent itself has vacillated (sinners are inconsistent, but not *perfectly* inconsistent). And even knowledge of the relevant information depends on the framework, reference points and governing schemes provided by a commitment of faith: whoever refuses to trust the God of Truth can see nothing in *exact* truth, and his or her darkened understanding always distorts in some way or other the *notitia* that was gained (demons do not

---

[16]John Calvin, *Institutes of the Christian Religion*, trans. Ford Lewis Battles, ed. John T. McNeill, Library of Christian Classics (Philadelphia: Westminster Press, 1960), 3.1.4.

[17]"Knowledge," "assent" and "trust." See John Murray's chapter on faith, *Select Lectures*, pp. 235-63.

know in truth; Jas 2:19). This comment is indebted to the Augustinian (and neo-Calvinist) insight that faith comes first and provides reason with its roots, orientations, horizons and criteria:[18] thus we must believe in order to understand.[19]

The other feature of faith that should be mentioned here is the personal bond it implies, a movement away from self toward another, who is the object of faith. Already, ordinary belief is characterized by the mediation of witness: I know what I believe because I trust a trustworthy witness, no longer relying on my own resources but making myself dependent on another. (And if the witness has a superior quality, the knowledge thus mediately obtained is *surer* than the knowledge I would gain from direct experience.) In matters of great existential import, faith implies adhering to a person, even a form of covenantal union.

SANCTIFICATION EXCLUSIVELY BY FAITH—SOLA FIDE

The vast majority of scholars would grant that sanctification, especially if a process, includes human behavior, acts, or *works*—and this at once raises a question. Since "by faith," when it qualifies justification, rules out human works[20]—if by faith, not by works (Rom 3:27-28; 4:5)—can sanctification be, with works, "by faith"? The answer of evangelical tradition is a resounding yes. Berkouwer claims and proclaims, "The Sola-fide is the only sound foundation of sanctification."[21] He insists that such an insight is a hallmark of Reformed theology. It is also found in Bavinck.[22] The Reformed Baptist Andrew Fuller preached, "For the accomplishment of the church's salvation it requires that it should be sanc-

---

[18]Physicist and philosopher Michael Polanyi called these the "fiducial framework," needed for all scientific endeavors.

[19]Augustine would quote Is 7:9b in support—in the old Latin translation he used (not very accurate). My brief summary cannot enter into important distinctions. Augustine also acknowledged the converse: we must understand in order to believe; his focus was on humility and on the purification of the human mind, that its mirror may reflect the light of the Logos. Later followers of Augustine emphasized other aspects.

[20]It is not possible to show here that "works" should not be restricted to works done in compliance with the Mosaic law, especially ritual works: Paul's logic requires the widest meaning.

[21]Berkouwer, *Faith and Sanctification*, p. 42 n. 3. See also p. 28: "The immediate consequence of the 'sola-fide' doctrine was exactly this indissoluble bond between faith and sanctification."

[22]Herman Bavinck, *Sin and Salvation in Christ*, pp. 248-49 (§480). See also the quotation from Calvin with which we started.

tified and cleansed by faith in the *word* of God," and "We are sanctified by the faith that is in him."[23]

Scripture offers sufficient warrant for such a proposition. It seems to follow from the message for the weak and despised who believe in him. Christ Jesus has become for us wisdom from God—wisdom expressed in a threefold way: righteousness (presumably in free justification), *and sanctification*, and redemption (1 Cor 1:30). Bavinck boldly writes, "They have received Christ not only as righteousness but also as ἁγιασμος (*hagiasmos*)— not holiness, as (ἁγιοτης) *hagiotēs* or ἁγιωσυνη (*hagiōsynē*), but sanctification—so that what is in view here is not the result but the progression of sanctification or consecration to God."[24] Faith appropriates what Christ is for us, and this is true whether we emphasize progress or not. Negatively, sanctification cannot be done "in the energy of the flesh," that is, with the nature with which we were born, for it is hostile to God and *cannot* please him (Rom 8:7-8). The new disposition implanted[25] by regeneration is not enough if isolated from God's actual activity in believers. Paul disclaims any adequacy (*hikanotēs*) in himself (2 Cor 3:5) and exclaims, "Who is weak, and I am not weak? Who is made to stumble, and I do not burn?" (2 Cor 11:29 HCSB). Paul is conscious that believers are in danger of falling back into the mechanisms of the "flesh" (Gal 3:3). When he legitimately boasts that he has worked hard, harder than the other apostles, he hastens to add, "Yet not I, but God's grace that [has been] with me" (1 Cor 15:10 HCSB). Even John, when he teaches that whoever is born of God does not sin (present tense), explains, "The One who was begotten of God [aorist, clearly designating the Son Jesus Christ] keeps him" (1 Jn 5:18). The paradox of sanctification is that, as we work, God himself works in us—through Jesus Christ—what is well-pleasing to him (Heb 13:21; cf. Is 26:12, "All our works, you have performed for us"). This receives the strongest expression in Philippians 2:13: "He is *God* the one who operates in you *both* to will and to operate, according to his

---

[23]Sermon on Eph 5:25-27, in *The Complete Works of the Rev. Andrew Fuller* (London: Henry G. Bohn, 1848), p. 721 (a and b). On cleansing, he adds (p. 721a): the term "frequently denotes the removal of sin, as to its condemning as well as its defiling influence. The blood of Christ operates in both ways; and the faith of him, in different respects, both justifies and sanctifies."

[24]Herman Bavinck, *Reformed Dogmatics*, vol. 4, *Holy Spirit, Church, and New Creation*, trans. John Vriend, ed. John Bolt (Grand Rapids: Eerdmans, 2008), p. 235; see also p. 250.

[25]The image in Jas 1:21.

good purposes."[26] This is why the marks of sanctification are the fruit *of the Spirit* (Gal 5:22-23). Salvation presumably embraces both justification and sanctification, it delivers us from both the guilt and the unclean slavery to sin, and "*through faith* were you saved" (Eph 2:8). Sanctification is *sola fide* because it happens "in Christ," through our clinging to him and our being conformed to him by that Spirit-enacted union with him, including concentration (focusing on our new identity in Christ) and "de-centration" (moving away from an egocentric perspective to one concerned with the other).

THE ROLE OF THE LAW

Since the apostle appears to make faith and law mutually exclusive (e.g., in Gal 3:12, "the law is not of faith"; and Gal 3:23-25; cf. Rom 3:21-22; 4:13-16; 10:5-6), the role of the law in sanctification (by faith) calls for clarification. Being a traditional bone of contention between Lutheran and Reformed theologians, the topic of the law has been abundantly revisited in recent decades, with a flood of learned literature generated by the "new perspective(s) on Paul." We cannot even begin to survey so complex a debate.[27] My view is this: Paul (and the whole New Testament agrees) teaches that the law, as a regime of justification, has been rendered obsolete for believers in Jesus Christ: in its "pedagogical" use.[28] It is in *that* sense that we are no longer "under the law." The "didactic" use, however, he retains— almost self-evidently. Paul is not without law (1 Cor 9:21); the law is "spiritual," a weighty qualification (Rom 7:14). He freely quotes from the Old Testament legislation, and the commandments have obvious normative force (Eph 6:2): there is no divergence between him and Matthew in this respect. The leading and rule of the Spirit (Gal 5:16, 18) does not operate through blind instinct, or emotional spontaneity, but with and through the Word, including the words of God's precepts. If we should ask about norms

---

[26]The emphatic position of *theos* in the verse legitimates my translation; however, it does not make it necessary, and most commentators ignore the nuance.

[27]Which was the object of a previous Edinburgh Dogmatics Conference; see Bruce L. McCormack, ed., *Justification in Perspective: Historical Developments and Contemporary Challenges* (Grand Rapids: Baker Academic, 2006).

[28]The role of the slave-attendant, *paidagōgos*, who led the boy to the teacher, Gal 3:24. By exposing our failure to satisfy the demands of divine righteousness, the law leads us to Christ. The change of covenant economy entailed also abrogates "fleshly," i.e., typical, ordinances, such as circumcision and sacrifices.

for behavior, Christ or the Spirit does not *replace* the law. Rather, Christ confirms, interprets and embodies the law, and the Spirit of Christ provides the energy toward Christlikeness.

At the same time, there seems to be, I think, a *reticence* on Paul's part—not Matthew's—about the binding authority of the law for believers. He is careful never to deny it,[29] but he prefers to speak of "commandments," of God's "will."[30] When he does mention the law, the manner is not straightforward: he preaches love and then comments that the whole law is thereby fulfilled (Rom 13:8, 10; Gal 5:14); he describes the components of the fruit of the Spirit, and continues, "The law is not against such things" (Gal 5:23); he feels more comfortable when he can add "of Christ" to the word *law*, though he would not drive a wedge between Christ's law and God's (1 Cor 9:21; Gal 6:2). Asked point blank to confess the normative authority of the law, he would consent,[31] but he usually says things in a different way. I suggest he does so because he discerned the danger of *legalism* infiltrating back into Christian devotion—and as Berkouwer rightly warns, "degenerate" forms of sanctification have plagued the history of the church through legalistic contamination.[32] Indeed, who can declare, "I am free of all legalistic infiltration as I pursue sanctification"?

LAW AND OBEDIENCE: FURTHER THOUGHTS

The legalistic temptation has been so present in history, even in our evangelical history, that we should pause to reflect on the phenomenon. One

---

[29] 1 Tim 1:9 might be taken as a denial of that authority, but attention should be drawn to the particular verb *keitai*: it suggests the promulgation of the law, its official establishment—not strictly the didactic use. As a guide for the righteous, as the precious expression of the Father's will, the law would not need an institutional establishment if there were only righteous people; it was "set up" because of the unruly and wicked, etc. The preceding verse (1 Tim 1:8) affirms the law's goodness and a right use (*nomimōs*, in accordance with the law's essence), presumably by Christian believers too. In any case, since believers remain sinners in this life, the pedagogical use of the law remains relevant also through their earthly career (a Lutheran insight).

[30] At other times, as in 1 Cor 6:12-19, he keeps even farther from mentioning the law: he refers to "usefulness," to the bondage experienced in sin (1 Cor 6:12, as something self-evidently to be shunned), to a kind of moral sensitivity that knows *porneia* is sinful, incompatible with being a member of Christ, a defilement of God's temple. All this depends on the normative validity of the law—but Paul refrains from saying it expressly.

[31] Actually, this is not so far from what we find in Acts 21:20-26.

[32] Berkouwer, *Faith and Sanctification*, pp. 118-20, 178. The symmetrical adulteration is antinomian (p. 164: Agricola could issue a vengeful "Let Moses be hanged!"); at root level, it has much in common with legalism.

could incriminate the remnants of our old sinful bent (Gen 6:5). More to
the point, we remember that life awarded to good works and death in-
flicted for evil doings is the simple logic of responsibility. Grace revolu-
tionizes this logic, without making it null and void: hence the perennial
threat that it might regain dominion. In sanctification, the logic of responsibility insists that grace does not operate without works, but *with* works.
As Berkouwer says, "In sanctification, can we still speak of 'sola-gratia'?
Are we not certain, on the way of progressive sanctification, to sense the
value of our effort, our struggle, our conquests?"[33] To sense the value, I
would say, may still be wholesome in itself, but it makes us vulnerable to
turning to self—usually under pious guises. The underlying structure, I
suggest, is the mystery of grace, which fulfills the mystery of our relationship to our Creator: total dependence (everything from him), *and yet*
a consistent role on our part vis-à-vis the Giver. Our response counts for
God—even though it comes from him and operates under his rule! Neither
monism nor *dualism* makes sense of this mystery. Monism infers that if
everything is from him and through him, then nothing else counts: thus
contradicting Scripture. Dualism confers at least a modicum of independence to creatures in order to make them important before God and
enable them really to exist: it thus also contradicts Scripture. The unique
biblical structure of the Covenant is *monergistic and yet dipleuric*.[34] It is
reflected in the fact that sanctification, as a pure gift of God in Christ, is
therefore *sola fide* and is at the same time a gift to be actively and respon-
sibly received by human beings (with works). Duality, but nonsymmetrical: all glory to God alone! The patterns correspond to the incarnation
of our Lord, in which the true duality of humanity and deity is preserved,
though nonsymmetrically.[35] Ultimately, the foundation of this mystery is

---

[33]Ibid., p. 123.

[34]Technical terms of classical dogmatics: *monergism* (opposed to synergism) affirms that salvation is the work of God alone; *dipleuric* applies to covenant as involving two distinct responsible
partners.

[35]Christ's human nature remains distinct, "without confusion or change"; it is not swallowed up
by deity: this corresponds to the "dipleuric" character of covenant, to what I call the "consistency" of the creaturely partner, and its role is essential in redemption. Yet deity is first; Christ's
humanity is said to be "anhypostatic," and this corresponds to monergistic grace. *Anhypostatic*
conveys the idea that with the incarnation the eternal Son of God assumed a particular human
nature, not an independent human *person*.

the mystery of God's triune being, whose ordered unity in distinction grounds creaturely dependence in distinction.

The consistency of our human response, under sovereign grace, may also help us elucidate a finer point about the law and our obedience. Roman Catholic ethics has been structured around a twofold categorization: first the commandments, *praecepta*, and then the counsels (of perfection), *consilia*. Drawn from Matthew 19:21—having obeyed all the commandments, "*if you wish to be perfect, sell . . .*"—the doctrine attached special merit to works not strictly required and instituted a two-storied piety and morality. Priests, monks and nuns would follow the counsels and thus tend toward perfection. The Reformers reacted vehemently against this scheme. Bavinck offers interesting comments. He associates "what Rome calls the 'counsels'" with a view that locates Christian freedom in the *adiaphora* ("things indifferent"), and writes, "Error begins in both schools of thought when the adiaphora and the counsels are located outside or alongside of, below or above, the moral law and are therefore detached from the moral life."[36] He reminds his reader of cases in which renouncing permissible things is a biblical *duty* (e.g., Rom 14:21, 23; 1 Cor 8:13; 10:23).[37]

The Reformers' critique of the disjunction is convincing. Nothing falls outside the *command* to love God with *all* one's heart and might. Logically, if anyone conceives of something to do that will please God more than something else, he or she is under "total love" obligation[38] to do it (and to say: we are unprofitable servants). Yet Paul himself distinguishes between what he feels compelled to do—to preach the gospel—and what he freely adds, his renouncing his right to financial support (1 Cor 9:12, 15-16). The "boasting" of this addition seems to dissolve under the rigorous logic of the argument I have just summarized. Is this logic humane? I suggest the following way of making room for Paul's distinction within total obedience. If indeed we were able to see all connections and weigh all actions, the rigorous logic would apply: *but we are not*. We hesitate, and hesitation is due in part to limitations not sinful in themselves. Thus a "margin" of decisions remains whose import, with regard to our expression of love, is not perfectly clear and assured. God,

---

[36]Bavinck, *Holy Spirit, Church, and New Creation*, p. 260 (§482).
[37]Ibid.
[38]Since total love is the requirement of the law, this is a *legal* obligation.

who "knows our frame," accepts and even values this margin; he does not attach absolute obligation to courses of action that belong to it—and this opens the possibility of choices that are "free" in the special sense of 1 Corinthians 9:12, 15. *Because of the consistency of a truly human response*, the duality of strict obligation and "freewill offerings" finds a place in the interplay of God's grace and his children's faith, in their sanctification.

SANCTIFICATION: NOT "BY FAITH" IN THE SAME WAY AS JUSTIFICATION

Sanctification, no less than justification, is *sola fide*, but not in the same way. With or without works, righteousness imparted or imputed: the difference is significant. Bavinck may lack due caution when he writes, "Christ is our holiness in the same sense in which he is our righteousness":[39] the same sense maybe, but not the same way. Or again: "Justification and sanctification, accordingly, grant the same benefits."[40] The strong distinction between imparted and imputed righteousness was maintained by Protestant orthodoxy in controversies with Roman Catholicism. That issue has been dealt with elsewhere,[41] and the changes in Catholic theology, mostly positive but complex indeed, would deserve full-length examination, which is not possible here.[42] I rather draw attention to a strain of evangelicalism that has patterned the message of sanctification after the message of justification, *faith* being the key word. It has, to be sure, exercised more influence on church life than on academic theology, yet my main concern will be with the theological issues it raises.

The Wesleyan imprint is obvious. John Wesley himself sharply separated sanctification from justification: "I believe justification to be wholly distinct from sanctification, and necessarily antecedent to it."[43] His doctrine of per-

---

[39]Bavinck, *Holy Spirit, Church, and New Creation*, p. 248 (§480).
[40]Ibid., p. 249 (§480). The sentence continues with words I find more satisfying: "Rather, the entire Christ; they only differ in the manner in which they grant him."
[41]See, again, the symposium in McCormack, *Justification in Perspective*.
[42]For a recent synthesis by a foremost expert in ecumenical dialogue, see Bernard Sesboüé, *Sauvés par la grâce: les débats sur la justification du XVIᵉ siècle à nos jours* (Paris: Editions Facultés jésuites de Paris, 2009).
[43]From his journal, Thursday, September 13, 1739 (about points of difference with other Anglican clergy), in *Wesley His Own Biographer: Selections from the Journals* (London: C. H. Kelly, 1891), p. 116.

fection, attainable in this life, then implied a special experience ushering in the superior state.[44] Benjamin B. Warfield recounts with great care and loyalty (though not sympathy) how the seed germinated in American soil, with the key role of Oberlin College and of its first president, Asa Mahan, and famous professor Charles Finney.[45] Mahan had a pioneer role; Warfield describes his influence on Finney: we have "seen Mahan imbuing him with his newly-found notion (borrowed ultimately from the Wesleyans) that sanctification is to be attained immediately by an act of faith, and indeed also with his mystical Quietistic explanation of how sanctification is brought about by faith."[46] Mahan had experienced a kind of second, fully liberating conversion and had thus discovered sanctification by faith, for which you must "cease wholly from man and from yourself, and trust Christ universally."[47] Although some statements are contradictory, he taught that some true believers can be justified and stay so without having any share in sanctification;[48] he called the second experience "baptism of the Spirit," with an association of power for ministry.[49]

The pattern having been thus established and variously elaborated, the contribution of such a teacher as William Edwin Boardman was to exert a lasting influence. "The 'Higher Life Movement' which swept over the English-speaking world—and across the narrow seas into the Continent of Europe—in the third quarter of the nineteenth century," Warfield writes, "was not without traits which derived from Oberlin. And Mahan lived to stand by the side of Pearsall Smith at the great Oxford Convention of 1874, and to become with him a factor in the inauguration of the great 'Keswick Movement,' which has brought down much of the spirit and many of the

---

[44]On Thursday, June 17, 1779, Wesley diagnosed the cause of the stagnation of the Edinburgh society as the muting of the old Methodist doctrine. He says (quoting another), "The doctrine of Perfection is not calculated for the meridian of Edinburgh," ibid., p. 500.

[45]Benjamin B. Warfield, *Perfectionism*, ed. Samuel G. Craig (Philadelphia: P & R, 1967).

[46]Ibid., p. 60.

[47]Ibid., p. 51; see also 42-43, 50-51, on that experience, dated 1836.

[48]Ibid., pp. 96-104. On p. 109 he says, "Here it is taught that, when we have been 'through the Spirit' 'convicted of sin,' and have exercised genuine 'repentance toward God, and faith toward our Lord Jesus Christ,' strange to say, nothing has been wrought in us by His Spirit."

[49]Ibid., p. 117: the label "Baptism of the Spirit" seems to have been applied first by John Morgan (1845–1846). According to ibid., p. 133: "Finney dallied a little with the idea of 'the baptism of the Spirit,' but did not really adopt it; he continued to confine the work of the Spirit to illumination and to deny all recreative functions to Him: He is our Guide, not our Regenerator."

forms of teaching of Oberlin Perfectionism to our own day."[50] Robert Pearsall Smith and his wife, Hannah Whitall, played a key role in spreading the movement into Europe. The Brighton Convention of May 1875, of which they were the keynote speakers, drew up to eight thousand earnest participants; the Keswick Convention followed,[51] and the Continent was also affected, especially with the Gemeinschaftsbewegung in Germany. What may be less widely known is that Abraham Kuyper attended the Brighton Convention, achieved "special consecration" and entered "higher life"; for him it was a "spiritual feast" producing "glorious and blessed moments of spiritual ecstasy."[52] He shortly afterward suffered nervous collapse—caused by overwork, and perhaps by post-Brighton turbulence in his soul—and had to rest outside of the Netherlands for fifteen months (mainly in the French Alps), at the end of which he recommitted himself firmly to the religion of his fathers,[53] and back home published a series of articles on perfectionism in *De Heraut*.[54] Some descriptions sound like personal confessions. He tells of the experience of receiving a blessing.

> It may [have happened] as a result of a marvellous in-working of God's sovereign grace which came over us suddenly when we hardly expected it any more. Not finding a listening ear anyway we had ceased to pray, only to experience such a release from the bonds of Satan, such an untying of the snares of sin, such showers of blessing on the dried-out garden of the self, such an anointing with fresh oil, such an awakening of our deadened listless soul, that it seemed we had all of a sudden made the leap of our life from a barren pit to the shores of the river of God and could not imagine any state of bliss more blessed than this one.[55]

But as Kuyper himself admonishes, beware of relying on such an experience rather than on the Word! Beware of imagining sin can be eradicated in this

---

[50]Ibid., p. 213.

[51]See Ian M. Randall, *Transforming Keswick: The Keswick Convention, Past, Present and Future* (Carlisle: O.M., 2000).

[52]James D. Bratt, ed., *Abraham Kuyper: A Centennial Reader* (Grand Rapids: Eerdmans, 1998), pp. 141, 162.

[53]Ibid., p. 156, excerpt from *Bedoeld noch gezegd* of 1885.

[54]Originally titled *Volmaakbaarheid* (March 17–August 4, 1878), reproduced in *Uit het Woord: Stichtelijke Bijbelstudien*, 3rd series (Amsterdam: Höveker & Wormser, 1879), four of which are published in English in Bratt, *Abraham Kuyper*.

[55]Ibid., p. 150.

life! "Those who are most advanced . . . no longer cling to the external but have been taught by their God to press deeper. And just there, in the depth of their existence, they discovered the loathsome essence, the scandalous root of sin and became acquainted with the demon who stirs up these ungodly realities from the depths of Satan."[56] Instructed by his own case, and by the evolution of the movement, Kuyper regretted the enthusiastic support he had first given it, and made a simple public confession.

> Herewith the author of these articles also acquits himself of this painful task, all the more readily and candidly inasmuch as he raised the hope among a wide circle that with this rustling of the wind of a day the breeze of the Spirit was bound to come. Whether the nervous exhaustion which shortly thereafter broke out in such serious illness may help to explain this misappraisal I leave to the judgment of the spiritually minded among God's children, above all to the judgment of Him who knows our bodies as well as our souls.[57]

The old story of the "sanctification by faith" wing of evangelicalism is also the prehistory of Pentecostalism, which was born of that tradition, with new elements added and a changed configuration.

Two special emphases of the Higher Life Movement may be singled out. The first one is the promotion of a pure act of faith, *not a work*, a pure trusting in one instant, a strict believing that one has received what one has asked for—entire sanctification. The motive is clearly to avoid legalism, a self-willed sanctification "in the energy of the flesh." Quite often one can scent a mystical longing for undifferentiated union in which the ego seems to dissolve in the flow of divine life.[58] The second feature is the separation introduced between the two benefits of the twofold grace Calvin spoke of,[59] justification and sanctification. It obviously entails that Christians are divided into two different categories. At conversion, a person is justified and "accepts" Christ as Savior; with the second blessing he or she receives sanc-

[56]Bratt, *Abraham Kuyper*, p. 160.

[57]Bratt, *Abraham Kuyper*, p. 163. Berkouwer, *Faith and Sanctification*, p. 61, mentions a questionable thesis from Kuyper's (later) *Gemeene Gratie* (Leiden: Donner, 1902), 2:323, on Rom 7: a central part of the soul would be sinless and already glorified, while the periphery is still fleshly, hence the painful struggle. Could this be a residue of Brighton perfectionism? It does not agree with what we have quoted above.

[58]Warfield, *Perfectionism*, p. 92, quotes remarkable phrases; e.g., Christ "as it were swallows us up."

[59]Calvin, *Institutes* 3.11.1.

tification, and *surrenders* to Christ as Lord. At conversion one enters the door, and later one starts on the way. Lower-class Christians live in Romans 7, but the second experience propels them into Romans 8. Some may say: at conversion we receive Christ, but the second blessing is the gift, or at least the baptism, of the Spirit. Again, we must acknowledge the motive: hunger for righteousness in life, thirst for the promised streams of Living Water—contrasting with the mediocrity of self-satisfaction.

An exegetical and theological critique unfolds easily. Apart from the ludicrous misreadings of 2 Corinthians 1:15 ("second benefit," in KJV) and Acts 19:2 ("since you believed" taken in a temporal sense), the separation of two decisive experiences lacks biblical warrant; acknowledging Christ as Lord is the *first* commitment, which makes the person a Christian. Faith receives *him*, and in him everything is ours. The commands to strive and make every effort gives the lie to the view of sanctifying faith described above. Christians are to work out their salvation *with fear and trembling* (Phil 2:12), and bring *spoudē*—"diligence"—that is, energetic concentration, to the task of sanctification (2 Tim 2:15; Heb 4:11; 6:11; 2 Pet 1:5, 10; 3:14; cf. Lk 13:24; Rom 12:11; Eph 4:3). And there are many other exhortations. Though I would still maintain that sanctification is "by faith," Scripture, as Warfield rightly observes, does not use these words and does not make the connection explicitly, even in Acts 15:9 and Acts 26:18[60]—a warning against drawing an artificial parallel with justification by faith.

Reflecting on the persistence of the temptation may bring more fruit. Though I know nothing about Asa Mahan's possible acquaintance with the writings of Fénelon, Quesnel or Madame Guyon, the kinship of some themes with quietism[61] should be pondered; some influences have crossed confessional barriers.[62] Quietism is a perennial temptation: much deeper than the attraction of a cheap device to lead a triumphant life, and even

---

[60]Warfield, *Perfectionism*, p. 335 n. 16.

[61]Quietism (from *quies*, "rest") was a seventeenth-century mystical doctrine and form of devotion initiated by the Spanish priest Miguel de Molinos, who found distinguished and influential followers in France. Madame Guyon was the most famous among them.

[62]It is little known that Watchman Nee, a Chinese representative of "higher life" spirituality (and in many respects an admirable servant of God), was influenced by Madame Guyon, to whose writings he was introduced by the missionary Miss Margaret Barber. My source: Olivier Baudraz, "De la sanctification selon Watchman Nee. Une analyse de son anthropologie et de sa sotériologie" (MDiv diss., Aix-en-Provence, Faculté Libre de Théologie Réformée, 1984).

distinct from the mystical urge toward fusion; a merely passive faith (its keynote) may look more authentic. The ugliness of legalism offers a negative confirmation. This particle of truth cannot be ignored: the first dimension of faith is passive, *Gott erleiden* ("to undergo God," a phrase from the *Theologia deutsch*, which was beloved of Luther), and there is indeed *quies*, a true resting, in the experience of God's grace. But quietism loses sight of the nonsymmetrical mystery to which I have already referred. Within dependence, or passivity, there is a consistent response: ours, though God energizes it—ours, since God energizes it as such. There is also the activity of faith—hence the striving for sanctification—and the toilsome effort that is paradoxically one with the *quies* of faith. And this, I suggest, Asa Mahan missed, as have many of his successors.

The other issue that arises from a consideration of higher life doctrine is the inscription of sanctification in *time*. If we do not preach the second blessing, are we to say that everything is enclosed in the first moment, when Christ and his fullness became ours? Is there anything more in other moments than the renewed actuality of the first one? If we affirm a meaningful progress, what shape does this progress take? Are there stages we should distinguish? A tendency among Lutheran theologians, especially, has been to deny progress, for it suggests that humans can "possess grace." Conversion, they say, takes place again every day. Among the Reformed, Hermann Friedrich Kohlbrugge scorned a process view of sanctification (in the interest of the grand objectivity of the cross).[63] Bruce L. McCormack, speaking as Barth's interpreter, writes, "I cannot look back on a date in my past and say, 'On that date I was justified.' God's justification of me is something that is new each morning; it is something that breaks in upon me in spite of my continuing unwillingness to live as one who is justified."[64]

And yet . . . Scripture does suggest that there is progress along the way. The image of *growth* is recurrent (Eph 4:15; Col 1:10; 1 Pet 2:2; 2 Pet 3:18). God promises to pursue to the end the good work of sanctification (Phil 1:6; 1 Thess 5:23). As the Thessalonians have been behaving in ways pleasing to God, they are to do so "more and more" (1 Thess 4:1). Timothy's "progress"

---

[63]Berkouwer, *Faith and Sanctification*, pp. 103-4.
[64]Bruce L. McCormack, "*Justitia aliena*: Karl Barth in Conversation with the Evangelical Doctrine of Imputed Righteousness," in McCormack, *Justification in Perspective*, p. 194.

should be manifest to all (1 Tim 4:15). Even more striking, degrees of advancement lead to making classes of Christians: still "fleshly" or more spiritual ones, infants in Christ or those more mature (1 Cor 2:6, 15; 3:1-3; Eph 4:14; Heb 5:12-14).

We are to handle the theme of progress carefully. Metaphors are not to be pressed, and the analogy of biological growth cannot be applied in a rigid manner: regression and pathological stagnation are (alas!) spiritually common! In the sense of covenant renewal, we start again and again on the Christian path: the mercies of God are new every morning (the beloved text of Lam 3:23), and each day Christ's disciple is to take up the cross assigned to him or her. Nevertheless renewal, or the confirmation of commitment, does not abolish the unique significance of the first moment and does not · negate continuity either. The analogy of growth actually illuminates experience. Like life in general, sanctification knows a combination of special moments, seasons of intense transformation, critical transitions as well as more linear continuity. If one claims to have had a second blessing we may rejoice but add that God also has in store a third, a tenth and a seventy-seventh blessing along the way.

The theological principle involved is the consistency of human response. We are temporal (though not only temporal, Eccles 3:11). In order to receive the gift actively, we need time. Even our sinless Lord had to grow in wisdom and grace (Lk 2:52). In him we receive the gift that is complete from the first moment, but subjectively, in order to apprehend its component parts and thus enter into their *enjoyment* in experience, we need time. The scheme of our apprehension in successive seasons of the Christian life shows patterns analogous to childhood, adolescence and maturity. It also varies from one individual to another. And it happens that some Christians apprehending at a later stage aspects of the gift of Christ that are subjectively very enriching or liberating to them load the experience with the wrong theological content; nevertheless we may give thanks for the experience itself.

FURTHER THOUGHTS ON SANCTIFICATION AND FAITH

Our emphasis on our active, productive response under the sovereignty of grace, within its all-embracing efficiency, is typically Augustinian. The question, then, could be raised (and it is by Catholic Augustinians) as to why it is so important for heirs of the Reformation to rule out *works* for justification: we include them for sanctification *sola fide*; we thereby show that their presence does not threaten the monergistic sovereignty of grace. The requirement of faith *as act* for justification expresses the importance, in God's eyes, of a human response—why then not add work to act?

The first part of the answer is well-known. Even our best Christian works, Spirit-assisted works, are still far below the standards of God's absolute holiness. Isaiah 64:6 (v. 5 in Hebrew) stands out as the impressive reminder of the purity that cannot stand the stinking deficiencies of our worthiest accomplishments. *If* they counted for our justification, we could not escape condemnation. We only stand before God under the "cover" of Christ's righteousness, and our works are accepted only because their deficiencies are similarly covered. From that gospel truth, freedom and assurance flow freely—while nothing that positive Catholic theologians are wont to celebrate is lost for us.

A suggestion may be added as a complement. Calvin seems to come close to it in his seventh sermon on Isaiah 53 (on Is 53:12): "Indeed, all the graces of the Holy Spirit are part of the spoil of our Lord Jesus Christ: God his Father gave him those riches because we had been deprived of them, and the devil prevented the power of the Holy Spirit from having a free course among men."[65] The devil, as the Accuser, could argue on the basis of God's holy justice that God could *not* send his Spirit into polluted lives, for he would thereby betray himself and deny his Word. The devil would thus block the work of the Sanctifier. Atonement, however, and its application in justification, is the new factor that removes such a hindrance. Justification opens the way for sanctification. I discern this teaching in the logic of Romans 8 (though Calvin's commentary does not introduce the thought). Paul *starts* with free justification and the condemnation of sin in the Substitute's flesh: this condition had to be met in order for the demands of the law (*dikaiōma*) to be fulfilled by human beings in their concrete behavior (Rom 8:4). What a paradox! The law, which focuses on obedience, is unable to secure that obedience; it is powerless as regards sanctification just as it is for justification. But faith that justifies without works makes sanctification possible

---

[65]CO 35:677-78.

and actual. The thought is again expressed in Romans 8:10: whereas the body is dead because of sin, the Spirit is life *because of righteousness*. The satisfaction of justice, the imputation of perfect righteousness, makes it possible for the Spirit to vivify and thereby for sanctification to take place.[66] In this way, the logical connection of the two benefits of salvation is brought to light.

When the biblical teaching on holiness and sanctification is looked at against the background of the common religiosity of humankind, the striking feature is the *moral* character of holiness. Already in the Old Testament, the Lord—Creator of heaven and earth, who fills the whole universe with his glory, for whom the nations are but a drop in a bucket (or "out of a bucket," *middĕlî*, Is 40:15)—abhors something! What is this monstrous violation of sacred rights? A measure that is not accurate, weights 2 percent lighter than they should be, instruments of common cheating (Deut 25:13-16; cf. Prov 11:1). The Holy One of Israel is unique in his ethical insistence. And the trait is even stronger in the New Testament. The division between sacred and profane[67] is abolished in *things*: to the pure all things are pure (Tit 1:15). The only true uncleanness is moral, as Jesus "scandalously" taught (Mt 15:10-20). The sacred is spelled out in terms of righteousness, to a degree unparalleled elsewhere.

The underlying foundation is theological, or, if you will, metaphysical (ontological). Among sinful humankind, the nearly universal division between sacred and profane is born of idolatry. When the *sensus divinitatis* is deviated and brought to bear on creatures, as Romans 1:18-22 describes, when elements or aspects of creation are divinized, these are set over against the other elements or aspects: a sacred realm is opposed to the impure part of reality—a part that is essentially identified with evil. Only the transcendence and ontological independence of the One Creator God frees us from idolatrous division. Since it proceeds from him alone, "every creature of God is good" (1 Tim 4:4). Uncleanness is not metaphysical, for evil is not a substance: it is ethical. I find this theo-logic in Psalm 24. Why does the poem celebrate the Lord's creative power and "metaphysical" sovereignty (Ps

---

[66]I would read 1 Cor 15:56 with the same thought in mind: the power of sin is the law because the law's condemnation forbids the release of healing energies into the sinner's life, and the sinner remains the slave and prisoner of sin. Warfield, *Perfectionism*, p. 100, offers a partially different interpretation: "Corruption is the very penalty of sin from which we are freed in justification; holiness is the very reward that is granted us in justification."

[67]See the masterly synthesis by Roger Caillois, *L'Homme et le sacré*, Idées (Paris: Gallimard, 1963).

24:1-2), before giving the ethical requirements for standing on the sacred hill (Ps 24:3-4)? Because the former are foundational to the latter. To the religiously minded, who thus seek the Lord's face (God's elect people, "Jacob"), the gift of righteousness, *tsĕdāqâ*, is granted (Ps 24:5-6)—through imputation and impartation.

The last verses of the psalm proclaim the triumph of the Lord of Glory, the Valiant One and the Victor, the Lord of all the powers of the universe. The metaphysical sovereignty of the Lord and the nonmetaphysical character of evil ensure (and they alone can ensure) that evil shall be defeated, that the whole mountain will be most holy (Ezek 43:12), that the whole earth will be filled with the knowledge of the Lord and all reality sanctified. The decisive battle has already been fought, evil has already been defeated by the Lord, our Champion: we have been sanctified by his once-for-all sacrifice (Heb 10:14). When facing secularism and atheism, which only *appear* to free human beings from idolatry and the sacred/profane division, we may confess the certainty of our hope; secular ethics not only fails to provide a legitimacy to its "values" but also can offer no sure hope.

On faith, two opposite opinions are worth considering together, one proposed by Abraham Kuyper and the other by Gerhard Ebeling. Kuyper highlighted the universal function of faith: nobody can abstain from believing something, and Christian faith is antithetical to idolatrous or apostate faith. Ebeling claims that "Christian faith is not a special faith, but simply faith"; when he speaks of "the faith," he means "Christian faith, with the implication that it is true faith, simply faith."[68] Leaving aside the rest of Ebeling's doctrine, I would take the two propositions as complementary. There is a universal function, a part of the human makeup as such. However, Ebeling's insight is valid: the *form* human "faith" takes can never be totally detached from its concrete direction, for the whole interest of faith is its object. In apostasy, with the wrong object, the nature of faith is damaged, distorted, adulterated; only Christian faith is true faith, simply faith.

Now if this is to be accepted, a final question for us arises: Is the nature of true faith manifest in sanctification? In justification, it is glaring! As a move away from self, in the decision to rely on Christ alone to receive a

---

[68]Gerhard Ebeling, *The Nature of Faith*, trans. Ronald Gregor Smith, Fontana Library (London: Collins, 1966), pp. 20-21.

iustitia aliena, the exercise of faith displays its purest nature. May we say the same of sanctification?

We may, I suggest, on two counts. Though the role of striving and works somewhat dims the traits that are evident in justification, faith in sanctification brings out two essential features of faith itself. First, the emphasis on the consistency of human response causes the *paradox* of faith, of renouncing oneself, to appear: losing oneself *in this way* is finding oneself, for good (Mt 16:26). When we cease relying on ourselves, we are truly established forever. We are energized as active, productive partners (sons and daughters), called to *energein*, in God's ongoing work. And second, it becomes clearer that the object of faith is not only the gift of righteousness but *Christ himself*, our Savior and Lord. Casting oneself on the mercy of God and believing the promise of free forgiveness means adhering to Christ, becoming united, *symphytoi* (Rom 6:5), with him; true faith thus entails being transformed into his likeness.

The fact that sanctification is *sola fide* reminds us that it is *sola gratia, solo Christo* and thus *soli Deo gloria.*

4

COVENANTAL UNION
AND COMMUNION

Union with Christ *as* the
Covenant of Grace

Brannon Ellis

The doctrine of union with Christ is today both widely celebrated and variously interpreted.[1] There are several live options for understanding the theme, even in my own Reformed tradition—and even when focusing particularly on the significance of union in the *application* of redemption.[2] In this context,

---

[1]I am grateful to Kelly Kapic and Jonathan King for their insightful comments on an earlier draft of this chapter. For the doctrine of union with Christ in general, see J. P. Baker, "Union with Christ," in *New Dictionary of Theology*, ed. Sinclair Ferguson, David F. Wright and J. I. Packer (Leicester: Inter-Varsity Press, 1988), pp. 697-99. For the variety of views among historical and contemporary Reformed theologians, see Richard A. Muller, *Calvin and the Reformed Tradition: On the Work of Christ and the Order of Salvation* (Grand Rapids: Baker Academic, 2012); John V. Fesko, *Beyond Calvin: Union with Christ and Justification in Early Modern Reformed Theology (1517–1700)* (Göttingen: Vandenhoeck & Ruprecht, 2012), pp. 381-84; Andrew T. B. McGowan, "Justification and the *ordo salutis*," in *Justification in Perspective: Historical Developments and Contemporary Challenges*, ed. Bruce L. McCormack (Grand Rapids: Baker; Edinburgh: Rutherford House, 2006), pp. 147-63.

[2]In the interest of brevity and clarity, I am giving close attention to the historical and contemporary discussion of these themes in the Reformed tradition. I leave it to the reader to draw wider implications and applications. It is also key in what follows to emphasize that I focus on union with Christ and related themes in the context of *applied* redemption. Considered most broadly, our being "in Christ," participation in his covenant people, and the certain goal and effectiveness of his redeeming work find their origin in the eternal purposes of God and will never find their end. I have written with a view toward this broadness, but keeping to applied redemption as a distinctive movement in the whole (and crucial for understanding the whole). For a helpful mapping of various significations of union with Christ—the predestinarian, the redemptive-

most have described union with Christ as one step in or one aspect of the *ordo salutis* (the logical order of the outworking of redemption), though differing over whether union or justification should be considered foundational for the whole process.[3] Others likewise have seen union as a moment in the application of redemption, but one functioning as the center in which all the saving benefits of Christ converge and from which they radiate.[4] Still others find in union with Christ a more thoroughly relational and participatory paradigm than many Protestant accounts that tend to give pride of place to legal categories (such as declarative imputation).[5] Despite these disagreements, there is much common ground as well—union with Christ is by faith, personal, spiritual, trinitarian, covenantal and absolutely vital.

Still, why and how the *doctrine* of union with Christ is crucial in Christian theology and practice remains an important issue to wrestle with. The variety of proposals and even the disagreements among theologians are not the primary issues I am concerned with here; I want to tackle these questions by suggesting that the doctrine of union with Christ *itself* is often part of the problem. That is, it is often treated—across a variety of interpretations—in such a way that its theological significance and role in applied redemption are much more strictly delimited than is biblically warranted. This may well surprise those familiar with the many quite richly textured accounts of union with Christ. My focus here, however, is not on the doc-

historical and the existential or applicatory—see Richard B. Gaffin Jr., "Union with Christ: Some Biblical and Theological Reflections," in *Always Reforming: Explorations in Systematic Theology*, ed. Andrew T. B. McGowan (Downers Grove, IL: IVP Academic, 2006), p. 275; cf. Mark A. Seifrid, "In Christ," in *Dictionary of Paul and His Letters*, ed. Gerald F. Hawthorne, Ralph P. Martin and Daniel G. Reid (Downers Grove, IL: InterVarsity Press, 1993), pp. 433-36.

[3]For the priority of justification or union as ground of the application of redemption, in addition to the post-Reformation figures explored in Fesko, *Beyond Calvin*, see Horton, "Union with Christ: Modern Reception and Contemporary Possibilities," in *Calvin's Theology and Its Reception: Disputes, Developments, and New Possibilities*, ed. J. Todd Billings and I. John Hesselink (Louisville, KY: Westminster John Knox, 2012), pp. 72-94. For a (rare) Reformed example of the *actual* priority of justification to every other aspect of applied redemption (even regeneration and faith), see Bruce L. McCormack, "What's at Stake in Current Debates over Justification?," in *Justification: What's at Stake in the Current Debates*, ed. Mark Husbands and Daniel J. Treier (Downers Grove, IL: IVP Academic, 2004), pp. 81-117.

[4]See Gaffin, "Union with Christ"; Gaffin, *By Faith, Not By Sight: Paul and the Order of Salvation*, 2nd ed. (Phillipsburg, NJ: P & R, 2013); Mark A. Garcia, *Life in Christ: Union with Christ and Twofold Grace in Calvin's Theology* (Milton Keynes: Paternoster, 2008).

[5]See, e.g., Julie Canlis, *Calvin's Ladder: A Spiritual Theology of Ascent and Ascension* (Grand Rapids: Eerdmans, 2010).

trine's theological depth or complexity, but its content and context. Much of the divergence regarding the proper relation between our belonging to Christ and our enjoyment of the manifold benefits of his work on our behalf arises because "union with Christ" or being "in Christ" is defined quite strictly in (individual) soteriological terms, and is therefore folded into the *ordo* as a specific aspect of or moment in it.

Taking a different approach to union than any of those mentioned above, some recently have described union with Christ as a key way of speaking about the *entirety* of our personal and communal participation in his accomplished redemption. J. Todd Billings, for example, observes that for Calvin union with Christ was not a "discrete locus" but a "cluster of related thoughts and images . . . related to participation, union, engrafting, and adoption." These all take on a strong corporate character, such that "[being] incorporated into Christ means being incorporated into Christ's body."[6] John Murray similarly suggested that "union with Christ is not simply one step in the application of redemption," but "underlies every step."[7] More directly, Michael Horton asserts that "union with Christ and the covenant of grace are not simply related themes, but are different ways of talking about one and the same reality."[8]

Here I pursue the claim that *being in Christ and belonging to his church are materially equivalent, as complementary ways of describing the whole of our participation in the very same covenantal reality.* Across the Pauline corpus—in many ways the wellspring of the doctrine of union with Christ—

---

[6] J. Todd Billings, "Union with Christ: Calvin's Theology and Its Early Reception," in Billings and Hesselink, *Calvin's Theology and Its Reception*, p. 50.

[7] As quoted by Gaffin, "Union with Christ," p. 275, based in part on notes from Murray's class lectures.

[8] Michael Horton, *Covenant and Salvation: Union with Christ* (Louisville, KY: Westminster John Knox, 2007), pp. 181-82, see further pp. 129-52; and Horton, "Union with Christ," p. 91. For the covenant of grace—understood as the eternally established purpose flowing from God's grace in Christ to gather redeemed sinners into communion with himself by the Spirit, temporally accomplished in his work of forming a people for his own possession from all the peoples of the earth, see Horton, *Covenant and Salvation*, chap. 2, as well as the magisterial treatments of Reformed federal theologians Francis Turretin, in *Institutes of Elenctic Theology*, trans. George Musgrave Giger, ed. James T. Dennison Jr. (Phillipsburg, NJ: P & R, 2003), 2:169-75; and Herman Witsius, *The Economy of the Covenants Between God and Man: Comprehending a Complete Body of Divinity*, trans. William Crookshank (repr., Phillipsburg, NJ: P & R, 1990), 1:163-324. Cf. in general Geerhardus Vos, "The Doctrine of the Covenant in Reformed Theology," in *Redemptive History and Biblical Interpretation: The Shorter Writings of Geerhardus Vos*, ed. Richard B. Gaffin Jr. (repr., Phillipsburg, NJ: P & R, 2001), pp. 234-67.

participation in Christ is spoken of in parallel terms and contexts with participation in the new covenant people of God. Appealing to typical Reformed categories, we might say that being united with Christ by faith is not a soteriological reality narrower than or antecedent to the ecclesiological reality of being a believing member of the covenant of grace. Being in Christ *is* participation in the new covenant through its life-giving Mediator, and belonging to the people of God *is* union with Christ our head in the Spirit-filled people who are his ecclesial body. So though Christ himself always holds preeminence as the head who gives life and identity to his body (Col 2:19), to be united to Christ is not therefore prior to or separable from being joined to one another. Put simply, union with Christ should not be thought of as something *within* the application of redemption—whether as a discrete stage in the *ordo* or as the ground from which other benefits flow. Being in Christ is a description of the *whole* of redemption applied individually and corporately by the Spirit who indwells the head as well as the body.

If this is the case, not only the character of union with Christ, but the relationship between union and the enjoyment of Christ's benefits in the application of redemption—both individually and corporately—should be revisited as well. My goal in this brief compass is to share two reasons why I think this is a faithful move to make, and to outline three significant doctrinal fruits of embracing this view (addressing a few key objections along the way).

LEX ORANDI, REGULA FIDEI, LEX CREDENDI: LITURGICAL AND EXEGETICAL TESTIMONY TO THE CHARACTER OF UNION WITH CHRIST

The adage *lex orandi, lex credendi*—"the rule of prayer is the rule of belief," or "as the church prays, so it believes"—traceable to the fifth century, has often been interpreted to mean that the liturgical practice of the church is what primarily determines (or should determine) the content and character of its theological reflection. Maxwell E. Johnson has called this interpretation into question, arguing that the original significance of this principle—directed against fifth-century semi-Pelagianism—was to urge that all soteriological claims regarding the identity of the Christian church and its mission should be deeply rooted in the scriptural witness to the gospel of

God's free grace. If the church daily prays for the forgiveness of sins—for itself and others—through God's mercy in Christ, in line with the Scriptures, then it *cannot* be faithful to describe anyone's participation in salvation as the result of something other than or apart from grace.[9] Tracing this insight further, we may say that *lex orandi* always points to *regula fidei*, the rule of faith, together flowing into *lex credendi*. I do not intend to suggest that the "flow" I describe here is unidirectional; the church's doctrine deeply forms its prayer as well, and the rule of faith as Scripture's own intrinsic sum and scope is constitutive of and normative for both the church's faith and worship.[10] But in circumstances where we ask if doctrinal claims are as consistent as they should be with the church's lived identity as formed by word and Spirit, this insight can be instructive. As the church prays, according to the Scriptures, so it believes.

I believe this is also a fruitful rubric for faithfully revisiting the contemporary doctrinal import of union with Christ. What does the church's corporate proclamation and worship say about what it means to be in Christ (*lex orandi*)? What is the stance of the biblical witness (*regula fidei*)? And how therefore should we articulate the truth of union with Christ (*lex credendi*)? Again, I focus my discussion on the Reformed tradition.

Lex orandi: *Baptism signifies and seals participation in the church no more or less than in Christ.* The *unitive* significance of being in Christ—of initially "putting on" Christ by faith (Gal 3:27), becoming one with him and coming to share his resurrection life in the Spirit—is brought to the fore in the sacrament of baptism.[11] The Genevan Catechism (revised 1545) describes baptism's meaning as comprising "two parts": "the forgiveness of

---

[9]The original statement, in an expanded form, is from Prosper of Aquitaine (d. ca. 455), who was dependent on the earlier thought of Augustine. See Maxwell E. Johnson, *Praying and Believing in Early Christianity: The Interplay Between Christian Worship and Doctrine* (Collegeville, MN: Liturgical Press, 2013). See further Paul De Clerck, "'Lex orandi, lex credendi': The Original Sense and Historical Avatars of an Equivocal Adage," *Studia Liturgia* 24 (1994): 178-200.

[10]Johnson, following others, helpfully argues for a mutually formative relationship between *lex orandi* and *lex credendi*; in *Praying and Believing*, chap. 5. For the rule of faith in general, see Kevin J. Vanhoozer, Craig G. Bartholomew, Daniel J. Treier, and N. T. Wright, eds., *Dictionary for Theological Interpretation of Scripture* (Grand Rapids: Baker Academic, 2005).

[11]For historical discussion of the practice of baptism among the early Reformed churches, and the significant liturgical difference from previous practice it usually entailed, see Philip Benedict, *Christ's Churches Purely Reformed: A Social History of Calvinism* (New Haven, CT: Yale University Press, 2002), pp. 493-94, 503-6.

sins" and "Spiritual regeneration."[12] The Scots Confession (1560) focuses on the benefit of being in the right before God in the righteousness of Christ: "By Baptism we are engrafted into Christ Jesus, to be made partakers of his righteousness, by which our sins are covered and remitted."[13] The Belgic Confession (1561) focuses on the benefit of transformative renewal, saying that in baptism

> our Lord giveth that which is signified by the Sacrament, namely, the gifts and invisible grace; washing, cleansing, and purging our souls of all filth and unrighteousness; renewing our hearts and filling them with all comfort; giving unto us a true assurance of his fatherly goodness; putting on us the new man, and putting off the old man with all his deeds.[14]

The Heidelberg Catechism (1563) aligns this twofold benefit of baptism with being cleansed through Christ's "blood and Spirit": washing in Christ's blood signifies and seals the forgiveness of sins, and washing in his Spirit our inner renewal and growth in sanctification.[15]

The benefits communicated to us in baptism, as these confessions describe them, come to us only because of Christ, but they do not come from a Christ who "remains outside of us," as Calvin urged.[16] Both the new status and the new birth signified and sealed in baptism belong to the Reformed emphasis on the "double grace" of justification and sanctification enjoyed in union with Christ. This is a hallmark of Calvin's account of the Christian faith and life.[17] As the Holy Spirit unites us to Christ by faith, we receive both the free forgiveness of sins through the imputation of Christ's righteousness and new life to walk faithfully by God's sustaining grace in that freedom that Christ has

---

[12]*The Catechism of the Church of Geneva*, trans. Elijah Waterman (Hartford, CT: Sheldon and Goodwin, 1815), C. 324, appealing to Eph 5:26 and Rom 6:4; cf. the French Confession (1559), article 35, in Philip Schaff, ed., *The Creeds of Christendom with a History and Critical Notes*, 4th ed. (repr., Grand Rapids: Baker, 1977), 3:379.

[13]*The Book of Confessions*, Part One of the Constitution of the Presbyterian Church, rev. ed. (U.S.A.) (Louisville: Office of the General Assembly, 2004), 3.21.

[14]Philip Schaff, *Creeds of Christendom*, 3:426.

[15]*Book of Confessions*, 4.070.

[16]John Calvin, *Institutes of the Christian Religion* 3.1.1. See further Canlis, *Calvin's Ladder*, pp. 139-47.

[17]J. Todd Billings, *Calvin, Participation, and the Gift: The Activity of Believers in Union with Christ* (New York: Oxford University Press, 2007), esp. chap. 4; Dennis E. Tamburello, *Union with Christ: John Calvin and the Mysticism of St. Bernard* (Louisville, KY: Westminster John Knox, 1994).

won for us.[18] Though Calvin's account was never the only Reformed exposition of union with Christ and the enjoyment of his benefits, Calvin's emphasis on the double grace of union expresses a shared Reformed accent.[19]
Murray summarized this classical Reformed conviction well: while
throughout the New Testament baptism is the means for cleansing from the
guilt of sin (justification) as well as the renewal of new birth for life in the
Spirit (sanctification), it encompasses both graces precisely because it communicates "union with Christ in his death, burial, and resurrection."[20]

At the same time, the Reformed tradition has emphasized the clear role
that baptism plays as a sacrament of initiation into the Abrahamic covenant
of grace under its new covenant administration (the church, inclusive of
Gentiles as well as Jews).[21] In baptism the many are incorporated into one
body (Eph 4:4) and begin to participate in the life of the age to come as those
who have put on the resurrected and glorified Jesus and are being conformed to the same image (Rom 4:11; 1 Cor 12:12-13). Entrance into new life
in Christ the head of his body is entrance into the life of the members that
receive life from and in their head (Eph 1:22-23; 2:21; Col 1:18). Though ex-
periencing baptism does not of itself save—and though the Spirit's effective
working through the sacrament is not limited to the time of its administration (so Westminster Confession of Faith 28.6)—Christian baptism is
never something merely nominal, nor is it legitimately administered beyond
the manifest realm of Christ's saving work and kingly rule.[22] It is not surprising, then, that Murray came very close to what I am arguing here regarding the material coextensiveness of union and new covenant membership: "Baptism is an ordinance instituted by Christ and is the sign and

---

[18]For Calvin this double grace is indeed ordered—theologically if not logically. For sanctification's dependence on justification for its character and power in Calvin's thought, see esp. Billings, "Union with Christ," pp. 59-60; Calvin, *Institutes* 3.11.1.

[19]See, e.g., the rich exposition of this theme by John Owen, in *Communion with the Triune God*,
ed. Kelly Kapic and Justin Taylor (Wheaton, IL: Crossway, 2007), esp. part 2.

[20]John Murray, *Christian Baptism* (repr., Phillipsburg, NJ: P & R, 1970), p. 3, see also pp. 4-5, 27,
31, 34, 43.

[21]See, e.g., Bullinger in the Second Helvetic Confession (1561): "Now to be baptized in the name
of Christ is to be enrolled, entered, and received into the covenant and family, and so into the
inheritance of the sons of God"; in *Book of Confessions*, 5.187.

[22]The Reformed agree with nonpaedobaptists on this last point, but commonly argue that the
children of believers are rightly considered to be included in that work and under that rule
(although through lifelong persistence in unbelief they may prove themselves not to be legitimate heirs of the inheritance promised them in Christ).

seal of union with him. This is just saying that it is the sign and seal of membership in that body of which Christ is the Head. The body of which Christ is the Head is the church (*cf.* Eph 5:23-30). Hence baptism is the sign and seal of membership in the church."[23]

Murray took his cue from the language of the Westminster Standards (1647), which in turn distilled a great deal of previous Reformed conviction:

> Baptism is a sacrament of the New Testament, ordained by Jesus Christ, not only for the solemn admission of the party baptized into the visible Church; but also to be unto him a sign and seal of the covenant of grace, of his in-grafting into Christ, of regeneration, of remission of sins, and of his giving up unto God, through Jesus Christ, to walk in the newness of life.[24]

The Reformed tradition should at least be able to say, therefore, that its historic confessional statements and liturgical practice argue strongly for the *inseparability* of mystical union and ecclesial inclusion. Baptism signifies and seals union with Christ *no more or less than* it is the sacrament of incorporation into the people of God. To be in Christ is to be in his church as well.

But should we say more, further unpacking the implications of this strand of Reformed baptismal confession and practice? There remains a good deal of doctrinal asymmetry in the Reformed tradition between incorporation into Christ and becoming a member of his new covenant community. Union with Christ is not usually allowed any *merely* external or visible significance, even though this signification is readily allowed for an individual's membership in the covenant community. The Westminster Standards, as seen above, speak of baptism being administered for entrance into the visible church, on one hand, and being given as a sign and seal of union with Christ and reception of his benefits in the covenant of grace, on the other. The Standards hold the two descriptions closely together, of course, but the phrasing suggests that being "in Christ" is only appropriately descriptive of those who *really*, internally participate in saving grace through true faith. Thus Billings observes that even amid deep continuity with the earlier Re-

---

[23]Murray, *Christian Baptism*, p. 31.
[24]Westminster Confession of Faith 28.1; cf. Larger Catechism 165 and Shorter Catechism 94 (*Book of Confessions*, 6.146, 7.275 and 7.094). Cf. Calvin's more compact affirmation: "[Baptism] is the initiatory sign by which we are admitted to the fellowship of the Church, that being in-grafted into Christ we may be accounted children of God"; in *Institutes* 4.15.1. His comment on Tit 3:5 is similar.

formed tradition, by the time of the Standards a quite specialized use of the language of union with Christ had become commonplace, reserved for speaking of redemption only as applied to *the elect* and in the context of their participation in the *invisible* church.[25]

My intention here is not to challenge the truth of participatory union as the temporal outworking of election in Christ, or the foundation of the covenant of grace in Christ's eternal mediation and temporal mission, or a certain invisibility of the church *sub specie aeternitatis*. What I am challenging is the conclusion that being "in Christ" should be *restricted* to a moment in the application of salvation in which each of the elect are incorporated into their Mediator by faith. I believe that in light of the broader *lex orandi*, this particular development—driven also by certain implications in the *lex credendi*, to be sure—needs to be submitted once again to a fresh engagement with the *regula fidei*.[26] Assuming for the moment that the specific doctrinal content of this restrictive understanding of union with Christ in applied redemption is still fundamentally correct, does this mean that the biblical language of being "in Christ" and enjoying intimate fellowship with him is likewise narrow in content and scope? What do we do with the thoroughly corporate quality of being in Christ that Paul maintains? What about the sheer *visibility* of those who are individually and corporately baptized into the church and affirmed to be "in Christ" and subject to his mediatorial representation, without qualification? In the Pauline corpus, as discussed below, being united to Christ by faith is not intrinsically distinct from believing participation in the tangible assembly of his called and gathered church. The mysterious internal realities of our salvation in Christ should not be set over against the explicit external realities of our ecclesial life, since they appear inseparable in Scripture. In short, our identity individually as "new creation" in Christ involves equally and together our identity as incorporated into his church, the temple of his Spirit, the earthly outpost of the kingdom of heaven, the firstfruits of the harvest of the age to come.

---

[25]See further Billings, "Union with Christ," pp. 66-67.

[26]Thus the truth of Regis Duffy's axiom, "A theology of initiation is inseparably linked to a theology of church." In *Systematic Theology: Roman Catholic Perspectives*, ed. Francis Schüssler Fiorenza and John P. Galvin (Minneapolis: Fortress, 1991), 2:213.

Regula fidei: *Paul's expansive use of "in Christ."* The extensive recent exegetical study by Constantine Campbell of Pauline occurrences of "in Christ" and related language presents a ready opportunity to revisit the exegetical moorings of a doctrine of union with Christ and the question of its relation with ecclesial communion.[27] Campbell suggests that the four interrelated themes of union, participation, identification and incorporation best encompass the depth and variety of Paul's "in Christ" language and its synonyms.[28] Campbell also settles on a number of key Pauline texts that are particularly relevant for union with Christ; these texts will prove a useful exegetical touchstone for my purposes. Whether these represent all the important texts or whether some are relatively more determinative than others, it is telling that none of them preclude a theological equivalence between the language of being in Christ and being a member of his body—indeed, collectively they lend support to it.[29]

Several of Campbell's key texts deal directly with the meaning or implications of baptism, the dual personal and communal resonance of which I have already described (Rom 6:3-5, 8; Gal 3:27-28; Col 2:12-13). Other passages do not mention baptism directly, but speak similarly of Christians' participation in Christ's death and resurrection by faith, so that in his death all have died and in his life all live and will rise again (Rom 7:4; 1 Cor 15:22; 2 Cor 13:4; Eph 2:5-6; Col 2:20; 3:3-4; 1 Thess 4:14; 5:10). Again, all these verses make corporate claims.

- "We have been baptized into Christ Jesus [and] into his death."

- "With Christ you [all] died."

- "In Christ shall all be made alive."

---

[27]Constantine Campbell, *Paul and Union with Christ: An Exegetical and Theological Study* (Grand Rapids: Zondervan, 2012).

[28]Ibid., pp. 29-30. Understandably, the lists of what Paul's language encompasses vary. Gaffin lists three categories of meaning for "in Christ" and its various synonyms (see note 2 above). Seifrid counts five categories, apart from this particular phrase's many synonyms (in descending order of frequency): (1) an instrumental use, pointing out the mediate agency of Christ in God's work of creation and redemption; (2) encouragement to or endorsement of attitudes and practices flowing from Christian identity; (3) reference to the "present state of believers in view of Christ's saving work"; (4) reference to particular persons or circumstances in their relationship to Christ's salvation; (5) descriptions of Christ's own character (e.g., Col 1:19; 2:9). "In Christ," pp. 433-36.

[29]Campbell, *Paul and Union*, pp. 424-35. In the next few paragraphs, I cite biblical chapter and verse ranges as Campbell gives them.

Statements such as these entail redemption's application to individuals, certainly, but are not exclusive to individual redemption. Nor, significantly, do these passages speak of our being-in-Christ strictly in the context of the individual outworking or application of eternal election. When speaking of the fruition of God's saving decree, even Ephesians 2:5-6 and 1 Thessalonians 5:9 are as corporate as they are individual in their use of the language of being-in-Christ.

Along these lines, a large number of other key union texts from Campbell are integral to the exposition of one or another of Paul's favorite metaphors for the relationship between Christ and his church as a whole. We are each and together

- God's children (Rom 8:17);

- God's temple (Eph 2:21);

- Christ's body (Rom 12:5; 1 Cor 10:16-17; Eph 1:22-23; 2:15; 4:15-16; Col 2:9-10); and

- Christ's bride (1 Cor 6:15-16; 2 Cor 11:2; Eph 5:29-32).

There are a few passages Campbell highlights as significant for union with Christ that are somewhat different in character from the above, focusing not so much on individual and corporate identification with our crucified and risen Lord, but on his accomplished work as personally appropriated and experienced (1 Cor 1:30; 2 Cor 5:17, 21; Phil 3:8-9).[30] These four passages emphasize Christians' enjoyment of a radically new identity in Christ through who he is and what he has accomplished for each and all. And it is again noteworthy that only one of these is explicitly *and entirely* focused on an individual's being-in-Christ (Paul himself, in Phil 3:8-9).[31]

Delineated in this way, we may appropriately affirm that in the Pauline corpus being in Christ and belonging to his people are materially equivalent—the theological significance of the language of "union, participation, identification, incorporation" in Christ is just as fittingly claimed for and

---

[30]One of Campbell's key texts is only indirectly related to the application of redemption (1 Cor 8:6).

[31]2 Cor 5:17 is grammatically singular, although intentionally generalized: "If anyone [*tis*] is in Christ. . . ." This is not to say there are no other deeply personal statements to this effect in the Pauline corpus (e.g., Gal 2:19-20); again, I am limiting myself to Campbell's key passages. In any case, these "I" statements from Paul are also representative claims from one who regularly encouraged his churches to imitate him in faith and life (e.g., 1 Cor 4:15-17; 11:1; Phil 4:9).

applied to the language of belonging to "the redemptive-historical people of God," of which Christ is head and husband, elder brother and chief corner-stone.[32] Being united to Christ is no less soteriologically essential (and inti-mately personal) when understood in this sense. Yet its scope is not limited to one aspect of the application of Christ's work to each individual who belongs to him—even if that aspect is central for all others—but encom-passes the whole of so great a salvation. I now turn to consider anew the rule of believing in light of the rule of praying and the rule of faith.

Lex credendi: *Three significant doctrinal fruits of the equivalence of union and covenant inclusion.*

Offers fresh answers to the classic problems of internal versus external and visible versus invisible participation. Why does it feel appropriate to say that all who are in Christ are (without qualification) members of the new cov-enant community, but not quite as fitting to say (again without qualification) that all who belong to the community are in Christ? Much of the reason, I have tried to show, seems to be because classical Reformed theology came to define union with Christ quite specifically, by aligning it more closely with the doctrine of particular election and its outworking in individual soteriology than with the doctrine of the church. After all, those who belong to the invisible church spanning all times and places only very rarely do not also become at some point in their lives members of the visible church in one or another of its concrete institutional forms; yet Scripture and expe-rience show that too often members of the visible church seem not to belong truly to the invisible church or really inherit God's promises. True union with Christ thus is seen as the applied soteriological outworking in time of God's promises purposed from eternity to be procured by and enjoyed in the Mediator, who together with his saving benefits is the substance of the covenant of grace. Thus also "internal" membership in the covenant of grace, eternally and temporally grounded in union with Christ, is synonymous with true membership in the invisible church.[33]

Certainly such an account makes good sense if the language of union

---

[32]The last-quoted phrase is Herman Ridderbos's; see in general his nuanced treatment of Pauline analogies for the relationship between Christ and his people in *Paul: An Outline of His Theology* (Grand Rapids: Eerdmans, 1975), chaps. 8-9, 11. See further Frank J. Matera, *God's Saving Grace: A Pauline Theology* (Grand Rapids: Eerdmans, 2012), pp. 74-80.

[33]Turretin, *Institutes of Elenctic Theology*, 3:11-26.

with Christ is reserved for the temporal out-working of a person's eternal election; in that case, belonging to the church—because this can be true of a person visibly while not being *necessarily* true invisibly—is allowed to remain a much more expansive conception (figure 1). I have suggested instead that the language of being in Christ is just as rich and expansive for Paul as his language of being in the church, and so it should be in our doctrinal exposition as well. Put differently, we should not speak more narrowly

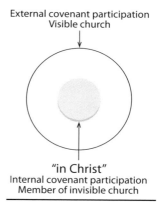

External covenant participation
Visible church

"in Christ"
Internal covenant participation
Member of invisible church

Fig. 1.

about being in Christ than Paul does. If for him this conveys both corporate and individual dimensions, and both an initial incorporation and an unfolding relationship, we should not pick and choose between these. When we do, we lose something. In my view, union with Christ is not narrower than or constitutive for participation in the covenant of grace; it is not the internal reality of which communion with the saints is an important, though not decisive, outward manifestation. Again, in Pauline terms, our being-in-Christ is no less outwardly administered (through the word and sacraments) than our being-in-the-church, and no less in need of fruitful communal expression (e.g., 1 Cor 11:17-33; 12:12-31).

If belonging to Christ and belonging to his covenant people are *both* internal and *both* external, then the typical Reformed mapping of what is internal and what is external needs to be expanded. Perhaps a more fitting way of putting things is in terms of union and participation being *either genuine or not* (as in figure 2). A person's identification with Christ and inclusion in his church can be authentic or inauthentic, but they are *always together* both true or both false. On one hand, this means that because true mystical union is

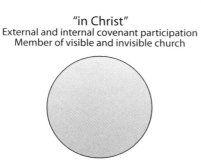

"in Christ"
External and internal covenant participation
Member of visible and invisible church

Either genuine or false

Fig. 2.

coextensive with true ecclesial inclusion, the Spirit who brings us into communion with one another is not doing something subsequent or supplemental to, or separable from, his work of bringing us into union with our Lord. On the other hand, being in Christ can be just as (merely) external or (merely) visible as belonging to his body. "Not all who are decended from Israel belong to Israel" (Rom 9:6) is, in Pauline terms, a warning no less relevant to incorporation in Christ than to community participation.

Upholds the corporate character of union and the personal and soteriological character of ecclesial communion. I hope it is quite clear in light of the discussion to this point that I am *emphatically not* saying there is no difference between Christ and the church, or between the individual and the community, or between soteriology and ecclesiology. What I am urging is that these pairs of themes should be mutual and inseparable *at every point* in doctrinal formulations of them, and a key to this is recognizing that we should recover a more variegated and robustly Pauline way of employing the language of our being-in-Christ as a rich description of the whole of redemption applied to Christ's people by his Spirit. Union with Christ is not the exclusive province of soteriology, while participation in the faith and life of the church belongs only to ecclesiology. Union with Christ is in reality—and should be in theology—thoroughly ecclesiological, and true inclusion in the covenant of grace is inseparable from the application and experience of redemption by grace through faith in Christ.[34]

This approach upholds the corporate, institutional and liturgical character of union with Christ. Too often Protestants, especially, understand our being-in-Christ in such a way that ecclesial life is deemed unnecessary for authentic personal religious experience or progress in faith and love. To understand being "in Christ" as a description of the whole of our participation in his accomplished redemption renders the ministry of word and sacrament essential to our participation in Christ, and recognizes applied redemption as inseparable from the Spirit's activity in including us in his people's holy worship, ministry and mission. Communion with

---

[34]So Barth: "The royal freedom of [a Christian's] faith is the freedom to stand in it as a brother or a sister, to stand with other brothers and sisters in the possession granted to [faith] and the service laid upon it. . . . There are no saints without the fellowship, but there is no fellowship without the saints." In *CD* IV/1, p. 751.

Christ's ecclesial temple and bride—embodied in local congregations and broader expressions of the communion of the saints, both charged with the ministry and mission of the gospel—is not a sometimes useful addition to our growth in union with him. Corporate worship cannot be a joint exercise in private devotions. *Growth in Christ is always growth in his body*, since believing apprehension of the infinite grace and glory of the Father in his Son is actually impossible apart from the cooperative doxology of "all the saints" (Eph 3:14-21).

At the same time, then, this approach maintains the personal, christological and pneumatological character of the new covenant community. Belonging to the people of God is just as concretely personal for each believer as belonging to Christ in whom we believe. A full-orbed approach to union does not allow individual applicative union with Christ *any* logical precedence over communal life with his members, yet it does so while upholding the particularity and dignity of *every* individual member (1 Cor 12:12-27) as well as the uniqueness and preeminence of the person and work of the one Lord of all (Eph 4:5).[35]

Provides clarity on the theological relation between union, justification and sanctification. Identifying our being-in-Christ with the whole of applied redemption also provides an opportunity to find greater clarity on several key issues involved in contemporary debates over the dynamics of union with Christ and the reception of his benefits by faith. The area where tensions arise perhaps most clearly in this setting is in an ongoing competition between union and justification—or, often, between incorporation and imputation—for the role of the foundation or antecedent ground of the application of redemption. On what immediate basis, or with respect to what direct consideration, does the Holy Spirit apply in the here and now the fruits of Christ's already accomplished redemption?

PROBLEMS WITH UNION AS THE GROUND OF APPLIED REDEMPTION

In his influential defense of the priority of union, Richard Gaffin endorses a maxim from Jonathan Edwards that neatly summarizes a key underlying

---

[35]See esp. Horton, *Covenant and Salvation*, pp. 181-215.

doctrinal concern of many who interpret our being-in-Christ as the ground of applied redemption: "What is real in the union between Christ and his people, is the foundation for what is legal; that is, it is something that is really in them, and between them, uniting them, that is the ground of the suitableness of their being accounted as one by the Judge."[36] Jonathan Edwards described this foundation or ground as the unitive "relation" of faith, and Gaffin as union with Christ by faith. Gaffin, like Edwards, does not want to undermine the "synthetic" character of God's verdict—it is always by free grace, and Christ's "resurrection-approved righteousness," not our own, is imputed to us by faith for justification within this relationship.[37] Sanctification, like justification, is grounded in and flows from this internal bond with Christ (as in figure 3).[38]

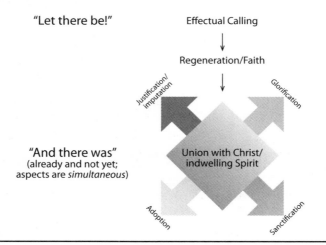

Fig. 3.

---

[36]Gaffin, *Resurrection and Redemption*, p. 132, quoting the works of Jonathan Edwards, vol. 19: *Sermons and Discourses, 1734–1738*, ed. M. X. Lesser (New Haven, CT: Yale University Press, 2001), p. 158. See further George Hunsinger, "Dispositional Soteriology: Jonathan Edwards on Justification by Faith Alone," *Westminster Theological Journal* 66 no. 1 (2004): 107-20; cf. Kyle Strobel, "By Word and Spirit: Jonathan Edwards on Redemption, Justification, and Regeneration," in *Jonathan Edwards on Justification*, ed. Josh Moody (Wheaton, IL: Crossway, 2012), pp. 45-70. Strobel goes so far as to claim that "Edwards's doctrine of justification stands or falls with his concept of union" (p. 61).

[37]Gaffin, *Resurrection and Redemption*, p. 132.

[38]In this approach, sanctification is related to justification insofar as they are both treasures hidden in Christ, and they both accomplish complementary purposes in the application of redemption; but sanctification is not *ordered to* justification. See the focused development of these themes in Gaffin, *By Faith, Not by Sight*.

There are many benefits of this model, including the inseparability of legal and transformative realities in redemption and the centrality of Christ, the Spirit and faith in its application. Still, "what is real is the foundation for what is legal" does not seem a suitably Protestant theological stance when seeking to describe the work of the one whose word will not return void, but accomplish all the purposes for which he sends it (Is 55:11), *especially* in the work of redemption, founded as it is on Christ and his vicarious work.

Again and again in Scripture, what is declared or accounted as such by God's pronouncement is foundational for, and indeed constitutive of, the actual effects of that pronouncement among and in his creatures. In the model endorsed by Gaffin, the justification of the ungodly appears to reverse the scriptural order: God accomplishes his work intrinsically, and then, upon seeing it, declares it to be (already) in existence. But God did not create all things and then confirm their being or meaning by his word; he spoke his word and all things came to exist through, and still find their meaning in, his word (the Word, Col 1:15-17). Abraham did not believe a God who first began to multiply his offspring before asking him to trust his promises; he entrusted himself to the God "who gives life to the dead and calls into existence the things that do not exist. . . . 'So shall your offspring be'" (Rom 4:17-18 ESV)— and it was counted to him as righteousness. This is the same God who through his Spirit creates faith by proclaiming the word of Christ (Rom 10:17). Indeed, it would be much closer to the scriptural logic of creation and of re-creation to assert that *what is legal is the foundation for what is real*.[39]

While God's creation of the natural order does not strictly correspond to redemption, then, there is an evident analogy and symmetry between the two in God's purposes that should inform the way we see the doctrine of union with Christ.[40] Both creation and re-creation involve the Father's declarative, effectual word bringing into existence what was not, through his Son and by

---

[39]Of course this should not be taken nominalistically, as a categorical absolute (appropriately applied to God as well as creatures). What I mean more specifically is that creaturely reality is grounded in the being and character of the triune God *manifested* in his will—in the Son perfectly expressing what is real of God, and by the Spirit truly bearing children with filial resemblance to their Father. So the legal basis is after all the law of love.

[40]In 1 Cor 8:6, for example, Paul explicitly encompasses the whole of reality—creation and redemption—in God's bringing "all things" to ultimate fulfillment in himself, in new creation. In Col 1:15-20, Paul attributes the totality of God's creational and redemptive work and purposes to the Son.

his Spirit. And for both creation and re-creation that performative act is the "legal" basis as the divine fiat, the declarative "Let there be!" calling forth what *therefore* "was" and was fruitful.[41] The comparison and contrast between our being "in Adam" or "in Christ" in Romans 5:12-21 is Paul's most developed parallel between creational humanity and redeemed humanity, and this passage also can be read as strong endorsement of the legal as the basis for the real in creation and redemption. Participation in the curse of sin and punishment unto death that is consequent on Adam's rebellion is placed in direct contrast to participation in Christ unto resurrection life consequent on his faithful obedience and death: "Therefore, as one trespass led to condemnation for all men, so one act of righteousness leads to justification and life for all" (Rom 5:18). Importantly, in this passage the ground of the participation of the sinful "many" in the curse of Adam's sin and death is his representative guilt, and likewise the ground of the participation of the righteous "many" in the grace of Christ's vindication and life is his representative righteousness (Rom 5:19). The expansive participatory consequences in both cases—death for all in Adam or life for all in Christ—come to pass because of an *imputed* status (cf. Rom 5:13 with Rom 5:20) adjudged by God for "all" on the basis of either Adam's "offense" or Christ's "righteous act" (Rom 5:16-18).

The often-used biblical image of marriage also offers a compelling illustration of the basis of the application of redemption in the effectual, declarative speaking of God. The foundation for marital union (actually becoming "one flesh") is the announcement before God and those present, "I now pronounce you man and wife." It is awkward to say that the marriage union itself is the basis of the marriage's legitimacy—in fact, union *before* pronouncement isn't properly "marital" at all! Being pronounced married is the legally legitimate context in which the one-flesh union takes root, and progresses from "just married" to "till death do us part."[42] The human analogy obviously falls short in certain respects, but the suggestiveness of marriage as a figure for

---

[41]For expositions of applied redemption that conscientiously attempt this stance, see Horton, *Covenant and Salvation*, pp. 216-66; McCormack, "What's at Stake," pp. 81-117.

[42]I am employing the typical language and forms of contemporary Western marriage in this example, but for the sake of this argument, the reality of marriage as a legally constituted covenant relationship (rather than a mutual "participation" that *thus* grounds its own legitimacy) is quite deeply rooted. See Ken Campbell, ed., *Marriage and Family in the Biblical World* (Downers Grove, IL: InterVarsity Press, 2003).

Christ's relationship with the church in Ephesians 5:25-32 is significant, as well as the number of passages that speak of the church being Christ's bride. So the nature of re-creation or "new creation" as a legally constituted relationship is an important context for understanding union with Christ, which, again, should not be taken in an individualistic sense—in a vitally personal sense, yes, but not an individualistic one.

Intrinsic to each of the biblical metaphors for our enjoyment of Christ's redemption just mentioned is that what is (legally) declared or "accounted" bears with it a new and very real existence, *not vice versa*. The point I want to tease out of this is that what Gaffin describes as necessary for ensuring that justification is not "arbitrary" but "according to truth," following Edwards, seems to derive much more from the necessities of certain commitments regarding the ontology of redemption's application than from the explicit stance of the biblical witness. The assumptions represented by Edwards's maxim are a quiet yet consistent backdrop against which Gaffin (along with many others) can assert that it is not "justification by faith but union with the resurrected Christ by faith . . . [that] is the central motif of Paul's applied soteriology."[43]

If being in Christ is indeed a way of speaking of being in the new covenant community with respect to its head, then this doctrine as such can hardly be applied redemption's "central motif" *as its antecedent ground*, at least not alongside a Reformed (and Lutheran) commitment to the justification of the ungodly on the sole basis of Christ's "resurrection-approved

---

[43]Ibid., p. 132; see along the same lines Sinclair Ferguson, *The Holy Spirit* (Downers Grove, IL: InterVarsity Press, 1996), pp. 100-113; Lewis Smedes, *All Things Made New: A Theology of Man's Union with Christ* (Grand Rapids: Eerdmans, 1970). While Campbell does not consider union with Christ to be the "center" of Paul's understanding of the application of redemption, he nonetheless concludes that union with Christ is the ground or basis on which redemption is applied to believers. Though Campbell's study is fruitful in many ways (as seen above), the limited usefulness of his inductive method for such doctrinal determinations becomes apparent when he argues that the multivalent and textured nature of Paul's use of "in Christ" language must *as a whole* govern any theological account of union with Christ—even though this language itself is often used to invoke quite distinct themes. Doctrinally, this will not do; it allows Campbell's prior exegetical, definitional and organizational commitments regarding which concepts should be mapped where—either as related to union, or describing union, or else themselves aspects of union—to supply the material content of the doctrine. Simply put, Campbell has given us much to enrich the doctrine biblically, but little to determine its theological role in the first place. See Campbell, *Paul and Union*, chap. 12.

righteousness."[44] I doubt very many arguing for the priority of union in the Reformed debates would want to suggest that belonging to the new covenant community is the ground of redemption in and among whom it is applied; but if the case I am building here holds any water, then in an entirely inadvertent sense that is what is implied. The covenantal matrix of applied redemption—being "in Christ" and belonging to his body—is not itself the ground of or motive for our participation in it.

PROBLEMS WITH THE TRADITIONAL LOGICAL *ORDO SALUTIS*

At the same time, the more traditional versions of a logical *ordo salutis* have their own problems (see figure 4), which I discuss here more briefly. Since Gaffin's paradigm is itself a vigorous biblical-theological evolution of a classical *ordo* approach, certain critiques of the priority of union in applied redemption apply here as well—first, in this context, the consideration that being "in Christ" is not best understood as a moment or aspect *within* the personal application of redemption. Further, the ontological assumptions at work in traditional orderings of the process of salvation are, like Gaffin's, often similarly inadequately "leavened" with the implications of the constitutive primacy of God's effective word in imputation and declarative justification. This can be the case regardless of whether union or justification holds logical priority.

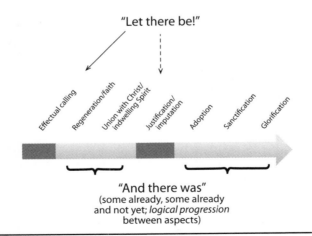

Fig. 4.

Horton has observed that "even if it is granted that justification is an exclusively forensic declaration, the rest of the *ordo* has sometimes been treated even in Reformed theology as the consequence of an entirely different event": the implantation of new life in regeneration.[45] This has had the unintended consequence of allowing the transformative aspects of applied redemption to operate according to a notably different ontological rationale than its legal aspects, rather than allowing the latter to be properly constitutive for the whole. In a traditional *ordo*, even if effectual calling and justification by imputed righteousness are seen as legally constitutive acts of God's gracious word, they nevertheless remain ill fitted to the intrinsic rationale of all the other aspects of applied redemption—which are rooted in "real" inward change for their ground and progress.[46] To this extent, *both of these approaches tend to make the legally declarative activity of God compete with intrinsic participation as the ground and motive of the application of redemption.*

AN ALTERNATIVE APPROACH TO THE *ORDO*

Understanding union as the covenantal relationship within which the Spirit applies Christ's redemption to us individually and corporately provides theological space to reconsider the foundational significance for applied redemption of God's declarative word—not only in effectual calling but also in imputation for justification. This is a needed corrective for the in many ways quite robust approach to Reformed participation from Julie Canlis, who grounds all our saving participation in Christ in the person of Christ himself by his Spirit, but does not give sufficient ontological weight to the declarative word that the Spirit bears in transformative power.[47] This is not to say that belonging to Christ our head or participation in his body is *subsequent* to justification; that would just be to narrow union's role again, merely assigning it an alternate position in the *ordo*. In brief, union is not a moment (either logical or temporal) within the order of salvation; it is a

---

[45]Horton, *Covenant of Salvation*, p. 216.

[46]See McCormack, "What's at Stake," p. 106: "In truth, forensicism (rightly understood!) provides the basis for an alternative theological ontology to the one presupposed in Roman and Eastern soteriology. Where this is not seen, the result has almost always been the abandonment of the Reformation doctrine of justification on the mistaken assumption that the charge of a 'legal fiction' has a weight which, in truth, it does not." Although McCormack may overstate the case in his alternative proposal, he has certainly raised the right questions.

[47]See esp. Canlis, *Calvin's Ladder*, pp. 245-52.

relationship spanning the outworking of redemption from beginning to end. This covenant is rooted in and continually motivated by the "righteous act" of the one on behalf of and in relation to the many freely given by faith, *proclaimed, secured and made fruitful* through the gospel of grace (figure 5).[48]

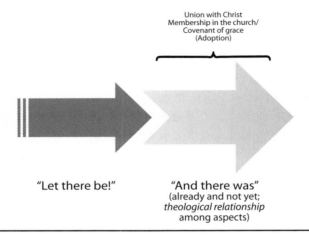

Union with Christ
Membership in the church/
Covenant of grace
(Adoption)

"Let there be!"   "And there was"
                             (already and not yet;
                             theological relationship
                             among aspects)

Fig. 5.

Thus I want to prevent a potential misapprehension of what I am suggesting. I am not advocating an externalization of our participation in Christ, abstracting the inner connection between him and each Christian into a mere "manner of speaking" about the reception of Christ's benefits within the community of faith. Put more pointedly, if being in Christ is speaking about the very same reality as being in his body, then what does it mean for *me* to be found in Christ (Phil 3:9), and for Christ to be formed *in me* (Gal 4:19)? My answer in many ways returns to the received doctrine: union is by the Spirit and through faith. In joining the church to Christ, the Spirit "is like a channel through which all that Christ himself is and has is

---

[48]There are elements of the model I suggest in fig. 5 that I simply cannot take up here (e.g., the regenerative nature of effectual calling, or the significance of adoption); again, I offer this as a preliminary proposal I hope will garner further dialogue and refinement. For a solid argument for effectual calling *as* regeneration, see Horton, *Covenant and Salvation*, chap. 10. Canlis and Billings also make a strong case for thinking of adoption as an overarching relationship applying to the whole of applied redemption (with respect to the individual believer as a child of the Father in the Son); see Canlis, *Calvin's Ladder*, passim; and J. Todd Billings, *Union with Christ: Reframing Theology and Ministry for the Church* (Grand Rapids: Baker Academic, 2011).

conveyed to us."[49] "For in one Spirit we were all baptized into one body—Jews or Greeks, slaves or free—and all were made to drink of one Spirit" (1 Cor 12:13). Yet the Spirit must not be thought of as *simply* the agent who makes possible the unitive relation between Christ and believers—he is Lord together with the Son, the constant "personal presence that constitutes the life of reconciliation."[50]

Faith, likewise, is not an external consideration, but a personal and intimate "closing with Christ" (as Edwards put it).[51] Yet hearing and believing the good news of Christ for our righteousness and sanctification is not a matter of *recognizing* a Christ who is already possessed by a faith previously given. Whether described biblically via marriage, or adoption, or new creation, or hearing by faith, or the justification of the ungodly, taking hold of salvation is hearing the good news of Christ *who is therefore my righteousness and sanctification*, possessed by faith, given by the Spirit in and with that effective word. Within this alternative paradigm, it seems to me, Canlis, Billings, Horton and McCormack—all appealing directly to Calvin—in their various insights supply a (mostly) complementary set of advances beyond many accounts of the character and role of union on both sides of the disagreement over the priority of participation or justification.

CONCLUSION

Union with Christ is that covenantal relationship within which Christ joins us to himself and one another by the Spirit through faith, as the communal fruition of God's effective word of forgiving and embracing grace. Being joined to Christ "the firstborn among many siblings" is also the realization of the eternal purposes of God in Christ to bring many sons to glory, the temporal horizon spanning calling, justification, sanctification and glorification (Rom 8:28-30). This spiritual matrix within which sinful saints are nourished on the gospel breathes faith, hope and love into the ungodly, as we put on the one who has become for us both sin and righ-

---

[49]Calvin, *Institutes* 4.17.12.

[50]Canlis, *Calvin's Ladder*, p. 148; and ibid., p. 156: "[The Spirit's] work must not be understood merely as the appropriation of the *beneficia Christi* but as their fulfillment within us." This is, in turn, a needed corrective to the somewhat thin account of union in McCormack, "What's at Stake?"

[51]*The Works of Jonathan Edwards*, vol. 21, *Writings on the Trinity, Grace, and Faith*, ed. Sang Hyun Lee (New Haven, CT: Yale University Press, 2003), p. 436.

teous, holiness and redemption, that we may become the righteousness of God (1 Cor 1:30; 2 Cor 5:21).

I have focused on a survey of the Pauline corpus both because it is the biblical locus of doctrinal discussion of union with Christ and because of length constraints. If the scope of this chapter allowed, or if future dialogue permits, these claims could be more deeply explored in Paul and extended to other New Testament writings (especially the Johannine corpus), as well as to other areas of the witness of the faith and life of the church besides baptism (especially the Lord's Supper).[52] Broader ecumenical engagement is of course deeply important. Be that as it may, I hope I have made a beginning of showing that according to the Pauline witness and supported in important ways by the liturgical significance of baptism in the Reformed tradition, being incorporated into Christ *is* becoming a member of his body, and vice versa. Baptismal union with Christ is a covenantal union, and the covenant of grace is a communion with Christ and one another in the life-giving Spirit of the age to come—a union finding its legal basis and power in, and in turn providing the living matrix for, the imputation of Christ's righteousness received, along with its transformative fruits, by faith.

---

[52]"The cup of blessing that we bless, is it not a participation in the blood of Christ? The bread that we break, is it not a participation in the body of Christ? Because there is one bread, we who are many are one body, for we all partake of the one bread" (1 Cor 10:16-17).

5

SANCTIFICATION AFTER METAPHYSICS

Karl Barth in Conversation with John Wesley's Conception of "Christian Perfection"

Bruce L. McCormack

Introduction

During the course of the academic year 1982–1983, I had a conversation with one of my professors at Princeton Seminary that made a lasting impression on me. Karlfried Froehlich was a medievalist who had started his career in New Testament and patristics, the subject matter taught by his *Doktorvater* in Basel, Oscar Cullmann. Froehlich had also taken several seminars with Karl Barth and knew his theology well. I was, at the time, a grad student preparing for my comprehensive exams and was only just beginning to get a handle on Barth's theology. I had been trained in conservative Reformed circles by teachers for whom seventeenth-century Reformed orthodoxy and its mediation by "old Princeton" theologians like Charles Hodge and B. B. Warfield provided the material standard for assessing all new theologies. And that made Barth rather strange. On this particular occasion, Professor Froehlich had come into the graduate study to retrieve a book, and I took the opportunity to ask him a question. I said to him, "I just don't get it. How does grace *work* for Barth?" He smiled and said, "Ah, you are asking an all too scholastic question." He then explained to me that the concept of grace implied in my question was not Barth's. "Grace" is not a quasi-substantial "something" that is infused into the soul. "Grace" is a person for Barth, the person of Jesus Christ in whom our salvation has been made real and even effective for us before we are made aware of it by the Holy Spirit. I was, at that moment, reading §63 of the *Church Dogmatics*—"The Holy Spirit and the Christian Life"—and suddenly everything I was reading made sense.

Now given all of this, it might seem strange for me to try to bring Karl Barth into conversation with John Wesley on the theme of sanctification. After all, Wesley understood sanctification in terms of divine surgery, a work of God in the individual in which the soul is cleansed of the contagion of original sin and, in this way, liberated from its power. Barth, however, understood sanctification christocentrically. For him, the "new creation" of which Paul speaks is something that happens in Christ. It does not first need to be "applied" to us before it can be effective. It is already effective in that it takes place in him. We need only to be awakened to its truth and efficacy, so that we can begin to live from and to it. So Wesley and Barth seem to be like the whale and the elephant meeting at the water's edge—an image that Barth used whenever he and an interlocutor could only stare at each other in astonishment and disbelief.

And yet, I cannot leave it at that. I cannot because I was, for the first sixteen years of my Christian life, a member of the Church of the Nazarene. And though I subsequently became a Presbyterian, I cannot agree that I ever ceased to be a "Wesleyan." The pursuit of holiness was too deeply ingrained to be set aside simply because I could no longer agree with the Arminian elements in the official theology of the Nazarenes. So in the essay that follows, I will be paying off a long-standing debt to the church that weaned me in Christian faith.

But I have another, more important reason for undertaking this task. It is at least possible that Wesley and Barth were saying the same things or at least quite similar things doctrinally, even though they were drawing on quite different philosophical resources in their attempts to explain themselves. Now the phrase "drawing on" needs some critical qualification if misunderstanding is not to arise here at the outset. Neither Wesley nor Barth did the work of philosophers. Their problems were not philosophical but theological in nature. In that they "drew on" philosophical resources, they did so not in a principled way but in a way pertinent to the explanation of theological subject matter. And even that was rare. Most of the time, philosophical influences were mediated by the theologians they engaged and from whom they learned. In any event, it is quite noticeable that they operated with different sets of philosophical commitments, however loosely held. And I do want to say something further about that.

John Wesley operated with a largely assumed rather than critically adopted ontology, one that had its origins in the classical Christian tradition. I do not think I do him any injustice if I describe it simply as a substantialist ontology that had its roots in cosmological speculation; my rendering of his doctrines of the new birth and sanctification will provide the justification for this claim. Barth operated with an actualistic ontology that was christologically rather than metaphysically grounded.[1] On the face of it, these can seem radically different—and they are when made to give answers to philosophical questions. But it must be remembered that both theologians were trying to explain the meaning and significance of biblical trains of thought and that they were working with the same biblical ideas and language. They were both constrained by biblical texts. That there should be a large amount of overlap should not be surprising.

And if I am right with regard to overlap, then we ought not to get overly excited by the substitution of an actualistic ontology for a substantialist one. In truth, Barth did not adopt his actualistic mode of thinking about questions of "being" in the final analysis because he thought that Kant had demolished classical metaphysics or because Hermann Cohen had treated the human "self" as task or because Hegel had inscribed "becoming" into the very being of God. He adopted it finally because he believed that the earliest Christian confession was that "Jesus is Lord" and that this conviction was set forth in the New Testament in the form of a narrated *history*. Kant, Cohen and Hegel—and even Schelling—all had their roles to play when it came to exposition, but they were not decisive. What was decisive was Barth's postmetaphysical, christological grounding of Christian doctrines—including those to be treated in this essay.

---

[1]The distinction between a "substantialist ontology" and an "actualistic ontology" can be explained as follows. The first locates divine "essence" in something that is fixed and complete in itself apart from and prior to any divine action directed toward that which is not God, so that divine action can be said to "express" divine being (though how far is left uncertain). The second understands divine "essence" to be enacted (rendered concrete and perceptible) in relation to Jesus Christ, so that revelation can no longer be understood as partial or incomplete.

In what follows, I am going to construct a conversation between Wesley and Barth on the twin themes of the "new birth" and "entire sanctification" (to use Wesley's language). Though Wesley understands these two concepts solely in terms of the work of God "in us" and Barth understands them preeminently (though not exclusively) as descriptive of the work of God "for us" in Christ, the two converge at the point of their appropriation of elements of New Testament apocalyptic—above all, the motif of "perfection." The essay will unfold in three parts, treating first of Wesley, then of Barth and concluding with some comparative remarks.

WESLEY ON THE "NEW BIRTH" AND "ENTIRE SANCTIFICATION"

John Wesley was born in 1703, just fifty-four years after the Westminster Assembly divines had concluded their work. He died in 1791, four short years after the publication of the second edition of Kant's *Critique of Pure Reason* and two years after the storming of the Bastille. His life thus spanned the whole of the eighteenth century. And, not surprisingly, he reflected in himself the leading interests and questions of the rapidly changing intellectual and religious conditions of that century. Lockean empiricism, Moravian pietism and Protestant theological commitments—all of these elements found a unique synthesis in him.

The last, especially, requires a brief comment. Understanding Wesley as a Protestant and, indeed, as a low-church evangelical, has been out of fashion in Wesleyan circles for quite some time now. In my view, however, such a development tells us far more about the aspirations of Wesleyan theologians over the last forty years or so than they do about Wesley. Wesley was self-consciously Protestant. On justification (the doctrine that made Protestantism to be Protestant), he wrote, "I think on justification just as I have done any time these seven-and-twenty years, and just as Mr. Calvin does. In this respect, I do not differ from him a hair's breadth."[2] The low-church element made itself felt in his views on the rites of the Christian churches. He regarded baptism as the sign of regeneration but also believed that regeneration rarely, if ever, accompanied baptism.[3] In adults, it does not; in infants,

---

[2]Letter to John Newton, May 14, 1765, cited by Kenneth J. Collins, *The Scripture Way of Salvation: The Heart of John Wesley's Theology* (Nashville: Abingdon, 1997), p. 86.
[3]See "The Marks of the New Birth," in *The Works of John Wesley*, vol. 1, *Sermons I: 1-33*, ed. Albert

it cannot—since infants are incapable of that repentance that, in Wesley's view, precedes the new birth. Moreover, Wesley's running debates with defenders of predestination constituted a fight over which strand of the Protestant tradition would reign supreme in the Church of England of that time—the hard-line Calvinism of his opponents or the Arminianism he preferred. But, of course, that was an in-house Protestant debate. Many have tried to portray Wesley as an "evangelical catholic" who was strongly influenced by the theology and spirituality of the ancient church. But that simply fails to convince.[4] He understood the atoning work of Christ along the lines of a penal substitution theory that fits badly with the *theosis* conceptuality with which many would like to link his doctrine of "Christian perfection." No, I find it impossible to understand Wesley as anything other than a low-church evangelical. I turn then to the new birth.

Wesley on regeneration. Since Wesley's treatment of the new birth presupposes his account of original sin, we would do well to begin with an account of the latter. In theory, at least, Wesley's account of original sin lacks for nothing from a Calvinist perspective. The consequence of Adam's fall is the "total corruption"[5] of human nature: "Everyone descended from him comes into the world spiritually dead, dead to God, wholly dead in sin; entirely void of the life of God; void of the image of God, of all that righteousness and holiness wherein Adam was created."[6] Indeed, Wesley says

---

C. Outler (Nashville: Abingdon, 1984), pp. 428-30: "Say not then in your heart, 'I *was once* baptized, therefore I *am now* a child of God.' Alas, that consequence will by no means hold. How many are the baptized gluttons and drunkards, the baptized liars and common swearers, the baptized railers and evil-speakers, the baptized whoremongers, thieves, extortioners? What think you? Are these now the children of God? Verily, I say unto you, unto whom any of the preceding characters belongs, 'Ye are of your father the devil, and the works of your father ye do.' . . . Lean no more on the staff of that broken reed, that ye *were* born again in baptism. Who denies that ye were then made children of God, and heirs of the kingdom of heaven? But notwithstanding this, ye are now children of the devil. Therefore ye must be born again."

[4]The most measured account of the largely indirect influence of a single strand of the Eastern tradition (that associated with Pseudo-Macarius) is to be found in David Bundy, "Visions of Sanctification: Themes of Orthodoxy in the Methodist, Holiness, and Pentecostal Traditions," *Wesleyan Theological Journal* 44 (2004): 104-36. Less restrained is Randy L. Maddox, *Responsible Grace: John Wesley's Practical Theology* (Nashville: Kingswood, 1994). Pseudo-Macarius was, in all likelihood, a member of the Euchite movement (in Syria), which was condemned by the Council of Ephesus in 431.

[5]John Wesley, "Original Sin," in *The Works of John Wesley*, vol. 2, *Sermons II: 34-70*, ed. Albert C. Outler (Nashville: Abingdon, 1985), p. 183.

[6]John Wesley, "The New Birth," in *Sermons II*, p. 190.

that there can be no natural knowledge of God[7] because original sin extends
to every "faculty" of the human soul.[8] And so he concludes, "Is man by
nature filled with all manner of evil? Is he void of all good? Is he wholly
fallen? Is his soul totally corrupted? [I]s 'every imagination of the thoughts
of his heart evil continually'? Allow this, and you are so far a Christian. Deny
it, and you are but a heathen still."[9]

Now it is quite true that this description of the natural state of the fallen
human is rendered null and void, for all practical purposes, by Wesley's account of prevenient grace. The effect of prevenient grace is to restore the
fallen human to something akin to Adamic (prefallen) liberty, the capacity
to receive saving grace such that the latter can no longer be deemed "irresistible." It is obvious that it is Wesley's desire to break the connection
between total depravity and unconditional election that has led to this conclusion.[10] But it is equally clear that, whatever we may think of this proposal,
it exercises no influence whatsoever on his account of the new birth. For
however true it might be that his affirmation of prevenient grace allows
Wesley to believe that the fallen human can, by God's assistance, prepare
himself or herself for the saving work of the Holy Spirit (through that "legal
repentance" that arises out of the spirit of fear[11]), it nevertheless remains true
that the "new birth" is worked in us by the Spirit alone and that what the
Spirit does in this work is to raise us from the dead and give us life. "New
birth" means life out of death, a "total change."[12]

The change in question can be best understood by means of a comparison
with justification. Justification and regeneration happen in the same instant
of time; they can be separated only for analysis and, when they are, Wesley
makes it clear that justification is logically prior to the new birth. "In order
of time, neither of these is before the other; in the moment we are justified
by the grace of God, through the redemption that is in Jesus, we are also

---

[7]Wesley, "Original Sin," p. 177.

[8]Ibid., p. 183.

[9]Ibid., pp. 183-84.

[10]I am, quite intentionally, refusing to embroil myself in the arguments that divide Wesley scholars
when it comes to the question of what it is precisely that prevenient grace is supposed to accomplish and whether it is irresistible in its working or resistible. For more on these disputed questions, see Collins, *Scripture Way of Salvation*, pp. 40-45; Maddox, *Responsible Grace*, pp. 83-90.

[11]See on this point, Collins, *Scripture Way of Salvation*, p. 55.

[12]Wesley, "The New Birth," p. 192.

'born of the Spirit'; but in order of thinking, as it is termed, justification precedes the new birth."[13] Justification, however, "implies only a relative, the new birth a real, change. God in justifying us does something *for* us: in begetting us again. The former changes our outward relation to God, so that having been enemies, we become children; by the latter our inmost souls are changed, so that sinners become saints. The one restores us to the favor, the other to the image of God. The one is the taking away the guilt, the other the taking away the power, of sin."[14] I will have more to say on the matter of regeneration taking away the power of sin in just a moment. For now, it is important to underscore the inseparability of justification and regeneration. The faith that receives the divine verdict in justification is itself worked in us by the regenerating power of the Holy Spirit. No justification, no regeneration, and vice versa!

But the new birth brings about in the believer not only the faith that receives justification but also a renewal of the image of God (in righteousness and holiness) that expresses itself in freedom from the *power* of sin. We touch here on Wesley's most important contribution, in my view, to the doctrine of regeneration: "From the moment we are born of God, we live in quite another manner than we did before; we are, as it were, in another world."[15] Wesley knows that regeneration is an eschatological event, the realization of the power of the future in time. *That* is his contribution. But he believes that the future is realized here and now *in* the believer. And here there is room for a bit of disagreement. But we will stay with Wesley a bit longer.

What happens in regeneration?

> Before that great change is wrought, although he subsists by Him, in whom all that have life "live, and move, and have their being," yet he is not *sensible* of God; he does not *feel*, he has no inward consciousness of his presence. . . .
>
> But when he is born of God, born of the Spirit, how is the manner of his existence changed! His whole soul is now sensible of God, and he can say, by sure experience, "Thou art about my bed, and about my path;" I feel thee in all my ways. . . .

---

[13]Ibid., p. 187.
[14]John Wesley, "The Great Privilege of Those That Are Born of God," in *The Works of John Wesley*, vol. 1, pp. 431-32.
[15]Ibid., p. 432.

> All his spiritual senses being now awakened, he has clear intercourse with
> the invisible world. . . . He now knows what the peace of God is; what is joy
> in the Holy Ghost; what the love of God which is shed abroad in the hearts of
> them that believe in him through Christ Jesus.[16]

Wesley's ontology of the human, to the extent that he has one, is dispositional
in nature; it is focused on the disposition of heart and soul out of which the
acts of an individual arise. He can also speak of "faculties" of the soul, so his
thinking on this subject is anything but well integrated. But dispositions
belong to the heart of his soteriologically grounded ontology. The consequence of regeneration, for Wesley, is that holy tempers take the place of evil
tempers; the fruit of the Spirit (Gal 5:22-23) replaces sinful dispositions like
pride, self-love and the lusts of the flesh, out of which acts of sin arise. And,
by this means, the power of sin over the individual is broken.

We do not have to await Wesley's treatment of "entire sanctification" for
the perfection motif to rear its head. It is already here in his treatment of
regeneration (where, I would say, it rightly belongs). In Wesley's hands, it is
closely connected with exegesis of 1 John 3:9: "Those who have been born of
God do not sin, because God's seed abides in them; they cannot sin, because
they have been born of God" (NRSV). Wesley understood this passage quite
literally, though he applied it primarily to externally observable acts of sin.[17]
The regenerated person, he believed, cannot commit willful sin—defined as
a voluntary transgression of a known law of God.[18] To be sure, he qualified
this in a decisive way—and had to do so, given his belief that the Christian
cooperates in his own sanctification. The person who "abides" in Christ,
who "keeps" himself through the practice of spiritual disciplines, cannot
commit willful sin.[19] But given his preoccupation with holy love as the basic
disposition of the regenerate, he also believed that the one born from above
has power over inward sin as well.[20] I think myself that he makes a mistake

---

[16]Ibid., pp. 433-35.

[17]Ibid., p. 436.

[18]Ibid.

[19]See on this point, Collins, *Scripture Way of Salvation*, p. 119.

[20]Wesley, "Marks of the New Birth," p. 419: "An immediate and constant fruit of this faith whereby
we are born of God, a fruit which can in no wise be separated from it, no, not for an hour, is
power over sin: power over outward sin of every kind; over every evil word and work. . . . And
over inward sin; for it 'purifieth the heart' from every unholy desire and temper." Cf. Wesley,
"On Sin in Believers," in *Sermons I*, p. 321.

here, not only in allowing room for cooperation in sanctification but also—
and especially—in failing to recognize just how *radically* eschatological the
claim made in 1 John 3:9 actually is. It is the eschatological subject of new
creation who *cannot* sin. If John also gives consideration to pastoral practice
in dealing with sin in believers in 1 John 1:8-9 ("If we say that we have no sin,
we deceive ourselves, and the truth is not in us. If we confess our sins, he
who is faithful and just will forgive us our sins and cleanse us from all unrighteousness" [NRSV]) and again in 1 John 2:1, this way of dealing with the
justified sinner in the present must not prevent us from seeing that this
subject has no future, that the "I" who sins does not stand on the other side
of a radical break with the "I" who is passing away. It is to Wesley's everlasting credit that he perceived the eschatological tension that cuts right
through the heart of the Christian's existence in this world; that he did not
flinch when confronted with a passage like 1 John 3:9 (see also Mt 5:48; 1 Cor
13:10; Phil 3:15) and would not let it be watered down.

But Wesley also believed that it was possible for a Christian to lose this
power over sin by not abiding in Christ, by failing to exercise the power
available to her. The "sin nature" is dealt a severe blow in regeneration, but
it remains. The remedy for that defect was to be found, Wesley believed, in
a "second blessing"[21]—the experience of "entire sanctification."

Entire sanctification. The new birth is, for Wesley, "initial sanctification."
Entire sanctification constitutes an "increase" in the former—and, indeed,
there is no experience of sanctification that could not be improved on.
Wesley writes,

> Christian perfection . . . does not imply . . . an exemption either from ignorance,
> or mistake, or infirmities, or temptations. Indeed, it is only another term for
> holiness. They are two names for the same thing. Thus everyone that is perfect
> is holy, and everyone that is holy is, in the Scripture sense, perfect. Yet, we may,
> lastly, observe that neither in this respect is there any absolute perfection on
> earth. There is no "perfection of degrees," as it is termed; none which does not
> admit of a continual increase. So that how much soever any man hath attained,

---

[21]On this point, see Collins, *Scripture Way of Salvation*, p. 157. It is sometimes held that Wesley did not lend his support to the idea of a "second blessing," that this was somehow the
invention of the American holiness movement. Collins gives us ample textual evidence to
prove the contrary.

or in how high a degree soever he is perfect, he hath still need to "grow in grace" and daily to advance in the knowledge and love of God his savior.[22]

Statements like these have led some Wesley scholars to claim that Wesley understood entire sanctification as a process rather than an instantaneous ("crisis") experience. That would be a mistake, in my view. It is true that there is a dynamism at work in Wesley's understanding of crisis moments. And that does justify speaking, as Albert C. Outler does, of a "perfecting perfection" rather than a "perfected perfection."[23] A perfecting perfection is ongoing; a perfected perfection is a given. But Wesley clearly also believed that the Christian can and sometimes does experience the removal of "inbred sin" in a moment. And therein lies the difference between "initial sanctification" and the "fullness" thereof: regeneration breaks the power of sin, while entire sanctification addresses the *being* of sin. It is the fact that entire sanctification has no permanency, no fixed character that renders the perfection in question to be a perfected rather than a perfecting perfection. That is the source of the dynamism in Wesley's thinking about the Christian life. Wesley regards the cooperative element in sanctification as the source of all backsliding—even a backsliding that allows that inbred sin that has been removed to regain a foothold, becoming inbred once more.

And yet, the possibility that "inbred sin" can be removed in this life must be taken with strict seriousness. To be "entirely" sanctified is to be perfected in love—love of God and love of neighbor. It is to be lifted above spiritual conflict; the believer "now 'feels' no contrary principle within."[24] No necessity of sinning remains.

Again, this does not mean that the believer will never sin again. Wesley never affirmed the possibility of a sinless perfection; in fact, he argued explicitly against it. What he did affirm was the possibility of a faith so "complete" that all that is left (for the time being, at least) is a heart full of love, joy, peace and so on. That he understood such an experience to be the product of a "crisis" that might need to be repeated takes nothing away from the importance of the experience. That Christians should settle for less than

---

[22]Wesley, "Christian Perfection," in *Sermons II*, p. 104.
[23]Albert C. Outler, "An Introductory Comment to Wesley Sermon 'Christian Perfection,'" in Wesley, *Sermons II*, p. 98.
[24]Collins, *Scripture Way of Salvation*, p. 175.

this was unthinkable to him. That they should do so willfully placed their souls in danger.

I think myself that Wesley has captured something here that is basic to the New Testament witness to the character of Christian existence in this world. Paul's writings especially (but not his alone) are shot through with eschatological expectation and a call to be holy as God is holy (1 Thess 5:23; cf. 1 Pet 1:15). The great issue raised by Wesley's doctrine of entire sanctification has to do with the location of the perfection described. Is it ever "in" the believer? Or is it something that takes place on our behalf in Christ— wherein it is kept for us, even as we are kept "in him"?

The only other comment I would wish to make is that Wesley's account presupposes throughout a conception of the soul and its powers that invites an understanding of grace as effective power or causality and of salvation in terms of cleansing or healing. It is this factor that has led numerous Wesleyans in recent years to compare Wesley's doctrine of sanctification with the Eastern soteriology of *theosis*. The great drawback to this comparison lies in Christology. Wesley understood the work of Christ along the lines of penal substitution and the threefold office[25]—in broad agreement with Calvin, then. So the attempt to order him to Eastern thinking is bound to disappoint sooner or later.

SANCTIFICATION AS EXISTENTIAL ENCOUNTER

In the second edition of his commentary on Romans, Karl Barth famously said, "A Christianity which is not completely and without remainder eschatology has nothing whatsoever to do with *Christ*."[26] But it is not just his early theology that was eschatologically oriented. The "Christocentrism" for which Barth would become famous after revising his doctrine of election in *Church Dogmatics* II/2 was equally so. In the early days, Barth could say, "By the Gospel, the whole concrete world is dissolved and established."[27] The center of Barth's attention was not yet the "there and then" of the earthly life, death and resurrection of Jesus of Nazareth but a concept of revelation that found its focus in the "here and now" of the believer. With his revision of election, his attempt to read all

---

[25]John Deschner, *Wesley's Christology: An Interpretation* (Dallas: Southern Methodist University Press, 1985).

[26]Karl Barth, *Der Römerbrief, 1922* (Zürich: TVZ, 1940), p. 298; ET: Barth, *The Epistle to the Romans*, trans. Edwyn C. Hoskyns (Oxford: Oxford University Press, 1968), p. 314.

[27]Ibid., p. 11; ET: p. 35.

doctrines through the lens of Christology emerged for the first time. When that occurred, the dissolution and establishing of the world by the proclaimed gospel would become the dissolution and establishing of humanity in Christ's death and resurrection—a realized eschatology that entailed the destruction of sinners and the creation of the new, eschatological subjects. In what follows, I want to show how Barth's revision of Calvin's doctrines of justification, regeneration and sanctification brought him, interestingly enough, within hailing distance of Wesleyan perfectionism—albeit, out of a center in Christology.

The meaning of "Christocentrism" as exemplified in justification. The charge of "a legal fiction" brought against the Protestant doctrine of justification by sixteenth-century Catholics has gained widespread acceptance today, especially among Protestants with a strong liking for the divinization soteriology of the Eastern churches. Basic to Calvin's answer to this charge was the claim that justification is never without regeneration as the initiating moment in the process of sanctification. The two take place in one and the same event or moment in the Christian's life. On this basis, he could then say that God does not merely impute Christ's righteousness to us; God makes us to be in ourselves what he declares us to be in justification: upright and holy persons. So God does not lie when he pronounces us "just"; he renders a judgment that looks forward to the completion of his work in us—an eschatological judgment in other words.

But there is a problem with this answer: it looks away from the ground of our justification in the alien righteousness of Christ and directs our attention instead to what God is doing in us. And the reason that this is a problem is that what God does in a sinner can never rise to the level of the basic content that Calvin himself assigned to justification. Calvin believed that justification is not merely pardon; it is *acquittal.*[28] And acquittal, as we all know, is a judicial verdict of innocence. No guilt is found in the accused, and she is rightly and justly set free. But Christ alone is innocent. He alone is without sin. So the basis of a verdict of acquittal can always and only be found *in him.* Only in him can it be true. To the extent that Calvin's struggle to address Catholic criticism led him to shift the focus away from Christ to what God is doing in us, to just that extent he failed in his efforts. For no

---

[28]John Calvin, *Institutes of the Christian Religion* 3.11.3, 6; cf. 2.16.5.

matter how changed and transformed a sinner may become, the fact that he was (and continues to be) a sinner means that he can never be made innocent in himself. He cannot be made in himself what God (according to Calvin) declares him to be in justification.

Barth's Christocentrism resolved this problem rather neatly. For Barth, too, acquittal is the basic meaning of justification. But for him, justification is effected in Christ alone, not in us. The distinction between redemption accomplished and redemption applied does not exist for him, as it did for Calvin and still did for Wesley. What Christ accomplishes is the reality of redemption, not its mere possibility. Not since John Owen had a Reformed thinker taken this axiom with the seriousness that Barth took it: the reality, not merely the possibility. The work of Christ is effective for us in being performed; it does not have to first be applied in order to become effective. And so it follows that justification is complete in him. But how does this work? How does it come about that *our* justification is complete in him?

Barth's answer is this: our justification is complete in Christ because we are already in him when he does what he does. We do not need to be "engrafted" into him later. We were there, present in him—by virtue of our election. Election, viewed from the side of its significance for theological anthropology, makes Christ the true, the royal human—the man who contains not only notionally but also in his very *being* as human the whole of the human race. That is why we do not need to be "added" later. Christ's work is not merely "for us"; it includes and embraces us even as it is taking place. And so, when he dies the death of the sinner, all sinners die. They are taken out of the way, set aside, rendered null and void, destroyed. When he rises from the dead, we rise with him—not as transformed sinners, mind you, but as completely new creatures. Thus the "I" that I am now has no future. The "I" that I am now has already died. And the "I" that I will be is not something I can be as a sinner in this world. It is not something I can be *in myself* at all. No transformative work of God in me can ever make me that. The "I" that I will be is the eschatological subject, the new creation.[29]

---

[29]It should be noted that the continuity of identity between the "I" who died and the "I" who is raised is guaranteed not by something in me (my "soul" as the putative guarantor of my identity, for example) but by what God determines in election and, on that basis, declares in the resurrection with respect to me. God's act of relating to me in the covenant of grace is the guarantee of my identity as dead and now alive.

Barth's answer to the charge of a "legal fiction" is more effective than Calvin's because it rises to the level required in making acquittal basic to the meaning of justification. What we will be is what we already are in Christ. In him, we are *rightly* judged innocent. We are the eschatological subjects no longer capable of sin.

Now, such an answer does raise questions about the significance of the Christian life. Why should it matter that we be awakened to faith and obedience in this life if, as those so awakened, we have no future? If it is only as those raised in Christ that we have a future? To answer these questions, I turn to Barth's account of regeneration and sanctification. Before doing so, let me just say that it is obvious that Barth has moved beyond Calvin's teaching on justification. But he has remained within the realm of forensic thinking. What is election if not a decision with ontological significance? It is an eternal declaration that is reiterated in time in the One who was raised for our justification (Rom 4:25). But it also has to be said that, in taking acquittal with even greater seriousness than did Calvin, Barth has moved closer to Wesleyan perfectionism. For what is innocence if not "Christian perfection"? The difference is that Barth locates Christian perfection in Christ, not in the believer in this world. But there is still a strong affirmation of perfection here.

The constitution of the Christian subject: Barth's version of "regeneration" (§63.1). Barth's account of regeneration requires no "healing" of will or even of mind; the absence of metaphysics from his thinking does not leave room for a "healing" of a substantially conceived soul or its "powers" (i.e., faculties). And, in any event, substantial "healing" presupposes that the individual who is healed is merely damaged and not truly "dead" in his sins and trespasses (Eph 2:1). In Barth's postmetaphysical understanding of the human (as grounded in the *history* of Jesus of Nazareth attested in Holy Scripture), regeneration is resurrection, not the resuscitation of a corpse, not the renewal of life in one who remains substantially what she was and is now given a fresh start. Resurrection means *new* creation. The self that we are, the self known to us as sinners, has already been set aside and destroyed. It has no future. The self that we will be is the self that we already are in Jesus Christ. Understood in this way, regeneration effects in an individual a radical decentering and recentering that has both psychological and ontological significance. Psychologically considered, the person awakened to faith by the power of the Holy Spirit is no longer "in control" of his life; he has surrendered control to Another. He is now made a witness to his true self in Christ. Ontologically, his true being, his *new* being, exists outside of himself. His being and existence is, henceforth, "eccentric."[30]

How does this take place? I already made mention of the awakening power of the Holy Spirit. Regeneration takes place not through divine surgery but through existential encounter with a Reality that is both indubitable and inescapable, a Reality that breaks into the circle of self-enclosedness in which the sinner finds herself and opens her up to a way of being in the world that was previously unknown to her. She is not given new faculties or capacities she did not possess before. Rather, as the human being she is, her life, her mode of existence in this world, is completely reoriented, redirected, and given a new telos.

This work of awakening is said by Barth to be "irresistible" (*unwiderstehlich*—that which we cannot stand against).[31] On the human side, the faith produced by this awakening is "a confirmation of a change which has already taken place, the change in the whole human situation which took place in the death of Jesus Christ and was revealed in His resurrection and attested by the Christian community."[32] As the act of *this* particular individual, faith "has no creative, but only a cognitive character. It does not alter anything."[33] As the act of the Holy Spirit who gives to faith its true object, however, awakening is indeed creative—but in a way and for a purpose that is not obvious to those accustomed to thinking in terms of a theological ontology that is not christologically grounded.

Classically, regeneration was understood to be the first moment in a series of moments that, taken together, constitute sanctification. Sanctification was then understood as a process, a movement from the lesser to the greater, from the provisional to the more complete, from a minimal to a greater acquisition of "grace." But "grace," for Barth, is not some *thing* that can be infused into us. "Grace" is a Person—Jesus Christ. He it is whose

---

[30]Barth, *CD* IV/1, p. 743.
[31]Ibid., pp. 752-53.
[32]Ibid., p. 751.
[33]Ibid.

being simply is his gracious activity for us. Moreover, where and when this gracious Person is powerful and effective in relation to us, there it is the Spirit of Christ that is at work. It is the person of the Holy Spirit who is this power, not a "grace" or "graces" abstracted from him as so many "gifts" that he bestows on us. What we are given is the Holy Spirit—not "gifts" that can be distinguished from his vital presence in us, as though we had acquired new predicates. He himself is the gift. What all of this adds up to is the fact that "regeneration" is not just the initial moment in a process but the divine side of a divine encounter with an individual that takes place moment by moment, in a history. Every moment of the Christian life is constituted by a transition from regeneration to sanctification. That also means that "conversion" (as the human side of the event of regeneration) is not something that takes place once and for all, an event that belongs to the past. It is an ever-present event, a converting that requires reenacting in each new moment.

Seen in the light of the foregoing analysis, "participation" in Christ is not to be construed metaphysically—in terms of the indwelling of a substantially conceived human nature. No human nature, Christ's included, is rightly understood if conceived substantially. What believers participate in is the history of Jesus' lived faith and obedience. That history is reiterated in them insofar as their existence is brought into conformity to that of Jesus. That is their "participation."

Examined more closely, the faith that is awakened in the individual by the work of the Holy Spirit is a human activity that Barth describes as taking place with a "profound spontaneity and a native freedom."[34] A human being does not need to acquire a new spiritual organ or capacity or faculty in order to exercise the freedom that is his in his humanness. It is his native freedom that is engaged and enlivened in that he is awakened to faith. That it also takes place with a certain "inevitability" is not to be denied. But this necessity is grounded in the reality of the new humanity in Christ, which is effective for all—even where it is not acknowledged and recognized as such. In Jesus Christ, "unbelief has become an objective, real and ontological impossibility and faith an objective, real and ontological necessity for all men

---

[34]Ibid., p. 744.

and for every man."[35] That some know nothing of this makes them "abnormal."[36] What is "normal" is the relation established in faith to our true humanity in Christ. In any event, "necessity" and "freedom" are here descriptions of our being in Christ and our being in ourselves; they are not conflicting (and perhaps irreconcilable?) descriptions of one and the same event in the life of any particular individual.

Faith is knowledge that is both theoretical and practical at the same time. It is "theoretical" in that it has definite cognitive content. It is "practical" in that it is engaged and participatory knowing. Barth is a bit uneasy about the classical definition of faith as *notitia, assensus* and *fiducia* since that ordering of concepts seems to imply that faith begins in "abstract knowledge"[37] of truths found in the Bible or formulated by the churches in response to biblical testimony. Christian faith, he says, is never abstract. It begins in "acknowledgment"—"a taking cognisance which is obedient and compliant."[38] We might say: it begins in an act of surrender to a Person, not in an assent to the truth of certain propositions. But, Barth insists, such acknowledgment entails and immediately gives rise to *recta cognitio*[39]—true knowledge of the being and activity of Jesus Christ as attested in Holy Scripture and proclaimed by the Christian community. If Calvin is right to say that "all true knowledge of God begins in obedience" (and Barth thinks he is), "then as the basic act of faith, this obedience is not an obedience without knowledge, a blind obedience without insight or understanding, an obedience which is rendered only as an emotion or an act of will."[40] Knowledge is contained in acknowledgment, but it is not the presupposition of acknowledgment. The two are given together, in the same moment.

Sanctification in self-denial, bearing one's cross and good works. We have already seen that "grace" is not a thing that can be infused into us or handed over to us, for Barth.[41] Therefore, there can be no "increase" of it—and sanctification does not consist in that increase. If there is a "more

---

[35]Ibid., p. 747.
[36]Ibid., p. 742.
[37]Ibid., p. 765.
[38]Ibid., p. 758.
[39]Ibid., p. 762.
[40]Ibid., p. 761.
[41]Ibid., pp. 624-25.

and more" to sanctification, it consists in the fact that living in humble self-denial—which was the constant feature of the life of Christ—is an increasingly frequent occurrence. It is becoming the pattern of my life and not merely episodic.

And so, not surprisingly, Barth's doctrine of sanctification finds its focus in a close description of what living the sanctified life looks like on the ground. Such a description begins, not surprisingly, with Christ, who is our sanctification (1 Cor 1:30).[42] He effects in himself "the conversion of man to Himself, His exaltation from the depths of his transgression and consequent misery, his liberation from his unholy being for service in the covenant, and therefore his sanctification." We are already sanctified in him before we know it. Our sanctification is already effective for us before we are made by God to acknowledge it. Those who have been awakened to this reality are "disturbed sinners"—those who now know that their sinfulness has been given a definite limit, that it has no future, that it is passing away. They are persons who now live *from* and *to* their sanctification in Christ, in "correspondence" to the "life-movement" of their Lord.[43]

Barth's description of this "correspondence" begins with "self-denial." "Self-denial" is exercised as freedom from the exaltation of certain "given factors" (e.g., possessions, fame, family and religion but also natural orders and historical forces)—anything to which our culture would give a quasi-divine status, thus placing them between God and ourselves as authorities to which we owe allegiance alongside of him.[44] Self-denial consists not in fleeing these things (in a world-denying mysticism or "inner emigration"[45]) but in public testimony to the fact that Christ has already decisively broken their power. In taking this step, in calling into question the reverence widely given to such "factors," the Christian will inevitably make herself unwelcome, a pariah, one who disturbs the peace.

The "fellowship of Christ's sufferings" spoken of by Paul in Philippians 3:10 does not entail a repetition of Christ's sufferings. The cross one takes up as the disciple of Christ (see Mt 10:38; 16:24; Mk 8:34; Lk 9:23; 14:27) is not

---

[42]Barth, *CD* IV/2, p. 515.
[43]Ibid., pp. 529, 533.
[44]Ibid., pp. 543-44.
[45]Ibid., p. 545.

Christ's. Jesus suffered rejection not only by men and women but also by God,[46] something Christians do not have to endure because he has taken it away in his passion and death. Still, to take up one's cross is to suffer the opprobrium that comes to those who are "aliens and strangers" in this world. "Things generally accepted as self-evident will never claim their absolute allegiance, even though they take on a Christian guise. Nor will they command their complete negation, so they can hardly count on the applause of the revolutionaries of their day."[47] However much solidarity Christians may find with the children of this world in relation to this issue or that, such solidarity has a definite limit: "They will never swim with the stream."[48] In any event, suffering furthers our sanctification insofar as we learn to trust ourselves to God's care in and through the experience of it.

And, finally, Barth's description of the sanctified includes a subsection titled "the praise of good works." The works of the sanctified are not good because those who do them are intrinsically good or because the works themselves are intrinsically good. It is because God accepts a work, that he takes it up as done in service to himself and gives it a share in his own missionary activity in this world that it is "good." Thus the praise of works looks in two directions: the works that contribute to our sanctification praise God and God praises them, thereby making them to be "good."

A Brief Comparison of Wesley and Barth on Sanctification

The point of convergence between Wesley and Barth has already been announced. "Christian perfection" is affirmed by Barth no less than Wesley. To be sure, Barth relocates that "perfection"—making it to be true of Christ and of the relation in which he stands to us. While that might seem to evacuate Wesley's doctrine of its content (given his interest in what is true of us), we would do well to pause and examine the matter more closely.

Barth was not any happier with the uses to which the Lutheran *simul* are often put than was Wesley, who saw *simul iustus et peccator* as an excuse, a rationalization on the part of the Christian for settling for a half-converted existence, a partial holiness that is no holiness at all. And if the *simul* were

---

[46]Ibid., p. 600.
[47]Ibid., p. 610.
[48]Ibid.

meant to say that the Christian is still "partially the old [man] and already partially the new,"[49] Barth wouldn't want anything to do with it either. If the *simul* is to be retained, it cannot be divided into a *"partim-partim"*[50] description of the Christian in this world. It is true only as two "total" descriptions. The whole Christian—not part of him but the whole—is wholly and completely the "old" and wholly and completely the "new." *What* he is as a Christian is defined by two "total determinations which are not merely opposed but mutually exclusive."[51] But there is no equality in the relation of these two determinations. The Christian is the "old man" only as that which is passing away, which has already been destroyed and rendered an ontological impossibility. In the *event* of faith, he is already—wholly and completely—what he will be when he sees Christ as he is (1 Jn 3:2). To put it this way is to acknowledge the eschatological character of Christian perfection both in its consummation and in its temporal actualization in this world. Every time a Christian achieves, by the grace of God and in faith, victory over temptation, a signpost is erected in this world of the world to come. In such events, the Christian is, even now, what he will be—not partially, but totally.

What Barth has done is to recast Wesleyan perfectionism in nonmetaphysical terms. Some might say that Barth's "actualism" is itself a "metaphysic"—but it is not. Barth has no *abstract* interest in history, in dynamism and relationality and no visceral reaction against the so-called fixed and static. His interest is not abstract because it is centered on a particular (and *concrete*) history, the narrated history of Jesus of Nazareth as attested in Holy Scripture—not actualism as such. It is because the New Testament tells us that Jesus Christ truly is who and what he is in the history of his self-revelation that Barth thinks this way, not because he has interpreted the New Testament in the light of a prior commitment to actualism.

Others have said that actualism is incoherent—that a disconnected series of random events cannot be productive of a coherent theological ontology. But the events of which I just spoke—the events in which the Christian is granted a victory over sin and, in doing so, experiences the power of the future—are anything but disconnected and random. The victorious events

---

[49]Ibid., p. 572.
[50]Ibid.
[51]Ibid.

of the Christian life are teleologically ordered by the perfection of Christ, which lies behind and before them and gives to them the character of a history that is moving toward a definite goal. The charge of "occasionalism" that has frequently been brought against Barth is thus without merit.

Conclusion

In this essay I have argued that Karl Barth's doctrine of sanctification is what Wesley's would have had to become had Wesley lived to see the possibility of elaborating a theological ontology that is not grounded metaphysically. And I must now confess, in conclusion, that I do think Barth's account to be superior to Wesley's—not simply because it does greater justice to the lived experience of Christians (though it does) but also because it does greater justice to the paradoxical nature of Paul's understanding of sanctification especially. I will conclude the essay with a brief illustration of this last claim.

Paul tells us in Philippians 3:12 that he has not yet obtained "perfection" (*teteleiōmai*). But then in Philippians 3:15, he includes himself among those who are "perfect" (*teleioi*). So Paul is and is not "perfect." What is going on here? Some have tried to resolve the tension between the two uses by giving the words different meanings. What Paul has not yet obtained is indeed "perfection"—and so what he is now is "mature" rather than "perfect." In adopting this strategy, Reformed exegetes are reacting against Wesleyan perfectionism. The goal is to remove the scriptural basis for the latter— which means that, to a significant degree, Reformed exegesis is controlled by Wesleyan doctrine. And that also means that the Reformed have remained blind to other possibilities. For it is also possible that Paul is saying that *in and of himself*, he is not perfect. But he has been given in Christ a "determination" for perfection such that he is already what he will be. Galatians 2:19-20 points, it seems to me, in the same direction. "I have been crucified with Christ; and it is no longer I who live, but it is Christ who lives in me. And the life I now live in the flesh I live by faith in the Son of God, who loved me and gave himself for me" (NRSV). I *have been* crucified. *I* no longer live. And yet, *I* am still here, living a life of faith in Christ. How is this to be explained? In my view, Barth's claim that the "I" that I was (the sinner) is already set aside and destroyed and that the "I" I will be is already here and present makes the best sense of this paradox.

PART TWO

Human Agency and Sanctification's Relationship to Ethics

6

"LET THE EARTH BRING FORTH . . ."

The Spirit and Human Agency in Sanctification

Michael Horton

The perennial debate over the proper relationship of divine and human agency often conjures the image of an old-fashioned scale. To the extent that God is identified as the agent in a particular event, the pan of human agency falls—and vice versa. In this essay I focus on two crucial coordinates that are often left out of the debate: (1) the analogical view of divine and human agency and (2) the trinitarian—specifically pneumatological—character of divine activity in the world. I will give the greater space to the latter here.

IDENTIFYING THE ANALOGICAL AND PNEUMATOLOGICAL COORDINATES

Especially in some popular versions of the Calvinist-Arminian debate, a false choice is pressed between a God who acts unilaterally upon the world and a self that is determined entirely by its own libertarian choice. For example, Clark Pinnock posed the options in stark terms: we worship either a God who does not want to "control everything, but to give the creature room to exist and freedom to love," or "an all-controlling despot who can tolerate no resistance (Calvin)." In Pinnock's view, we must choose between open theism and divine "omnicausalism."[1]

---

[1]Clark Pinnock, *Most Moved Mover* (Grand Rapids: Baker, 2001), p. 4.

It is easy to challenge this caricature of classic Calvinism. Regardless of one's judgment concerning its coherence, Reformed theology has consistently rejected what Pinnock calls "omnicausalism." With ancient and medieval precedent, Reformed theology has traditionally embraced an analogical view of the relation between God and human beings. Even when both agents are involved in the same event, they do not trip over each other, as it were. God's activity does not coincide univocally with human activity at any point. God is not only quantitatively greater than us, but qualitatively different.

Ironically, Arminian and hyper-Calvinist views agree with each other at a crucial point: namely, that agency is univocal. Consequently, the only real disagreement is over the way this liberty is divided. Both agree that God's freedom is original and that whatever freedom creatures receive is a gift. Nevertheless, both assume more of a quantitative than qualitative distinction between divine and human agency. Like a pie divided unequally between the host and guests, free agency is something to be negotiated or rationed. The chief difference with the hyper-Calvinist, then, is the ratio of divine and human freedom.

Following patristic sources, as well as Thomas Aquinas, Reformed orthodoxy has traditionally affirmed that the Creator-creature relation is analogical. In an analogical perspective, strictly speaking, God does not have freedom; he *is* freedom, since attributes and existence are one in the simplicity of God's being. God therefore cannot restrict his freedom or give it away to others. On the contrary, this divine freedom is the ground of that dependent liberty that God gives freely to creatures. Precisely in this difference, God allows creatures to exist in a mode of freedom that, although dependent, is entirely their own. Even when acting in the same sphere, or even in the same event, divine and human agency do not collide, because God is not simply one agent among others. To paraphrase St. Paul's citation of Epimenides, "In God we live and move and have our freedom."

The second coordinate in this essay is the Spirit's agency in the external works of the Trinity. In treating the God-world relationship, it is crucial to distinguish not only divine and human agency in qualitative terms, but also the qualitative difference between the personal agency of the Spirit in relation to the Father and the Son. While affirming the unity of essence is crucial for maintaining the ecumenical doctrine of the Trinity, we should be as wary even of an implicit modalism that downplays the personal distinctions.

Typically, debates over divine sovereignty and human freedom focus on the impact of one divine subject on the creaturely world. The persons are simply collapsed into "God," as if divine agency could be reduced to one mode. Usually, this mode is causal: God acting on the world. This image is reinforced by the tendency to correlate the activity of each person with various works. One Calvinist writer puts it this way: "Each of the three Persons of the blessed Trinity is concerned with our salvation: with the Father, it is predestination; with the Son propitiation; with the Spirit regeneration."[2]

Although common in some popular defenses, this is far from classic Reformed theology, which affirms the Cappadocian formula, namely, that in all of the external works of the Godhead everything is done from the Father, in the Son, by the Spirit. In one of his own variations of this formula Calvin writes, "To the Father is attributed the beginning of action, the fountain and source of all things; to the Son wisdom, counsel, and arrangement in action, while the energy and efficacy of action belong to the Spirit."[3] In every external work of the Godhead all three persons are engaged (*opera trinitatis ad extra indivisa sunt*). Though engaged in every external work, each person is engaged differently. "In the doctrine of the Trinity," wrote Herman Bavinck, "beats the heart of the whole revelation of God for the redemption of humanity." As the Father, the Son, and the Spirit, "our God is above us, before us, and within us."[4]

Too often in contemporary debates, the Spirit comes into the economy too late and leaves too early, making a cameo appearance in personal regeneration. If we do not recognize the Spirit's distinct agency in creation, providence, the incarnation and redemption, these doctrines will be rather different in content. An implicit unitarianism threatens the christological shape of creation, providence and the new creation. However, my concern in this chapter is with the tendency to overlook the Spirit's agency, whether by collapsing the Spirit into the Father or the Son.

So more clearly analogical and more robustly trinitarian coordinates will be fleshed out by a partial but hopefully suggestive survey.

---

[2]A. W. Pink, *The Sovereignty of God* (Grand Rapids: Baker, 1984), p. 72.

[3]John Calvin, *Institutes of the Christian Religion*, trans. Lewis Ford Battles, ed. John T. McNeill, Library of Christian Classics (Philadelphia: Westminster Press, 1960), 1.13.18.

[4]Herman Bavinck, *Reformed Dogmatics*, vol. 2, *God and Creation*, ed. John Bolt, trans. John Vriend (Grand Rapids: Baker Academic, 2004), p. 260.

THE SPIRIT'S AGENCY IN CREATION AND PROVIDENCE

The world does not emanate from God's being. *Ex nihilo* creation safeguards God's sovereignty—and difference—from creation. At the same time, it safeguards human freedom. In pantheistic or panentheistic schemes, a univocity of being threatens both divine and human liberty. A free word that is freely spoken issues in a cosmos. It is a personal word: the speech of the Father. Yet it is also spoken in the Son, who is the only divine person who can—and will—become flesh in the union of God and human natures. The Logos, by whom the worlds were made, is not a silent principle or semidivine demiurge, but the second person who is eternally spoken by the Father in the Spirit. Further, this word is brought to fruition by the work of the Spirit within the cosmos thus brought into being. It is the Spirit who molds, fructifies and fashions the matter into the temple of covenantal communion. The Spirit of God (*rûaḥ 'ĕlōhîm*), who hovered over the watery depths to create dry land for the creature whom he, with the Father, and the Son, would animate as "a living soul" (*nepeš*), is none other than the Holy Spirit, who regenerates those who are "dead in the trespasses and sins" (Eph 2:1).[5]

Colin Gunton brought to our attention the intimate connection between the Trinity and creation with considerable skill.[6] In this trinitarian economy, God is transcendent and immanent simultaneously, utterly distinct from creation

---

[5]See Robert Jenson, *Systematic Theology*, vol. 2, *The Works of God* (New York: Oxford University Press, 1999), pp. 11-12. "If this phrase were to be translated 'wind from God,' as some modern versions do," Jenson observes, "again the narrative would be mythic," but such a translation just indicates the translators' prejudice. There is no reason to believe that by *ruach Elohim* the Spirit of God was not intended.

[6]Colin Gunton, *The Promise of Trinitarian Theology* (Edinburgh: T & T Clark, 1997), pp. 142-58. Regarding creation, see "Atonement and the Project of Creation" in the last appendix. See also Colin Gunton, "Relation and Relativity: The Trinity and the Created World," in *Trinitarian Theology Today*, ed. Christoph Schwöbel (T & T Clark, 1995). In this essay, Gunton points out that both Plato and Kant have a world and timeless ideas, but Kant's is "an inversion of Plato's. The concepts are, indeed, both timeless and, in a sense, objective. But their locus is not reality, 'out there,' so much as the structures of human rationality. The human mind replaces exterior eternity as the location of the concepts by means of which reality is understood. Both proposals . . . are idealist, and, indeed, systems of transcendental idealism" (p. 92). They are just different in where they locate the transcendence: one objective, the other subjective (ibid.). Gunton argues for a trinitarian theology of creation. Following Irenaeus, this means that because the Father created the world through the Son, "it is real and good," which the incarnation reaffirms in its connection of creation and redemption, and the eschatological Spirit guarantees its future consummation (p. 97). God's creation of the world is wholly voluntary. "He does not need to create, because he is already a *taxis*, order, of loving relations" (p. 97). To enter into relationship freely in no way implies some necessity on God's part.

yet actively involved in every aspect of its existence and preservation. Gunton elaborates: "[God] is clearly 'without' in the sense of being other, transcendent. He is creator and not creation, but he is also, in realisation rather than denial of that transcendence, one who in Christ becomes part of that creation, freely involved within its structures, in order that he may, in obedience to God the Father and through the power of his Spirit, redirect the creation to its eschatological destiny."[7] Gunton's point, especially concerning the Spirit as the one who directs creation to its eschatological destiny, is highlighted by the special relation of the Spirit to the last Adam's fulfillment of the trial and entrance into the everlasting Sabbath as our forerunner. It is also evident in the prophets, where the Spirit is identified with the arrival of the "last days" of this present age and the beginning of the age to come (e.g., Joel 2).

Especially when wedded to a strong affirmation of transcendence and sovereignty, a unipersonal deity is easily construed as being related to the world as the ultimate cause or unmoved mover. The analogy is that of a person exercising force, acting on an object. By contrast, trinitarian faith acknowledges that the world exists from the Father, in the Son and by the Spirit. As God's external works are always the agency of these three persons, such action can never be reduced to external cause and effect.

Not only is God's external agency constituted by these three agents who work on, for and within creatures; but the triune God also works through creaturely media even to accomplish the intended effects.

It is significant that the biblical doctrine represents God's living speech as the means by which the Trinity creates the world. How unlike the analogy of physical force applied to a particular object, a clever watchmaker, or a world that causes itself, is the analogy of the Father speaking in the Son and bringing the effect of that speech to fruition through the agency of the Spirit. As a result of this trinitarian speech-act the creation itself answers back in its own voice of praise (Ps 19:1-4). The psalmist moves easily back and forth between the testimony of nature and that of God's historical revelation (Ps 19:7-14). Unlike the hypostatic Word, this performative word of God cannot be identified with God's essence, nor placed merely on the creaturely register. It is the energy of God. Like creation and the new creation, Scripture is identified

---

[7]Colin Gunton, *The Triune Creator* (Grand Rapids: Eerdmans, 1998), p. 24.

as "breathed out by God" (2 Tim 3:16) because it is the product of God's own speech. So God's works are neither God's essence nor merely a creature, but are God's energies, and the primary analogy for such *energeia* is the word.

This powerful word always comes from the Father, in the Son. In Christ the whole creation was created and holds together (Jn 1:1-3; cf. Col 1:15-17), and in him a new creation comes into being out of nothing but sin and death (Jn 1:9-14; cf. Col 1:18-20). It is significant that in these references from John's Gospel and Colossians both points are made in the same breath. Further, the word spoken by the Father in the Son is brought to pass in time through the personal agency of the Spirit. The Spirit is at work within creaturely reality so that this word will not return to the Father empty, but will accomplish its purpose. Yahweh is the Alpha and Omega, not as a solitary actor but as the Father, the Son and the Spirit. The eternal Son is the mediator in his essence, while the freely spoken word—the sacramental word—is the medium of this trinitarian work in God's energies.

> The mighty one, God the LORD,
>> speaks and summons the earth
>> from the rising of the sun to its setting. (Ps 50:1)

Notice the covenantal language for these communicative actions: "speaks" and "summons." Creation is in its very existence and from the very beginning covenantally ordered. God speaks the world into existence, and the world answers back in a symphony of praise, each species chirping, barking, bellowing or otherwise communicating its delight and dependence on God and each other. Yet it is human beings who are created as communicative partners in covenant.

Through this performative word, the Father speaks (the locutionary act), the Son is the propositional content (illocutionary act) and the Spirit is the one who brings about the perlocutionary effect. This appeal to speech-act theory is simply another way of expressing the formula that Calvin derived from the Cappadocians: "To the Father is attributed the beginning of action, the fountain and source of all things; to the Son wisdom, counsel, and arrangement in action, while the energy and efficacy of action belong to the Spirit."[8] In every divine work, the Spirit is the person who brings about within

---

[8]Calvin, *Institutes* 1.13.18.

creatures the "amen" to the word of the Father in the Son. The Father's word does not merely cause a state of affairs, but accomplishes this state of affairs through the mediation of the Son and the perfecting agency of the Spirit. (It is not surprising, then, that in the prophets the sending of the Spirit is identified with "the last days" and eschatological consummation.)

At the outset, then, the act of creation cannot be identified with God's essence but rather with God's energies. Like many radical Protestants from Jakob Böhme to Schelling and Hegel, Jürgen Moltmann draws on the kabbalistic doctrine of *ṣimṣūm*. According to this doctrine, creation is a contraction within God's own being, making space for finite reality. In a panentheistic scheme, this contraction is immanent and necessary to God's being. Although evangelical Arminians typically deny this necessity, they often speak of human existence and freedom as predicated on God's voluntary self-limitation.[9] However, both of these views—as well as the implications at least of Jonathan Edwards's speculations (discussed below)—so identify divine and human agency that neither agent seems finally to possess real freedom to be who they are.

By definition, God's act of *ex nihilo* creation is unique. Yet even in this singular case of unilateral divine agency, the Son is the mediator and the Spirit is the perfecting agent. In Genesis 1 itself we encounter two distinct types of divine declarations: the fiats of *ex nihilo* creation: "Let there be . . ." (with the report, "And there was . . .") and God's command to creation to put forth its own powers with which he has endowed it and within which the Spirit is operative: "Let the waters under the heavens be gathered together into one place, and let the dry land appear" (Gen 1:9); "Let the earth sprout vegetation, plants yielding seed" (Gen 1:11). In fact, it is reported, "The earth brought forth vegetation" (Gen 1:12). God adds, "Let the waters swarm with swarms of living creatures, and let birds fly above the earth across the expanse of the heavens" (Gen 1:20), and "Let the earth bring forth living creatures according to their kinds" (Gen 1:24). Furthermore, God commands the fish and fowl, as well as humans, "Be fruitful and multiply" (Gen 1:22, 28). We may put these two types of speech-acts in the form of "Let there be . . ." and "Let it become what I have 'worded' it to be."

---

[9]Keith D. Stanglin, "Arminius and Arminianism: An Overview of Current Research," in *Arminius, Arminianism, and Europe: Jacob Arminius: 1559–1609*, ed. Th. Marius van Leewen, Keith D. Stanglin and Marijke Tolsma (Leiden: Brill, 2010), p. 10. This is drawing in particular from Richard Muller, *God, Creation and Providence in the Thought of Jacob Arminius: Sources and Directions of Scholastic Protestantism in the Era of Early Orthodoxy* (Grand Rapids: Baker, 1991), esp. p. 268.

Thus far I have offered a fairly traditional defense of analogy and concursus in the "let the earth bring forth" category of God's speech.[10] However, I am also encouraging a more explicitly trinitarian—indeed, pneumatological—as well as communicative emphasis than is sometimes found in traditional Roman Catholic and Protestant accounts. For example, the Protestant orthodox spoke of a continual creation (*creatio continua*) that was nevertheless distinct from the original creation (*creatio originalis*).[11]

With the Enlightenment, this analogical view of the God-world relationship, involving the doctrine of concursus, began to unravel. Modernity has pressed on us a false choice between antisupernaturalism and hypersupernaturalism. The debate between Gottfried Leibniz (1646–1716) and Nicholas Malebranche (1638–1715) anticipated many contemporary controversies.[12] We cannot go into detail here; it will suffice for our purposes to point out that according to Malebranche's position, known as *occasionalism*, every creaturely action or event is directly and immediately caused by God.[13] God's agency is real, whereas creaturely agency is merely apparent. Arguing that every event is an *ex nihilo* act of divine creation, Malebranche collapsed providence (*creatio continua*) into miracle (*creatio originalis*). Malebranche argued that every event was an *ex nihilo* creation: a direct and immediate act of God. Although Leibniz is sometimes listed in a more deistic direction, the basic drift of his arguments was consistent with Protestant orthodoxy: in upholding the creation, God works through ordinary means and natural processes revealing the gifts with which the Creator has endowed it and continues to call forth its flourishing.[14]

---

[10]*Concursus* ("running together") affirms the reality of divine and human agency rather than seeing them in an antagonistic relation. It is closely related to the position of compatibilism in debates over free will and divine sovereignty.

[11]Charles Hodge provides an excellent summary with numerous citations in his *Systematic Theology* (Grand Rapids: Eerdmans, 1946), 1:577-78.

[12]On this debate and the respective views regarding creation see Nicholas Rescher, *Leibniz: An Introduction to His Philosophy* (Totowa, NJ: Rowman & Littlefield, 1979); G. H. R. Parkinson, *Logic and Reality in Leibniz's Metaphysics* (Oxford: Oxford University Press, 1965), pp. 98-110; G. W. Leibniz, *Philosophical Papers and Letters*, ed. and trans. Leroy E. Loemker (Dordrecht: D. Reidel, 1989); Nicholas Malebranche, *Dialogues on Metaphysics and on Religion*, ed. N. Jolley, trans. D. Scott (Cambridge: Cambridge University Press, 1997).

[13]Nicholas Malebranche, *The Search After Truth/Elucidations of the Search After Truth*, ed. and trans. T. M. Lennon and P. J. Olscamp (Columbus: Ohio State University Press, 1980), p. 658.

[14]G. W. Leibniz, *Philosophical Papers and Letters*, ed. and trans. Leroy E. Loemker (Dordrecht: D. Reidel, 1989), p. 499. At the end of the day, however, Leibniz seems to have held an almost

Reacting against deism's antisupernaturalism, Jonathan Edwards sometimes argued in terms that were virtually identical with Spinoza, and at other
times closer to the slightly less extreme views of Malebranche. "Therefore
the existence of created substances, in each successive moment," he wrote,
"must be the effect of the immediate agency, will, and power of God. . . . It
will certainly follow from these things, that God's preserving of created
things in being is perfectly equivalent to a continued creation, or to his
creating those things out of nothing at each moment in their existence."[15]
The falling of a leaf, in this view, is not a natural event in which the triune
God was involved in his own distinct agency, but is simply the effect of God's
direct fiat.[16] The "Let the earth bring forth . . ." type of speech-act vanishes
into the sea of *ex nihilo*, "Let there be . . . !" fiats.

While Arminians and deists restrict God's involvement in the preservation and government of the world, occasionalists collapse providence into
ex nihilo creation, Charles Hodge observes.[17] In the occasionalist view,
"There is no power, no cause, no real existence but the efficiency and causality of God." Recall that this is precisely the view that Pinnock identified
with Calvin and his heirs, and while it is certainly a caricature of traditional
Calvinism, it is difficult for me to see how Edwards might exonerate himself
from that charge. Hodge notes that "the strange doctrine of Edwards" on
this point owes much to Platonic realism/idealism, which reduces worldly
agency to mere appearances.[18] "Between this system and pantheism," he
judges, "there is scarcely a dividing line."[19] I share John Cooper's conclusion

---

deistic picture of continual creation as the effect of nothing more than the "mechanism of the
world" running as it was created to operate—without any divine involvement along the way. "I
consider it sufficient that the mechanism of the world is built with such wisdom that these
wonderful things depend on the progression of the machine itself, organic things particularly,
as I believe, evolving by a certain predetermined order."

[15]Jonathan Edwards, *Original Sin* 4.3, in *The Works of Jonathan Edwards* (Edinburgh: Banner of
Truth Trust, 1834), 1:223.

[16]Jonathan Edwards, Miscellany 1263 in *The Philosophy of Jonathan Edwards from His Private
Notebooks* (Eugene: University of Oregon, 1955), p. 185. Edwards even refers to these divine acts
as "arbitrary," not in relation to God's own nature, but in relation to natural laws. However, it is
difficult to see how there could even be such a thing as natural laws in this system.

[17]Hodge, *Systematic Theology*, 1:576-80.

[18]Ibid., 2:220-21. Hodge elaborates his objection to this view here in his treatment of Edwards's
view of original sin, which lodges guilt and corruption in the real (numerical) identity of human
substance in Adam.

[19]Ibid., 1:580. If Hodge's judgment is too severe, the more recent conclusion of Michael James
McClymond seems entirely appropriate: "The concept of God as known, as manifest, as visibly

that although Edwards was a fairly traditional Augustinian Calvinist in his theology, his philosophical proclivities were panentheistic.[20] For his own part, Hodge found the traditional Reformed appropriation of Thomist concursus more satisfying: "It is best, therefore, to rest satisfied with the simple statement that preservation is that omnipotent energy of God by which all created things, animate and inanimate, are upheld in existence, with all the properties and powers with which He has endowed them."[21]

This classic Thomist-Reformed interpretation of concursus goes a long way in integrating the analogical thread of my thesis. According to Aquinas, "When the free will moves itself, this does not exclude its being moved by another, from whom it receives the very power to move itself."[22] God's sovereignty is the source rather than the antithesis of creaturely freedom.[23] Hence, writers like Calvin and Francis Turretin can affirm simultaneously divine sovereignty and the freedom and contingency of creaturely agency.[24] At this point, Edwards and Pinnock can be seen to have arrived at very different conclusions based on a common presupposition: namely, the univocity of being, which forces the equally problematic choice between "omnicausalism" and libertarian free will.

Yet as helpful as Aristotle's causal category (primary and secondary) has been in the history of theology, it may at least be supplemented by a communicative approach: a point that has been explored fruitfully by Kevin Vanhoozer.[25] We have seen that God characteristically brings about his purposes through speech. "The LORD . . . who executes his word is powerful" (Joel 2:11).

---

glorious, proved so decisive a factor in Edwards's thinking that it gave birth to idealist metaphysics." Michael James McClymond, *Encounters with God: An Approach to the Theology of Jonathan Edwards* (New York: Oxford University Press, 1998), p. 34. For a different appraisal see Oliver D. Crisp, "How 'Occasional' Was Edwards's Occasionalism?," in *Jonathan Edwards: Philosophical Theologian*, ed. Paul Helm and Oliver D. Crisp (London: Ashgate, 2003), pp. 61-77.

[20]John W. Cooper, *Panentheism: The Other God of the Philosophers* (Grand Rapids: Baker Academic, 2006), pp. 74-77.

[21]Hodge, *Systematic Theology*, 1:581.

[22]Thomas Aquinas, *Summa theologica* (New York: Benzinger Brothers, 1947–1948), I, q. 83, art. 1, p. 418.

[23]See Ernan McMullin, "Evolutionary Contingency and Cosmic Purpose," in *Finding God in All Things*, ed. Michael J. Himes and Stephen J. Pope (New York: Herder, 1996), pp. 140-61.

[24]Calvin, *Institutes* 1.16.9; Francis Turretin, *Institutes of Elenctic Theology*, trans. G. M. Giger, ed. J. T. Dennison Jr. (Phillipsburg, NJ: P & R, 1992), 1:499.

[25]Kevin J. Vanhoozer, "Effectual Call or Causal Effect? Summons, Sovereignty and Supervenient Grace," chap. 4 of *First Theology: God, Scripture and Hermeneutics* (Downers Grove, IL: InterVarsity Press, 2002), 96-124.

Not only in creation but also in providence it is God's lively speech that is at work: "He upholds the universe by the word of his power" (Heb 1:3). So instead of the familiar analogy of the invisible hand, we should think in terms of the audible word. God does not simply operate *on* the world, causing its history and human actions, but *in* the world and *within* its manifold creatures. He is not only the Father but also the Son and the Holy Spirit. As Calvin notes, "The Son of God doth suffer not only with us, but also in us," bearing us up and provoking within us by his Spirit the cry, "Abba, Father," even in our misery.[26] So we need to resist the false choice between divine action on the world in a fiat declaration and a purely naturalistic account. As God, the Spirit works within creaturely reality so that it does truly "bring forth" what is consistent with the sort of creature it has been "worded" to be.

THE SPIRIT'S AGENCY IN REVELATION AND REDEMPTION

The same motifs and presuppositions could be applied to the doctrine of revelation, where the false choice of naturalism and hypersupernaturalism recurs. Here as well there is a basic agreement (at least implied) that divine and human agency are univocal. In this scheme, to the extent that revelation shows evidence of human mediation (including finitude, weakness, limited cultural horizons, etc.), its origin in God is discredited. The only real disagreement, then, is whether to highlight or suppress this human mediation. This conundrum is only possible and problematic because of a univocal view of divine and human agency. Furthermore, to the extent that the doctrine of revelation is established on any foundation other than the Trinity, the same concerns will arise that we have identified with regard to creation and providence.[27] Basing inspiration one-sidedly on the Father as *cause* can lead to a mechanical theory; basing it one-sidedly on the Son as the *content* fosters a canon-within-a-canon model, while Spirit-centered views are susceptible to *enthusiasm*: the separation of the Spirit from the word.

Sometimes in Scripture we encounter the fiat sort of decree: "'Let there be . . . ' And there was." This corresponds to the examples, especially in the

---

[26]John Calvin, *Commentary upon the Acts of the Apostles*, trans. Henry Beveridge (Grand Rapids: Baker, 1974), 2:297.

[27]This danger is especially evident when the doctrine of revelation is treated as "prolegomenon," without already appealing to trinitarian coordinates.

prophets, where we read, "And the word of the Lord came to me, saying . . ." or "Thus says the Lord: . . ." But in many other instances, we find biblical writers drawing on eyewitness testimony, cultural contexts, and peculiarities in personality, emphasis and manners of speaking.

The interaction between Mary and the angel provides a clear example of double agency. Troubled in heart at the annunciation, she asks, "How will this be, since I am a virgin?" (Lk 1:34). After the most basic explanation ("The Holy Spirit will come upon you, and . . . the child to be born will be called holy—the Son of God" [Lk 1:35]), she replies, "Behold, I am the servant of the Lord; let it be to me according to your word" (Lk 1:38). In this event, we have all of the relevant pieces of the argument I am making. First, it is trinitarian: the Father speaks (through the embassy of his angel), the Son is the content and the Spirit is the one who will bring the word to pass. The Holy Spirit will "come upon" her, as the same Spirit hovered over the waters in creation in order to make fruitful the Father's command, in the Son. Mary's response is basically to say "Amen!"—a response that the Spirit engenders within her just as he would now bring about the incarnation in her womb. Wherever we encounter not only the Father's speech in the Son but also the Spirit's "bringing forth" of inspired speech from human witnesses, the new creation dawns.

So far we have seen that in creation and providence as well as in revelation, the Spirit is the person who is at work within creaturely reality, bringing about its voluntary consent to God's word even through that word itself. There are fiat declarations, "'Let there be. . . .' And there was." But there are also declarations that empower the creation to "reply" appropriately, to say "Amen!" to what it has been "worded" to be by the Father in the Son.

The same pattern is evident in Christ's incarnation and ministry. Not even in the incarnation did Jesus' humanity become overwhelmed by his deity; rather, he attributed his mission to the Father and his success—including the miracles—to the Holy Spirit. Unlike his conception, there is nothing miraculous about his birth, and unlike in the Gnostic Gospels, he is not a child prodigy. "And the child grew and became strong, filled with wisdom. And the favor of God was upon him" (Lk 2:40). "And Jesus increased in wisdom and in stature and in favor with God and man" (Lk 2:52). "Although he was a son, he learned obedience through what he suffered" (Heb 5:8). The incarnation itself was of the fiat variety: "'Let there be!' . . . And there was." However, his natural birth, life and ministry were more along the lines of "'Let the earth bring forth.' . . . And the earth brought forth." And where we are prone to identify the Spirit with invisible operations apart from creaturely means, in Scripture it is precisely within creation: separating the waters in creation and the exodus and baptism; bringing about the incarnation within the watery depths of Mary's womb; leading by pillar and cloud, inhabiting the temple and uniting us to Christ, the true sanctuary, through the preached gospel, ratifying this union by the Eucharist.

Precisely in his personal obedience to the whole will of God did Jesus recapitulate the trial of the first Adam and win our right, in him, to eat from the Tree of Life. Yet it was always in dependence on the Spirit, even from the moment that the Spirit led him into the wilderness for his temptation.

Having departed the earthly sanctuary, this Spirit of glory now fills the eschatological end-time temple: the church as Christ's body. If the Son is the place in God where covenant community is created, then the Spirit is the one who turns a house into a home. The inbreathing of the Spirit that makes humanity a living being in Genesis 2:7 reappears throughout redemptive history, as in the temple-filling episode in Ezekiel 37, as well as Mary's annunciation (Lk 1:35), culminating in the prophetic anticipation of Pentecost, when Jesus breathed on the disciples and issued his performative utterance, "Receive the Holy Spirit" (Jn 20:22).

Echoing the original creation, the Father and the Spirit issue their heavenly benediction on Jesus in his baptism (Mk 1:11), repeated by the Father at the transfiguration (Mk 9:7), testifying from heaven. Yet by themselves the words and signs of the Father, the Son and the Spirit would not have won the consent of those who are "dead in the trespasses and sins" (Eph 2:1) apart from the Spirit's ministry of testifying *within us* to the word of Christ *outside of us*. Even after spending three years at Jesus' side, the disciples' understanding of, much less testimony to, Christ's person and work depended on the descent of another witness from heaven: the Holy Spirit. The Father does not merely act on us, but with us (in the Son) and within us (by his Spirit), so that the word spoken will effect its design without any coercion.

Christ's ascension opens a fissure in history where the Spirit—for the first time in redemptive history—will not only lead, guide and light above or on the temple people, but will also permanently indwell them (Jn 14:16-18). Jesus Christ indwells believers and the church, but by his Spirit, not immediately in the flesh (2 Cor 1:22; cf. Rom 8:17, 26; 1 Cor 3:16; Gal 4:6; Eph 5:18). Because of the ascension, the church on earth is not triumphant and must wait for the bodily return of its head in the future for the renewal of all things. Christ's resurrection inaugurates the age to come, and the Spirit's descent at Pentecost is evidence that we are living in "these last days," as prophesied in Joel 2 and confirmed by Peter's Pentecost sermon in Acts 2. It is the Spirit who causes us to recognize the Jesus of history as the Christ of faith (2 Cor 5:16-17). Thus the great divide is not between the original events and our own horizon, but before and after Pentecost.

This Spirit bridges the eschatological distance between the already consummated Jesus history (the age to come) and our existence in the last days of this present age. The Spirit takes what belongs to Christ and gives it to us, so that our Lord's absence in the flesh from earth does not stand in the way of our identity being located even now "with [Christ] in the heavenly places" (Eph 2:6). The Father speaks the liturgy of grace, while the Son is himself its embodiment, and the Spirit then works in "the sons of disobedience" (Eph 2:2) to create a choir of antiphonal response that answers back its appropriate "amen" behind its glorified forerunner (2 Cor 1:19-22). "He who has prepared us for this very thing"—immortality—"is God, who has given us the Spirit as a guarantee" (2 Cor 5:5).

The Spirit's presence announces that the epochs are turning: this present age is giving way to the age to come. In fact, as Paul teaches, the Spirit is not only sent *among* believers but also *into* them, to indwell them, as a deposit (*arrabōn*) of their final redemption. It is precisely because we "have the firstfruits of the Spirit" that "even we ourselves groan within ourselves, eagerly waiting for the adoption . . . the redemption of our body" (Rom 8:23 KJV; cf. Gal 4:6). As the *arrabōn* (down payment) of our final redemption, the Spirit gives us the "already" of our participation in Christ as the new creation, and it is the Spirit within us who gives us the aching hope for the "not yet" that awaits us in our union with Christ (Rom 8:18-28; cf. 2 Cor 1:22; 5:5; Eph 1:14). The *more we receive* from the Spirit of the realities of the age to come, the *more restless we become.* Yet it is a restlessness born not of fear but of having already received a foretaste of the future.

The new creation is neither an improvement of the old creation nor its destruction. Rather, the Son has entered into creation as the firstfruits of the new order, and the Spirit is now uniting the children of disobedience to the last Adam. In addressing union with Christ, the *historia salutis* meets the *ordo salutis*.

THE SPIRIT'S AGENCY IN APPLYING REDEMPTION

If anywhere, it is in the famous "I" of the Calvinist "TULIP"—"irresistible grace"—where the suspicion of coercion seems justified at first blush. However, this term—indeed, the TULIP acronym itself—is of fairly recent origin.[28] Traditionally, Reformed theology speaks of effectual calling or regeneration, and the exposition of this doctrine in our confessions and standard systems is often rather different from what one might hear on the ground in more popular presentations.

Effectual calling is based on the corruption of nature rather than on any inherent defect of nature itself. Reformed theology applies a useful distinction between *natural* and *moral* ability from our discussion of original sin. In Adam, we freely choose our alliance with sin and death. The fall has destroyed not our natural ability to reason, observe, experience and judge but our moral ability to reason, observe, experience and judge our way to God as our Lord and Redeemer. The Second Helvetic Confession teaches, "Therefore, in regard to evil or sin, man is not forced by God or by the devil but does evil by his own free will, and in this respect he has a most free will." In "heavenly things," he is bound in sin. "Yet in regard to earthly things, fallen man is not entirely lacking in understanding." While passive in this initial regeneration, those who are regenerated work actively in good works. "For they are moved by God that they may do themselves what they do. . . . The Manichaeans robbed man of all activity and made him like a stone or a block of wood. . . . Moreover, no one denies that in external things both the regenerate and the unregenerate enjoy free will," as in deciding whether to leave the house or remain at home. However, with respect to salvation, their will is bound by sin until God graciously acts.[29]

---

[28]See Kenneth J. Stewart, *Ten Myths About Calvinism: Recovering the Breadth of the Reformed Tradition* (Downers Grove, IL: IVP Academic, 2011), pp. 75-96.

[29]Second Helvetic Confession, chap. 9 (Free Will), in *The Book of Confessions* (Louisville: PCUSA, 2004), p. 65.

More precisely, the Westminster Confession states, "God hath endued the will of man with that natural liberty that it is neither forced, nor by any absolute necessity of nature determined to good or evil." Before the fall, the will was entirely free to choose good or evil, but after the fall, humanity "has wholly lost all ability of will to any spiritual good accompanying salvation," rendering every person "dead in sin . . . not able, by his own strength, to convert himself, or to prepare himself thereunto."

When God converts a sinner and translates him into the state of grace, he frees him from his natural bondage under sin and, by his grace alone, enables him freely to will and to do that which is spiritually good; yet so as that, by reason of his remaining corruption, he does not perfectly or only will that which is good, but does also that which is evil. The will of humanity is made perfectly and immutably free to good alone in the state of glory only.[30]

Such statements reflect a basic Augustinian consensus, filtered through the Reformation. The Westminster divines add that God is pleased "in his appointed and accepted time, effectually to call, by his Word and Spirit," all of the elect "out of that state of sin and death in which they are by nature, to grace and salvation by Jesus Christ." He accomplishes this by "enlightening their minds, . . . taking away their heart of stone, . . . renewing their wills, . . . and effectually drawing them to Jesus Christ; *yet so as they come most freely, being made willing by his grace.*"[31]

The Synod of Dort affirmed that God's inward calling always meets with success. However, just as the fall "did not abolish the nature of the human race" but "distorted" it and led to spiritual death, "so also this divine grace of regeneration does not act in people as if they were blocks and stones; nor does it abolish the will and its properties or coerce a reluctant will by force, but spiritually revives, heals, reforms, and—*in a manner at once pleasing and powerful*—bends it back."[32] The will is liberated, not violated. "If it be compelled," says John Owen, "it is destroyed."[33] As I have argued elsewhere, the classic

---

[30]Westminster Confession of Faith, chap. 11, *The Book of Confessions*.

[31]Westminster Confession of Faith, chap. 12 (Effectual Calling), *The Book of Confessions* (emphasis added).

[32]Canons of the Synod of Dort (1618–1619) in *Ecumenical Creeds and Reformed Confessions* (Grand Rapids: CRC Publications, 1988), pp. 135-36 (emphasis added).

[33]John Owen, *The Works of John Owen*, ed. William H. Gould (Edinburgh: Banner of Truth Trust, 1965), 3:319.

terminology of effectual calling already indicates a more communicative model of divine action than causal grammars (like "irresistible grace") imply.[34]

One might argue that only within a truly trinitarian framework can such distinctions be maintained so that divine agency does not flatten out human agency. Nowhere do we see more clearly that in every external work of the Godhead the Father acts in the Son and by the Spirit. To repeat Calvin's invocation of the patristic formula, "To the Father is attributed the effective principle of what is done, and the fountain and wellspring of all things; to the Son, wisdom, counsel, and the ordered arrangement of what is done; but to the Spirit is assigned the power and efficacy of the action."[35]

If God were merely one person, sovereign and transcendent, his relationship to the world might easily be conceived in terms of action *on* the world: brute force. However, God is tripersonal, and this triune God's relationship to the world is covenantal and communicative. The triune God accomplishes everything that his speech intends (Is 55:11). When God says, "Let there be light," whether in the first creation or the new creation, it is so. Nevertheless, he also commands, "Let the earth bring forth. . . ." The new birth, in which we are passive recipients, yields to conversion, in which we respond in Spirit-given repentance and faith. In fact, this is how actual instances of conversion are described in the New Testament, as in the case of Lydia: "The Lord opened her heart to listen eagerly to what was said by Paul" (Acts 16:14 NRSV).

Christ is not only promised; he *is* the promise. "For in him every one of God's promises is a 'Yes.' For this reason it is through him that we say the 'Amen,' to the glory of God" (2 Cor 1:20 NRSV). Those who by nature "suppress the truth in unrighteousness" (Rom 1:18 NASB) are swept into the story that God is telling the world. Thus regeneration is attributed to the Father's speech, the Son as the content—clothed in his gospel—and the Spirit as the perfecting agent. They find themselves "born anew, not of perishable but of

---

[34]For further elaboration of the following argument see Michael Horton, *Covenant and Salvation: Union with Christ* (Louisville, KY: Westminster John Knox, 2007), pp. 216-42. See also Vanhoozer, "Effectual Call or Causal Effect?" Employing the traditional Aristotelian categories, Reformed theologians affirmed that the Holy Spirit is the *efficient cause* of regeneration. While I agree with this point, I share Vanhoozer's appreciation for speech-act theory as a conceptual resource that is actually more congenial to the position that Calvinists wish to defend.

[35]Calvin, *Institutes* 1.13.18.

imperishable seed, through the living and enduring word of God. . . . That word is the good news that was announced to you" (1 Pet 1:23, 25 NRSV). More like being overwhelmed by beauty than by force, the call is effectual because of its *content*, not because of an exercise of absolute power independent of it. And yet apart from the Spirit's regenerating work we would never answer this gospel with our own "amen" of faith.

It is the Spirit who brings this new creation about, but through means. The proclamation of the gospel is specifically and repeatedly identified as that medium (Rom 1:16; 10:8-17; Eph 1:13-14; 1 Thess 1:5; 1 Pet 1:23, 25; Jas 1:18). It comes to us from outside of ourselves, announcing our salvation by the work that Christ accomplished for us, outside of ourselves. And yet, this external word becomes verified and embraced by us because the Spirit is at work within us, winning our consent to this word (1 Thess 2:13; cf. Rom 8:14-16; 1 Cor 2:4-5; 4:12-13; 2 Cor 4:13; Eph 1:17; Gal 3:2; 1 Thess 1:4; Tit 3:4). "It is the Spirit who gives life; the flesh is no help at all," yet Jesus immediately adds, "The *words* that I have spoken to you are spirit and life" (Jn 6:63, emphasis added).

Far from canceling creaturely agency, the Spirit empowers it within us and does so through the means of preaching and sacrament. Therefore, it is not simply a sovereign display of power from a distance, God acting on the creature as one might on a piece of wood. Precisely because the triune God works through such accessible means, creaturely agency is evident on every hand. Commenting on Romans 10:17 ("Faith comes from what is heard, and what is heard comes through the word of Christ" [NRSV]), Calvin writes, "And this is a remarkable passage with regard to the efficacy of preaching; for he testifies that by it faith is produced." There is no antithesis between God's work and the work of the ministry; rather, it is through this ministry of sinners that Christ accomplishes his work. It remains an utterly human ministry with myriad frailties, Calvin acknowledges, "but all these things are no hindrances, that God should not work effectually through the voice of man, so as to create faith in us through his ministry."[36]

Against both the medieval doctrine of justification according to infused

---

[36]John Calvin on Rom 10:17 in *Commentary on the Epistle of Paul the Apostle to the Romans*, ed. and trans. John Owen, Calvin's Commentaries 19 (Edinburgh: Calvin Translation Society, 1843–1855; repr., Grand Rapids: Baker, 1993), p. 401.

habits and the Anabaptist emphasis on a direct and immediate work of the Spirit within us, the Reformers insisted on the mediation of the word—specifically, the gospel. "For faith and the Word belong together," Wilhelm Kolfhaus notes concerning Calvin's view. "The foundation of both expressions is always the faith produced by the Spirit through the Gospel."[37]

Regeneration is a unilateral act of liberation—belonging to the fiat, "Let there be . . ." type of performative utterance. Yet conversion and sanctification are no less the work of the triune God when this word of the Father, in the Son, by the Spirit declares, "Let the earth bring forth fruit . . ."

As noted above, Reformed theology has emphasized that sin is accidental rather than essential to human nature. J. Todd Billings has observed that Calvin's *Bondage and Liberation of the Will*, responding to Pighius, is especially interested in defending the Reformation teaching from patristic sources. "Thus, citing Irenaeus in his favor, Calvin affirms that redemption heals and restores the original 'good will' and 'good nature' of Adam. . . . Although the reception of faith involves the voluntary assent of believers, and the assent 'is properly called ours,' it does not 'derive from us' in exclusion from God, but is a work of the Spirit."[38]

In regeneration we are passive. We hear the gospel, and the Spirit creates faith in our hearts to embrace it. However, in conversion we are active. We have seen that the Spirit is the sanctifier not only in the narrow sense (viz., progressive growth in Christ), but in every external work of the Trinity. The Spirit is identified in the prophetic writings as the harbinger of the future. And now the Spirit is at work within us, causing us to bear the fruit of the Spirit and to grow up into Christ with his body.

In spite of the fact that the Corinthian church had become filled with immorality, strife, division and immaturity, Paul begins both letters to this body by addressing them as "saints" (holy ones) and reintroduces the wonder of the gospel. To be united to Christ by the Spirit through the word is not only to be justified; it is also to be renewed and to be conformed gradually to Christ's image. The Corinthian saints are holy because of the

---

[37]Quoted and translated by Dennis Tamburello, *Union with Christ: John Calvin and the Mysticism of St. Bernard* (Louisville, KY: Westminster John Knox, 1994), p. 86.

[38]J. Todd Billings, "John Calvin: United to God Through Christ," in *Partakers of the Divine Nature: The History and Development of Deification in the Christian Traditions*, ed. Michael J. Christensen and Jeffery A. Wittung (Grand Rapids: Baker Academic, 2007), p. 202.

fiat declaration of justification, which Paul compares with *ex nihilo* creation (Rom 4:17), so now they may bear the fruit of righteousness: "Let the earth bring forth. . . ." Just as the Spirit is at work in our hearts to bring about faith in Christ through the gospel, the Spirit is at work in us "both to will and to work for his good pleasure" (Phil 2:13). The same point can be discerned in John 15:3, where Jesus says, "You are clean because of the word that I have spoken to you," and only then calls them to bear fruit that is consistent with this forensic declaration.

In Romans 4:17, God's work in justification is compared to his work in creating the world out of nothing. Justification is the fiat declaration, "Let there be righteousness!" even where, at present, there is nothing but guilt and unrighteousness in the sinner, because Christ's righteousness is imputed through Spirit-given and gospel-created faith. As in creation, only after God's declarative word of justification ("Let there be. . . . And there was . . .") can there be an appropriate creaturely response ("Let the earth bring forth . . ."). Only with the final fiat declaration of glorification, in the resurrection of the dead, will the empirical ambiguity of our justification and the already–not yet tension of our sanctification be resolved publicly.

The mediated character of the Spirit's work in uniting us to Christ is evident in the sanctification of the most natural elements of ordinary life: human speech, water, bread and wine. In the covenantal economy, the Father, the Son and the Spirit have freely bound themselves in their ordinary operations to these creaturely elements and actions. It is not merely by acting on creation, or making it possible for creation to act, but by working within creation (even with creaturely media) that the Spirit gives us faith and confirms that faith throughout our pilgrimage. Just as creation began with a command, "Let there be. . . . And there was . . . ," so too does the new creation originate in the womb of the word. Hence, creation echoes are heard in the apostolic witness to the new birth (1 Pet 2:9; 2 Cor 4:3, 6). By speaking righteousness into a condition of unrighteousness, God brings into existence a new creation, which refers not only to justified and renewed individuals but also to a living community: his church.

There is no contrast drawn here between divine and human action: the human signs are sanctified as divine signs that communicate the reality signified. Within the appropriate covenantal context, the words of commissioned representatives actually bear God's word, accomplishing that of which it speaks. Paul could even identify himself—and even Timothy—as God's coworkers (2 Cor 6:1), not in any synergistic sense, but in that analogical sense of creaturely mediation of God's word of reconciliation (2 Cor 5:11-21).

As Bonhoeffer argued, the form as well as the content of preaching is crucial for the creation of the kind of new society of which it speaks.

> If there were an unmediated work of the Spirit, then the idea of the church would be individualistically dissolved from the outset. But in the word the most profound social nexus is established from the beginning. *The word is social in character, not only in its origin but also in its aim.* Tying the Spirit to the word means that the Spirit aims at *a plurality of hearers* and establishes a visible sign by which the actualization is to take place. The word, however, is qualified by being the very word of Christ; it is effectively brought to the heart of the hearers by the Spirit.[39]

Even baptism and the Lord's Supper derive their efficacy from this proclaimed gospel. From beginning to end, the church always remains a "creation of the word." Bonhoeffer observes,

> To summarize, the word is the sociological principle by which the entire church is built up . . . both in numbers and in its faith. Christ is the foundation upon which, and according to which, the building of the church is raised (1 Corinthians 3; Eph. 2:20). And thus it grows into a "holy temple of God" (Eph. 2:21), and "with a growth that is from God" (Col. 2:19), "until all of us come to maturity, to the measure of the full stature of Christ" (Eph. 4:13), and in all this growing "into him who is the head, into Christ." The entire building begins and ends with Christ, and its unifying center is the word.[40]

The preaching creates the community, while the Supper, by evoking personal acceptance through faith, makes that community in some sense visible—or better still, audible.[41] "We hear the word of God through the word of the church, and this is what constitutes the authority of the church."[42] Only because of this

---

[39]Dietrich Bonhoeffer, *Sanctorum Communio: A Theological Study of the Sociology of the Church,* Dietrich Bonhoeffer Works 1, ed. Joachim von Soosten, English edition ed. Clifford J. Green, trans. Reinhard Krauss and Nancy Lukens (Minneapolis: Fortress, 1998), p. 158 (emphasis added).
[40]Ibid., p. 247.
[41]Ibid.
[42]Ibid., p. 250.

does one owe obedience to the church, submitting private opinions to her tutelage, yet never contrary to the Word itself.[43] Insofar as the church speaks God's Word its authority is not illusory or an exercise in arbitrary power.

In this interpretation, the Spirit's agency has priority over both that of the church and of the individual believer, since both are creatures of the word. Yet precisely because of this fact, the Spirit's work is mediated through creaturely agency. Far from talking over us, the Spirit gives us our voice back, to answer the "amen" to the word. It is not a question of what the word and sacraments do within us, or what the individual does with them, but what the Spirit does through them, that makes these creaturely actions means of grace.

The Spirit's distinguished career in the economy of grace is especially evident in the consummation. The new creation is not an *ex nihilo* creation. It is not a return to the beginning, but the everlasting Sabbath that was forfeited by the first Adam. The Spirit is associated throughout Scripture with bringing about the *fulfillment* of God's plans: in creation, redemption and the consummation. Every gift we receive through union with Christ here and now is a morsel of the age to come, which the Spirit brings to us like the dove that brought Noah a leafy branch as the harbinger of life after the deluge. There is no better proof of the Spirit's role in bringing about the perlocutionary effect of the word than this identification with the consummation.

THE SPIRIT'S AGENCY IN CULTURE

I do not have the space to do justice to this aspect of the Spirit's agency in bringing about the perlocutionary effect of God's speech. Therefore, I will have to settle for some intimations.

Given the preponderance of biblical passages, it is not surprising that we associate the Spirit's work with saving grace. Nevertheless, it is important also to observe the Spirit's role in common grace. The Spirit's canvas is larger than the church. No greater evidence of the effectual but noncoercive operations of the Spirit is possible than in the lives of those who do not trust in Christ.

---

[43]Ibid., p. 251.

If radical Protestants could not conceive of creaturely media as the tools through which the Spirit dispensed Christ and his benefits, they certainly could not allow that the Spirit is at work in common society. Against the "fanatics," Calvin refers to the truth, goodness and beauty even among the pagans as the gifts of the Spirit. To reject these gifts, wherever they are found, is "to dishonor the Spirit of God."[44] Even in its fallenness, the world—including humanity—reflects God's wisdom and goodness, truth and justice, beauty and love.

John Murray writes, "Special grace does not annihilate but rather brings its redemptive, regenerative and sanctifying influence to bear on every natural or common gift; it transforms all activities and departments of life; it brings every good gift into the service of the kingdom of God. Christianity is not a flight from nature; it is the renewal and sanctification of nature." This approach has always challenged ascetic versions of spirituality. "And its practical outlook has been, 'For every creature of God is good, and nothing to be refused, if it be received with thanksgiving: for it is sanctified by the word of God and prayer' (1 Tim. 4:4, 5)."[45]

By extending the horizon of the Spirit's work to its biblical limits, the dangers of separating nature (ostensibly autonomous) from a purely extrinsic grace that acts on the world rather than within it may be obviated while retaining the valid distinction between its common operations in providence and its operations in the economy of salvation.

My goal has been to highlight some categories that are often missing from discussions of divine and human agency. I have focused here on analogy and the work of the Spirit. "Now the Lord is the Spirit, and where the Spirit of the Lord is, there is freedom" (2 Cor 3:17). This essay is hardly a destination, but I hope that it at least identifies some crucial coordinates for the voyage.

---

[44]Calvin, *Institutes* 2.2.15.
[45]*Collected Writings of John Murray* (Edinburgh: Banner of Truth Trust, 1991), 2:295.

7

SANCTIFICATION AND ETHICS

Oliver O'Donovan

It may seem at first glance that though the two words in my title are distinct, and have distinct meanings, their reference is the same, namely, the active life of the redeemed. The association of sanctification and ethics may then be thought to be a synthetic proposition: what looks from one angle like a work done by God *for and in* the redeemed (sanctification) looks from the other angle like a practical obligation that the redeemed must undertake (ethics). In the light of some such proposition as this it may seem an obvious decision to invite a moral theologian to contribute to a discussion among dogmaticians on the theme of sanctification; if justification, or the sacraments, or the being of God were in question, the moral theologian would have been encouraged to keep quiet. On the estate of sanctification he is allowed to hold an ancestral tenancy, a farmer with a knowledge of the soil, unable to rival the landlord's comprehensive understanding of the estate as a business, but with some useful insights with which to complement it. So much for impressions at first glance. I shall do my best to shatter them, and prepare the ground for a more satisfactory account of the relation of these two spheres of inquiry.

Let us identify three related problems. The first is internal to the study of doctrine: how to define the sphere of sanctification in relation to the proximate sphere of justification? The second concerns the relation of doctrine to ethics: how to place the work of moral theology on the patchwork quilt of dogmatic topics. And when we have briefly outlined the scope of these two problems, the third will emerge in its due time.

JUSTIFICATION AND SANCTIFICATION

The distinction between justification and sanctification has sometimes seemed under threat of redundancy. Classically it has been spoken of as a contrast between the beginning and the continuance of the Christian life, a conception too biographical to be quite above suspicion. In the New Testament the term *hagiasmos*, translated "sanctification," does not always seem to have the connotations of continuance in contrast to a distinct beginning. This, at any rate, we must take as a starting point: the difference between justification and sanctification, wherever it may lie, does not lie in a difference of agency, for God is the primary agent in both. As Barth writes finely, "As God is the active subject of reconciliation in general, so he is the subject of man's conversion."[1]

We should go further. There is no difference between the two in the role assigned to human agency, either. We may be tempted to allow that God's work in sanctification evokes a corresponding human activity, while to God's work in justification we will assign no human activity at all, only passivity. Luther's famous contrast between *iustitia passiva* and *iustitia activa* (passive and active righteousness) may seem to offer us a good ground for making the distinction in this way. But it would be a mistake. It is quite clear in Luther's case, and a fortiori in other magisterial Reformers, especially the English, that the dialectic of passive and active righteousness is conceived as internal to justifying faith. Active righteousness, that is, lies within the territory of justification together with, though secondary to, passive righteousness; it is not to be shoved off into the territory of sanctification. It is to Luther that we owe the resonant declaration of the 1522 *Preface to Romans*: "Oh it is a vital, active, busy and effective thing, this faith! Impossible it should not incessantly be doing good!"[2] "Justification by faith," as the Reformers understood it, was a doctrine about what pleased God in a human life, which is to say, about what made human activity *truly*, as opposed to only *apparently*, good, for pleasing God was the only serious sense they could give to the word "good." An active life was pleasing to God precisely because it was rooted in a faith that was primarily receptive, and found its moral energy in what it received. "Faith is the life of man," as William

---

[1]Barth, *KD* IV/2, §66.1, p. 566 (ET: *CD* IV/2, p. 500).
[2]Martin Luther, *Preface to Paul's Epistle to the Romans* (WA, Deutsche Bibel 7.10).

Tyndale writes, "out of which life the pleasantness of all his works spring";
that is to say, it is the one foundational undertaking of human existence
within the terms of an alien righteousness extended to us, which must un-
derlie and make sense of all the undertakings that will, in the event,
command God's good pleasure.[3] If, in speaking of justification by faith, we
speak not of our passivity only, but of our activity too—of activity in second
place, because faith is first of all receptive, but necessarily, because faith is
the life-source of activity pleasing to God—then the distinction of passive
and active righteousness is no frontier that can demarcate justification from
sanctification or faith from love; it is a dialectic polarity that constitutes the
redemptive dynamic of justification by faith itself.

Barth at any rate does not attempt to distinguish justification from sanctification in terms of passive as opposed to active righteousness. The doctrine of justification is defined, for him, by its account of God's self-humili-
ation in approach to humanity, the doctrine of sanctification by its account
of God's elevation of man to share his glory—both equally passive and
equally active from humankind's point of view. And in proposing a threefold
cord of justification, sanctification and vocation (on which more shortly),
and aligning it with the theological virtues of faith, love and hope (always
in that order, the default order in the New Testament, departed from only
at 1 Cor 13:13), Barth recognizes that talk of justification has already ventured
on the ground of the Christian virtues.[4]

THEOLOGICAL ETHICS AND DOGMATICS

That brings us to the second of the two questions I identified, whether and
how ethics as a theological discipline may be located within a scheme of
doctrines. For ethics cannot renounce its interest in any of the three theological virtues, the implication of which, if we follow Barth's alignment, must
be that ethics lays claim to a view of all three doctrines of salvation, namely,
justification, sanctification and vocation.

On this subject I myself put some promissory notes into circulation a

---

[3]William Tyndale, *Exposition of Matthew 5,6,7*, in *Expositions of Scripture and Practice of Prelates*
(Cambridge: Cambridge University Press, 1849), p. 125.
[4]This proposal forms the architecture of volume IV, the great unfinished symphony of the twentieth
century, and is expounded in the introductory §58.

quarter of a century ago when I proposed that the proper location of ethics lay with the doctrine of the *resurrection of Christ*, in which the created order, to which our active life was bound, was vindicated and delivered from threat of dissolution.[5] The question I was trying to answer was how moral teaching could be evangelical, not an appendage to faith in the gospel but integral to it. If the work of Christ were understood solely from the point of view of the cross, as negation of the world, or from the point of view of the ascension, as transcendence of the world, or even from the point of view of the incarnation, as assumption of the world into the being of God, moral norms, which have *human* action in view within the created world, could not be conceived evangelically. They could be a law that condemned us, an old order that we left behind, or a precondition for realizing the birth of God; but only when salvation was conceived as gracious restoration of the world from threat of dissolution could moral norms be a gift that made the path before our human feet a celebration of the coming of God. In locating ethics at that moment in Christology, what I argued, in effect, was the centrality of this moment. That said, and said truly so far as it goes, there remains to be explored the relation of the Holy Spirit to ethics, of the church, of the doctrine of the last things. For redeemed action is not solely a matter of *world*-redemption, but also of the redemption of subjectivity and of time.

I have to correct, then, any inference that might be drawn from my proposal that theological ethics (alias moral theology) relates to dogmatics at this sole point in the dogmatic scheme. To put it another way: moral theology does not locate itself by reference to a distinct dogmatic theme. Ethics is a reflective mode of *practical reason*, that is, thought undertaking not to conclude in *knowledge* but in *action*. Ethics is doctrine existentially situated, extended into the living of life.

One very important implication of this, it seems to me, is that we should avoid any suggestion that doctrine, whether in whole or in part, may be *ethicized* in the manner favored a century or so ago under the influence of Albrecht Ritschl. Ethics cannot replace, or improve on, dogma. Dogmatic statements must simply be grasped and believed—by a moral theologian as by any other Christian. (And it is well to remember that "moral theologian"

---

[5]Oliver O'Donovan, *Resurrection and Moral Order* (Grand Rapids: Eerdmans, 1992).

is not the designation of a distinct class of person, merely of an academic specialism.) What ethics can do is reflect on how those statements, once believed, shape and transform practical reason. It thinks, as it were, *around* dogmatic statements and *out from* dogmatic statements, but not *about* dogmatic statements. And since the revelation that dogma attests is essentially a single truth of God's action, not a series of truths, ethics is in no position to choose among dogmas and declare itself more at home with one (let us say, creation or the incarnation) than another (let us say, Christ's heavenly session at God's right hand). There may, however, be a *route through* the one truth of God's action that is especially conducive to pursuing the questions that arise in reflection on practical reason. Even dogmatics, after all, does not always follow the trinitarian order of the Apostles' Creed. And that is how my proposition in *Resurrection and Moral Order* is best understood, I now think: as identifying *a dogmatic starting point* that will allow moral theology to unfold in a comprehensible and ordered way.

SANCTIFICATION AND VOCATION

I gave warning of a third preliminary question, and that has already begun to emerge. The implication of the ground covered so far is a definition of sanctification not only in relation to justification but to vocation as well. Is this proposal more than an arbitrary complication generated by the ever-fertile mind of the twentieth century's greatest theologian? Past generations, influenced too much, perhaps, by the biographical way of distinguishing justification from sanctification as the beginning and the continuance of the Christian life, found the twofold division sufficient. Is there a conceptual advantage in a threefold one, which means, in effect, partitioning the ground traditionally occupied by sanctification? I think there is. Early in my career I briefly acquired a reputation in some circles as a Barthian; the only reason I can imagine for this is that I never missed an opportunity to criticize the great dogmatician for the manifest weaknesses in his treatments of ethics. Now, having long since shed that reputation, I have the pleasure of recommending a Barthian formula with some enthusiasm, and suggesting how his proposal to give substance to the threefold cord of justification, sanctification and vocation through the theological virtues of faith, love and hope is potentially very fruitful for ethics, though Barth's own attempts at execution, it must be said, are a disappointment.

Sanctification understood biographically has given encouragement to a belief in progressive and incremental moral improvement, to be attained with maturity and age. One of those attractive poems that form a minor part of the literary legacy of the incomparable C. S. Lewis catches the idea wittily.

> By now I should be entering on the supreme stage
> Of the whole walk, reserved for the late afternoon . . .
> Now, or soon now, if all is well, come the majestic
> Rivers of foamless charity that glide beneath
> Forests of contemplation . . .
> If storms arose, then in my tower of fortitude—
> It ought to have been in sight by this—I would take refuge . . .
> Light drops of silver temperance, and clovery earth
> Sending up mists of chastity . . .
> I can see nothing like all this. Was the map wrong?[6]

The map was indeed wrong. It confused the work of God, who sanctifies old age as he sanctifies childhood, youth and maturity, with the more attractive features that may decorate the progress of years through unaided nature. Unaided nature can also bestow some very unattractive features on progressing years. Standing at the threshold of old age myself, I have every reason to hope that age, too, may have its distinctive forms of holiness, but every reason to know that nothing can be taken for granted about these, and that the settlement and fixity of advanced years can as easily be a hindrance to as a support in God's service. The doctrine that the elect commit no post-baptismal sin is generally known as heresy; why, one wonders, has indulgence been accorded to the doctrine that the elect commit only venial sins after the age of fifty? The incremental concept is responsible, I suspect, for the deeply antithetical relation that arose between justification and sanctification in the Protestant thought of the seventeenth century, leading to the steady eclipse of justification by a sanctification that presumed too much on the natural assets of maturity and lost sight of the risk that the workings of grace incur at every stage of life. "*Today*, if you hear his voice, do not harden your hearts" (Ps 95:7-8). Barth complained of a "this-worldly, immanentist, not to say bourgeois" air about a Protestant ethics based only on faith and

---

[6]C. S. Lewis, "Pilgrim's Problem," in *Poems*, ed. W. H. Lewis (London: Bles, 1964), pp. 119-20.

love, in need of vital appropriation of the divine promise as the object of hope.[7] (No, *not* "bourgeois," but the point should be acknowledged all the same!) The conceptual importance of the doctrine of vocation lies in correcting the complacency to which sanctification is otherwise exposed, reminding us of a summons to decision and risk that stretches beyond recognized patterns of attainment, while not considering them irrelevant or misleading. "I count not myself to have attained" then becomes a structural rule for all talk of ethics, not a modest afterthought.

SANCTIFICATION AND THE VIRTUE OF LOVE

With these preliminaries behind us, let us venture on a sketch of the moral content of sanctification that sets it in counterpoint to vocation. As an organizing proposition I suggest the following thesis: *sanctification is the gracious work of God in our human living that leads out the gift of righteous agency in Christ into reconciled participation in the world, shaping within us the multifaceted virtue of love.*

Three initial comments of an explanatory nature will clear the way for an exploration of what is said here under two main headings, "Love as Motion and Rest" and "Love as Cognition."

1. I speak of righteous agency in Christ as "led out," an expression that intends to capture what is understood by Paul's articulation of "faith working through love" (Gal 5:6) and James's "faith operative with works and brought to completion by works" (Jas 2:22 my translation)—between the force of Paul's *energein* ("work in") and James's *synergein* ("work with") only the more pedantic style of lexicographer will be in a hurry to drive a wedge. In each of these expressions faith is not passive, leaving all the action to love; but neither is it one activity among others, so that one might say, as James imagines someone saying, "You have faith and I have works" (Jas 2:18). Faith lies behind; it gives rise to every activity that could be pleasing to God. It is "led out" into love in the sense of being "carried through" or "elaborated." Already an *active* response to God's quickening voice, it takes form in the vast array of activities that we may undertake in obedience to God; it is the root from which they draw their moral coherence. Without faith going

---

[7]Barth, *KD* IV/1, §58.2, p. 118. The standard English translation renders *bürgerlich* by "middle-class" (*CD* IV/1, p. 109).

before them those activities cannot be pleasing to God; they lack a root, a center, an integrity; no restored and revivified agency performs them. But without the works of love coming after it faith is not faith at all, but "dead" (as James puts it), not as a living thing is dead when its life is done, but as a stillborn is dead without having lived. Faith is the root of action that must flower, and as faith in God's work is one and invariable, so the flowering into which it is led out is of many kinds, though all comprehended within the unifying coherence of love.

2. The many kinds and the embracing coherence of love reflect the multiplicity in unity that belongs to the creation in which we are given to participate. Creation is one ordered and coherent good with many goods contained within its order and coherence. Love, too, which responds to creation given back to us in Christ's resurrection, is both one and various. For love is a reconciliation to the real world in its beauty, and a reconciliation to the God who is its Creator and Redeemer. Love consists of admiration for the one and worship of the other.

3. If faith must be "led out" into love, love in its turn must be "led out." Admiration and worship are not fully realized until they have expression in particular actions done at particular moments of time, together making up our path through life. Vocation corresponds to sanctification as the gracious work of God in our human living, which in turn leads out the gift of reconciled participation into the discovery of the opportune time and occasion for action. Vocation shapes within us the virtue of *hope.*

Love as motion and rest. With these prefatory explanations I comment first on love as the motion and rest of the soul. Love has traditionally been spoken of in spatial metaphors either as a movement or as a position, as it is wished to characterize it as an event or as a settled state. The traditional terms *inclination* and *attachment* apply the spatial imagery in these two complementary ways. It is, of course, unnecessary to insist that the spatial reference of these expressions is *purely* metaphorical. The soul's "movement" and "rest" are its faith, love and hope; there is nothing else that the soul does by way of self-propulsion! The soul of an agent is understood as self-moving because it is capable of self-disposal in relation to the objective world. What is accomplished by the use of the metaphor is to highlight that aspect of love that exceeds the purely cognitive and so, in turn, to distinguish two kinds of cognition: an emotive cognition and a merely theoretical one. It was a mistake, however, which Locke did something to popularize, to understand the relation of the cognitive and the emotive as a distinction of separate "faculties" or "powers" of the soul.[8] On the implications of this mistake more will be said shortly.

What shall we say, then, of the motion to which, by God's sanctification of us, we are excited? It is *self*-movement, though it is God that excites us to make it. It is movement in which we reach out to the good, to the world as the handiwork of God and as the sphere of his action and self-giving. In reaching out to the world as good we are reconciled to it, as those who have previously found it deceptive and opposed to any good of our existence. Now we can enter it with joy as the sphere of our existence, in which we have been granted to act and to live. Humankind quickened from death is given life—so much we may say in speaking of faith—but quickened from death to life humankind is then given a place to live, a worldly context stamped with the resurrection of Christ, opened in hospitality to the service God's people are called to render. Love is the leading out of restored agency in worldly activity. Of an agent quickened to God in a faith *not* led out in love (an unreal abstraction, but to James a useful counterfactual, and so not to be spurned by us) we might say that it was unclear whether he or she would have any life in the world, or whether his or her only calling would be to mortify the flesh and die to the world. But as the world is given back to us again no longer as a broken world but as a world repaired, we are drawn in love toward God and into the world in one motion, for it is as the work of God's redemption that we receive the world's good.

And so, too, we are drawn back to ourselves, in gratitude that we, too, are part of, and benefit from, the worldly work that God has persisted in. As the movement of love is directed both to Creator and to creature, so love realizes the inner unity that God would confer on the soul. We may accept the point on which Edwards insists, that movement toward "divine things" (by which

---

[8]Cf. Jonathan Edwards, *A Treatise Concerning Religious Affections* 1.1, in *The Works of Jonathan Edwards*, vol. 2, ed. J. E. Smith (New Haven, CT: Yale University Press, 1959), p. 96: "The affections are no other, than the more vigorous and sensible exercises of the inclination and will of the soul. God has indued the soul with two faculties: one is that by which it is capable of perception and speculation. . . . The other faculty is that by which the soul . . . is in some way inclined with respect to the things it views or considers."

he means not only divine being, but all that God has wrought within the world) is primary, and movement to self is secondary. But that is an order of theological logic, not of experience. It is God's deed alone that makes us tolerable company for ourselves, but the good that God is, and does, "for me" cannot be separated out experientially from the good that God is and does "in himself."[9] The "for me" necessarily accompanies our admiration of the good "in itself"; if we cannot say "good for me," we cannot say "good" at all. There will be no sanctification, no recovery of love for others and for God, without the reflexive acceptance of the self's own place within the scheme of "divine things" to which we are moved. Every attempt to eliminate self-reference on principle, which is to postulate a good for which I am not bound by my very existence to be grateful, ends in nihilism.

Love as the motion of the soul is not motion of the body. It is not an act in the world. To become an act love needs to be led out into the sphere of *time*, for otherwise it cannot take form as *decision*. Love in itself is devotion, not action. The peculiar moral weakness we call "indecision" is not a weakness of love; it cannot be countered by a relentless ratcheting up of the affections. It is a weakness in discerning and hearing a call to act, a weakness in observing a practical possibility given in the shape of the moment, and that is a weakness of hope, for hope discerns in the light of God's promise what is given to us to do. Where love attends to the "today" that has come to be out of the past, the "today" of the world around us, hope attends to the "today" that has not yet come to be, but opens out in front of us, the "today" of opportunity. Hope presides over the venture of action and focuses deliberation on its possibility.

Love as cognition. How, in the second place, shall we speak of love as *cognition*? This is not different from love as the soul's motion and rest. There are not two loves, one moving and the other knowing, but one love, which moves as it knows and knows as it moves. We can never love the wholly unknown, but only that which in some degree or another we know. In faith and love motion is led by knowledge, faith by the knowledge of the self with which we are confronted in the presence of God's saving work, love by the knowledge of the world, which attracts us to itself and to its Creator and

---

[9]Edwards, *Treatise* 3.2, p. 240.

Redeemer. Love is the fulfillment of faith; the soul reaching out to grasp what it does not understand yet is satisfied in part with the understanding of love. Love, as Augustine spelled it out, exists in the half-light of an imperfect knowledge, always accompanied by a faith that is urgent to know more, yet never in the darkness of total ignorance. We love St. Paul as a figure we can imagine, he tells us, though we do not know the sound of his voice or the cast of his features. Yet love can speak *of* its object and *to* its object, not shooting its arrows into the mist, but achieving a focused reference to it. We should not, of course, envisage this knowledge as objective and distanced. The knowledge of love is participatory and celebratory. It is a glad knowledge that evokes our capacity for action, which discovers us in a situation of service. Sanctification is seen, therefore, in a comprehension of the ordered structure of the world and the ordering of human action with it, as the grasp of a moral *law*, which norms action fittingly to the world.

This comprehension structures not only individual actions but also the whole life of individual human beings and the shape of human communities. Human life is sanctified complete with its naturally ordered temporal development through maturity to the frontier of death. Sanctification thus involves the acquisition of *wisdom* over the course of years; in this aspect, but in this aspect alone, we may think of it as incremental, as the experience that develops wisdom is incremental. Yet since wisdom is never more than participation in the world, not transcendence of the world, sanctification is most refracted at this point through the worldliness of our being with all its hazards and qualifications. The wisdom of age is the wisdom of weakness and of partial experience, not the wisdom of God.

Love in its cognitive aspect needs "leading out" in its turn. It needs to be led on from what it knows to what it does not yet know, to what can only be known through promise and grasped by hope. Hope, too, is a motion, but not a motion led by what it knows. Hope is of things not seen. It leads obedience beyond love, over the edge of knowledge into the darkness of ignorance. It confronts the future, which is not visible or comprehensible, and confronts it with a promise of God, a promise that love has learned of in its attention to the work and words of God but that it is not in a position to grasp of itself.

Promise is our access, and our only access, to an eschatological moment beyond the reach of the wisdom given before death. Death is the decisive moment for hope, because death refuses to be integrated wholly and satisfactorily into the shape of a holy and fulfilled life. At whatever point of maturity death may come, it never comes without rupture. Hence the sonorous prayer of the Church of England Burial Service, "In the midst of life," in praying, "Suffer us not at our last hour for any pains of death to fall from thee," is not to be suspected of a morbid anxiety unable to grasp the truth of justification. It responds, rather, to a distinct challenge to obedience, a temptation different in kind from any that we have had to overcome in the course of our lives.[10] It recognizes that the soul has a destiny that exceeds the world, and it prays for the realization of that destiny in the hour of passing from the world. A Protestantism that thinks it has nothing to do in the face of death but be thankful for the life of the deceased has come perilously close to accepting the horizons of worldly life as ultimate, and so perilously close to the frontier with atheism, since it is a short step from absolutizing the horizons of worldly life to treating God's presence in the world as a mere manner of speaking. The falsity in this view of death can be measured by our inability to find a sympathetic understanding for world-weariness, that exhaustion with the sameness of the world's repetitive circles by which nature reconciles us to our death and which bulked very large in the pietists' understanding. We are not likely to sing, "Then, world, farewell! Of thee I'm weary. Only my Jesus do I seek."[11] World-weariness may extinguish even love, for love must die and be reborn, but hope can call even through world-weariness and summon us to a service beyond the limits of this world, insisting, when nature would have us let everything go, that God's service may be held on to.

In reflecting on the ground we have covered so far one point deserves underlining. The confusion and recrimination that arose over the relation of faith and works, or faith and love, is symptomatic of a deeper confusion of moral conceptuality that had taken hold of the Christian intellectual tradition by the time of the Reformation. C. S. Lewis observes "how tragically narrow is the boundary between Tyndale and his opponents, how nearly he means by faith what they mean by charity."[12] But this confusion was not an

---

[10]Cranmer based his prayer on the medieval hymn *Media Vita*, transmitted through a German hymn by Luther and translated into English verse by Miles Coverdale.

[11]Herzog Ernst-Ludwig von Sachsen-Meiningen, "Trauerode."

[12]C. S. Lewis, *English Literature in the Sixteenth Century* (Oxford: Oxford University Press, 1954), p. 189.

innocent and accidental tragedy. It was born of a failure in the tradition to keep the dynamic progress of the perfection of human being clearly before its eyes, and indeed, it not only concerned the relation of faith to love but also the relation of both faith and love to hope. Tyndale's achievement was to see how "these three, inseparable in this life, have yet separable and sundry offices and effects."[13] The tradition had connived at a collapse of faith, love and hope into a single disposition that it called "love" and that purported to be the moral disposition of the soul without reference to its source and destiny, an aspiration and attachment to the good shorn of responsibility and of focused action.

The pervasive sentimentality of modern talk about love and the pervasive aggressiveness of modern talk about the will both have their cause in this inward collapse of the understanding of the Christian moral life. What makes faith, love and hope distinct from one another is the different ways in which motion relates to cognition in each. The immediacy of faith's active discovery of self and God is cognition only implicitly, containing no experience of the world. It gains this only as it is mediated through the worldly experience of love. But this in turn must be surpassed by the knowledge of future things, exceeding worldly experience, on which hope fixes its famous anchor within the veil. The mistake that confused them arose from the attempt to take knowledge out of moral analysis in the belief that the good and evil of human action could be located in self-motion alone. As David Hume put it: "I am more to be lamented than blam'd, if I am mistaken. . . . No one can ever regard such error as a defect in my moral character."[14] Or, even more famously, Immanuel Kant: "It is impossible to think of anything at all in the world, or indeed even beyond it, that could be considered good without limitation except a *good will*."[15] The name we give to such a moral disposition conceived as without cognitive content is "the will," and the philosophy of ethics that promoted this conception we conveniently designate as "voluntarism." Of its sources there is still much to be learned. Despite the readiness with which the *illuminati* of the eighteenth century pro-

---

[13]Tyndale, *Exposition of Matthew*, p. 14.

[14]David Hume, *Treatise of Human Nature* 3.1.1, ed. L. A. Selby-Bigge (Oxford: Oxford University Press, 1888), pp. 459-50.

[15]Immanuel Kant, *Grundlegung zur Metaphysik der Sitten* 4.393, trans. Mary Gregor, *Practical Philosophy* (Cambridge: Cambridge University Press, 1996), p. 49.

claimed the focus on the will as their own special discovery, it is more than clear to historians that they drew on a long tradition going back at least to the beginning of the scholastic era in the West, and perhaps earlier in the East. If I understand the seventh-century monothelite controversy correctly, this is what Maximus Confessor thought was at stake in resisting the attribution of a simple, undifferentiated will to the person of Christ, a cause for which he was prepared to suffer the most extreme torture and humiliation.

What we call, inadequately, "morality," and in earlier ages, no more adequately, "virtue," has everything to do with the truth with which we comprehend the world, not merely with the energy of motion with which we hurl ourselves at it. With that realization the triadic relation of faith, love and hope regains its significance. These three moments constitute the dynamic of the redemption and perfection of human agency. In articulating the dialectic between justification and sanctification, between faith and love, the Reformers pointed the way to a recovery of the meaning that voluntarism threatened to take away. But without the third member of the triad their gesture was incomplete, and their reconception of morality, therefore, was ineffective and lacked successors.

THE GREATEST OF THESE IS LOVE

A concluding matter remains, however, to be raised. Paul follows his most famous mention of the threefold shape of virtue with the observation, "The greatest of these is love" (1 Cor 13:13). Granted that we cannot and must not collapse the three into an agapeic monism, how may we speak of the *preeminence* of love? I identify two points that will be essential ingredients of any answer.

We must, in the first place, respect the *eschatological context* of this utterance. Prophecies, knowledge, tongues shall pass away. Life and action within the world must reach their term. When the perfect appears, what is partial passes away. Speech, purposes and conceptions appropriate to childhood are left behind by adults. Love's preeminence is final, not initial. In the second place we observe that faith and hope do not yield before love as the so-called gifts do. "Now, faith and hope, and love abide, *these three*" (1 Cor 13:13). Love is not the unique content of morality, not even in its state of final accomplishment. Its triadic structure, its awareness of self, world and time, is crowned in the primacy of love. We are not destined to become creatures of feeling and vision without energy and purpose. The primacy of love is not the final vindication of quietism. Yet there is a point of view from beyond the moments of active faith, love and hope, and in that point of view love commands. Love endures beyond its genesis in virtue, and participates in eternity. So argued Augustine.[16] How can we understand it?

The contribution of love to action is its *objectivity*; in love we are turned outward to a reality that presents itself to us, not inward to our own emotions. Love is the reflective moment in which practical reason takes stock of what there is, including its own relation to what there is, the "for me" of every good communication. We may, therefore, express the final preeminence of love by saying that reflection on reality is not *expended*, and thus *superseded*, in being the ground from which we proceed to deliberation and action. As deliberation bears fruit in action, it acquires greater reflective scope. The relation with the real world forged in love is irreversible, and through action continually strengthens itself. A preeminent love crowns action by reflection. As moral reason passes from faith to love and on through hope into action, so it passes back to love again.

In this reflux of active motion we see how the bare idea of "action" is articulated into "rest" and "work." Rest is conceivable only in relation to action, a moment that crowns work. It is not simply a reversion from action to contemplation, the final victory of theory over practice. One may contemplate many things that one has not done, but only in contemplating what one *has* done can one attain rest. Agency continues to be present in reflection on action; action remains "our" action when we rest, that through which we ourselves are engaged with world and time. All that has changed is the relaxation of the tension of care and striving. In Jewish and Christian moral thought the Sabbath was a moment of accomplishment of work, not an interruption of it. "God saw all that he had made, and behold, it was very good" (Gen 1:31). Our action can answer our agency only if it has the blessing of accomplishment in view. The end of agency is the satisfaction of work in rest.

---

[16]For Augustine's carefully balanced statement on this, see *De doctrina Christiana* 1.37.41-38.42. For the best English translation, see Augustine, *On Christian Teaching*, trans. R. P. H. Green (Oxford: Oxford University Press, 1997).

Only in beholding God is rest perfected. Our satisfaction in our work needs intellectual substance, the consciousness of a true object to rest *in*. To reflect on our work is to reflect on a penultimate object, a pane of glass through which, as Herbert understood, we "then the Heav'n espy." When we understand our work truly, we see it set within the whole purpose of God, a moment within his work of bringing to perfection all he has made. It was that which made our work purposeful in the first place, rather than merely an act of self-positing. As John Donne puts it:

> The ends crown our works, but thou crown'st our ends,
> For at our end begins our endless rest;
> This first last end now zealously possess
> With a strong sober thirst my soul attends.[17]

The Sabbath, then, is a moment of praise in which our completed work is passed through the prism of God's work. But there is a provisional Sabbath on earth as well as a final Sabbath in heaven, and from this far horizon we must turn to something nearer at hand. If love will take its complete form as objective delight in God present in the completion of his works, there is an anticipatory shadow, prefiguring the final delight as the weekly Sabbath prefigures the end of world history. In the course of our active lives we may know already what it is to pass from a love that generates hope and action to a final love that can simply rest in what it sees. And that is because God's complete works are provisionally shown us in the body of Christ. To contemplate the works of witness that members of that body are given to perform affords a delight beyond any satisfaction we may take in our own works. For as we see those works of witness performed by others, we know that our own works are merely a small part of what God is doing; we are freed from that stifling sense that God may somehow be dependent on the success of our own enterprises.

And so it is that the whole thrust of the famous chapter of 1 Corinthians to which all talk of faith, love and hope comes back in the end turns on delight in other people's doings. The "partial," which gives place to the "perfect," consists of those performances in which one is different from others, where

---

[17]John Donne, "La Corona," in *Divine Poems,* ed. Helen Gardner (Oxford: Oxford University Press, 1978), pp. 1-2.

the capacity to speak, the capacity to understand, the capacity for ecstasy, the capacity for service, all have expression in differentiated variety. But "the transcendent way" (*kath' hyperbolēn hodon*) to which Paul beckons his readers has gone beyond personal gifts and personal accomplishments. It has acquired the patience and humility that takes joy in others' gifts and accomplishments. It is without jealousy and self-importance. This love stands on the far side of hope. For hope leads the emotive cognition of love out into particular actions, responds to a vocation constituted by unique gifts and unique circumstances and affirms the self-standing right of different services. But now love, in its turn, leads hope out into the attachment of many members within one body, a solidarity experienced in the church of Christ as a foretaste of the unity of redeemed humanity in Christ. Only this transcendent way permits us to think of sanctification not only in terms of individual holiness but also of community, in which the virtues of one member match the virtues of others in a mutually delighting coexistence.

The English language preserved until quite recently a distinct term for the transcendent love that, in this way, had the last and final reflection of practical reason. It called it "charity." As so often, theological baggage most quickly discarded as excess weight soon proves to have carried some indispensible insight. Charity is love as a balanced and reflective fulfillment, shorn of that pressing need to act which constantly turns us back into ourselves, which finds the work we have been given to do offered back to us a thousand times enriched through the work and life of other people with other gifts than ours. Imagine, for example, a theologian, used to sharing thoughts with fellow theologians and to receiving stimulating thoughts in return, encountering one day a believer who, though having no head for disciplined theology, has nevertheless received and entertained just one small thought from the flood that issues perpetually from the theologian's mouth, and has been inspired by it to perform some act of witness—of courage, perhaps, or of sacrificial generosity, or leadership—that no mere theologian would ever be likely to prove capable of. Such a theologian may well think himself shown the transcendent way. God, he will surely conclude, has set a crown on his ends more spectacular than anything his works could have anticipated.

8

ON BAVINCK'S THEOLOGY OF SANCTIFICATION-AS-ETHICS

James Eglinton

Herman Bavinck (1854–1921), the great dogmatician of the Dutch neo-Calvinist revival that crossed the late nineteenth and early twentieth centuries, offers a rich and nuanced understanding of the relationship between sanctification and ethics. Recent years have seen a renewal of interest in his life and work, particularly outside his native Netherlands. Various theologians working as part of this Bavinck revival have paid close attention to his dual identity as both systematician and ethicist: the disciplines of theology and ethics were, according to Bavinck, "organically linked." The latter gave shape to the former. Further, his participation in both disciplines is now being increasingly recognized. Exploration of the relationship of dogmatics and ethics in Bavinck's thought centers on his theology of sanctification. As will be seen, his is a theology of sanctification-as-ethics.

BAVINCK IN CONTEXT

Although the general details of Bavinck's life are now relatively easy to access in the English-speaking theological community,[1] it is perhaps nonetheless useful to begin by plotting some basic points in his life, particularly where

---

[1]Bavinck had two primary Dutch biographers, Valentijn Hepp and R. H. Bremmer. Valentijn Hepp, *Dr Herman Bavinck* (Amsterdam: W. ten Have, 1921); R. H. Bremmer, *Herman Bavinck en zijn Tijdgenoten* (Kampen: J. H. Kok, 1966). An English-language biography has more recently been published: Ron Gleason, *Herman Bavinck: Pastor, Churchman, Statesman and Theologian* (Phillipsburg, NJ: P & R, 2010).

contextual influences would go on to shape his views on sanctification.

Herman Bavinck was born in December 1854. His father, Jan Bavinck, was a pastor in the conservative, separatist Christian Reformed Churches (*Christelijke Gereformeerde Kerken*)—a denomination with its roots in the ecclesiastical Separation (*Afscheiding*) of 1834. His parents both represented their own upbringings in rural, pietistic Calvinist circles. As a young man, Bavinck studied theology at his denominational seminary in Kampen, where his father was a pastor, for one year. Following this, he made the contextually scandalous choice to transfer instead to Leiden University. The theology advocated at Leiden, an antisupernatural, mechanical deism, stood at the opposite polar extreme to that of his upbringing.[2] Bavinck chose to study at Leiden because he wanted a more "scientific" training than could be offered (at that time) in Kampen. This was a move in search of an academically credible approach to theological study. In general, his decision was not well received in his own denomination. Although his parents supported him, many within the Christian Reformed Churches simply assumed that he had abandoned his orthodox upbringing.

While at Leiden, he was taught by well-known nineteenth-century Dutch theologians including Johannes Scholten, Lodewijk Rauwenhoff and Abraham Kuenen. Kuenen was perhaps the most famous of Bavinck's professors outside the Netherlands, though the likes of Scholten and Rauwenhoff were of considerable influence within their own country. Their shared theological vision was one of a new Christianity for a modern world, a Christianity knowing neither virgin birth nor bodily resurrection. Their denial of the supernatural was accompanied by a strong emphasis on Scripture as a human text and the notion that the church could offer nothing useful to society not already provided by the secular state.

Bavinck was educated within the Leiden school, and much of his theology should be read as a reaction against its various emphases. The Leiden school seems to have produced two principal streams of graduates: first, those who followed its belief that Christianity offers nothing distinctive and who, accordingly, abandoned the church (the prominent nineteenth-century Dutch minister-turned-journalist Allard Pierson

---

[2]For an overview of the Leiden school, see James Eglinton, *Trinity and Organism: Towards a New Reading of Herman Bavinck's Organic Motif* (London: T & T Clark, 2012), pp. 13-18.

being the best known, though there were many less famous Leiden graduates who also gave up their ministries); and second, those who formulated a reinvigorated Christian orthodoxy, also known as the neo-Calvinists, among whom Herman Bavinck and Abraham Kuyper are the most recognizable theologians.

Following his undergraduate studies, Bavinck remained at Leiden to write a doctoral dissertation on Zwingli's ethics. After this, he was ordained a pastor in his own denomination in Franeker. Having been a pastor for one year, he was appointed theology professor at Kampen. There, he wrote his magnum opus, *Gereformeerde Dogmatiek*, and began to write its companion, *Gereformeerde Ethiek*—a work that never saw completion. That Bavinck was also employed there to teach ethics is an oft-neglected fact. At the start of the twentieth century, he moved from Kampen to the newly established Vrije Universiteit in Amsterdam, where he became Kuyper's colleague. He remained there for the rest of his life. While teaching at the Vrije Universiteit, he wrote widely on ethical issues, although he never published his own Reformed ethics.

Bavinck's wider engagement with the application of Christianity to society was seen in his close involvement with Kuyper's anti-Revolutionary Party, the Netherlands's first modern political party. In this capacity, he engaged with issues of enfranchisement,[3] was active in the development of Reformed education in the Netherlands and wrote widely, with publications ranging from the Christian family, the Christian and war, and the subconscious.[4] Suffering a heart attack while preaching at Synod in 1920, his health began to fail from then on, and he died in the following year.

Various features in this brief biographical sketch will come to the fore as one examines the place of sanctification in Bavinck's developing thought: the pietistic Calvinism of his parents, the weak account of human agency taught by his Leiden professors, his doctoral studies in Christian ethics and his own writings on ethics all contribute to a somewhat ignored picture of Bavinck as ethicist.

---

[3]Niels van Driel, "The Status of Women in Contemporary Society: Principles and Practice in Herman Bavinck's Socio-Political Thought," in *Five Studies in the Thought of Herman Bavinck: A Creator of Modern Dutch Theology*, ed. John Bolt (Lewiston, NY: Edwin Mellen Press, 2012), pp. 153-95.

[4]For a complete summary of Bavinck's publications, see Eric Bristley, *Guide to the Writings of Herman Bavinck* (Grand Rapids: Reformation Heritage Books, 2008).

With that in mind, this chapter begins by considering various aspects of Bavinck's handling of sanctification viewed against the wider backdrop of mainstream nineteenth-century Dutch theology, and within his own life context.

HUMAN AGENCY AND SANCTIFICATION IN NINETEENTH-CENTURY DUTCH MAINSTREAM THEOLOGY

Although Bavinck's own background was in a stream of separatist, pietistic, non-"scientific" Calvinism, his primary local conversation partners were the rival mainstream schools in Leiden and Groningen. Although these schools took up very different positions regarding the importance of the church in the modern world, their ideas concerning sanctification and human agency were not dissimilar. In Leiden, as has already been noted, the church was seen as a wholly outdated human institution. Bavinck's Leiden professor Rauwenhoff once quipped, "What actually lay in the beautiful dream of the Kingdom of God on earth can be fulfilled in and through the State."[5] The church can offer no miracle; it cannot offer a God who speaks or who can be known. Its only tangible ministry deemed credible by the Leiden school—its diaconal ministry to the poor—could be better organized and administered by the secular state.

Theirs was a world of passive, optimistic, mechanical and evolutionary thought typical of the nineteenth century. In that world, humanity was set to march on, progressively increasing in moral superiority with every passing generation. The absolute determinism of Johannes Scholten, in particular, emphasized that there is no true freedom in human agency. Rather, his insistence was that humans act as (divinely initiated) processes of cosmic cause and effect determine that they will act. Human, and in particular Christian, agency, according to the Leiden school, was as such weighted toward passivity. Scholten's most significant work, the *Leer der Hervormde Kerk* ("The doctrine of the Reformed Church"), has no section devoted to sanctification or human agency.[6] Rather, it is structured to encourage the human simply to accept one's lot in life.

---

[5]L. W. E. Rauwenhoff, cited in Cornelius Augustijn, "Kerk en Godsdienst 1870–1890," in *De Doleantie van 1886 en haar Geschiedenis*, ed. Wim Bakker (Kampen: Kok, 1984), pp. 58-62.

[6]Johannes Scholten, *De leer der Hervormde Kerk in hare grondbeginselen: uit de bronnen voorgesteld en beoordeeld*, 2 vols. (Leiden: P. Engels, 1848–1850).

There is no need for a dedicated account of active Christian agency, as Scholten's confidence was in the ongoing, predetermined self-betterment of humanity (wedded to an understanding of the Bible's presentation of good triumphing over evil in the eschaton).[7] When Scholten's wider oeuvre touches on topics like prayer, for example, the conviction expressed is that prayer should be a passive acceptance of the predetermined circumstances of one's present experience. The one who uses prayer to express discontent with providence, or to ask God to change his circumstances, is an *egoïstische bidder*: a "selfish supplicant."[8]

There was no active struggle against sin. There was, rather, the assurance that the twentieth century would be marked by the march toward world peace. Humanity's ever-increasing humanity to humankind would be the hallmark of the future. Jesus, a morally superior human being, could serve as a useful example of the inevitable goal of human moral evolution, but whether humans were connected to the church was of no crucial significance in that regard.

The Groningen theologians took a similar position in terms of the prevailing culture of nineteenth-century optimism.[9] Although their ecclesiology was different, in that they espoused a national church (*volkskerk*)[10] within which all Dutch people would be nominal members, they also embraced the idea that Christ would lead by example as humanity strode on toward moral perfection. However, their intense nationalism (often verging on xenophobia toward foreign theological influences) meant that the *volkskerk* remained a key element in their model of Dutch culture. Thus Christ would lead through the church as humanity arrived at its inevitable, passively acquired moral destination. In the case of the Groningen theologians, their understanding of how humanity would progress to moral superiority was different to the Leiden ideal (in that it acknowledged, rather than excluded, the church). However, it was nonetheless another manifestation of the Zeitgeist. Both looked to the twentieth century with the same passive optimism regarding the goodness of human nature.

---

[7]Ibid., 1:32.

[8]Johannes Scholten, *De Vrije Wil* (Leiden: P. Engels, 1859), p. 261.

[9]For an overview of the Groningen school, see Eglinton, *Trinity and Organism*, pp. 6-11.

[10]Karel Blei, "Volkskerk," in *Christelijke Encyclopedie*, ed. George Harinck (Kampen: Kok, 2006), 3:1819.

This optimism no doubt strikes the reader in the early twenty-first century as naive and one-sided: the present-day reader is conscious of a twentieth century marked by Auschwitz and Dachau. However, that the mainstream Dutch theologians of that era wrote within such a worldview goes some way to explaining the underdeveloped, or often absent, handling of sanctification in their writings.

BAVINCK'S ACCOUNT OF HUMAN AGENCY

Against that backdrop, the priority Bavinck placed on human agency becomes particularly interesting. Perhaps the most important statement made in *Reformed Dogmatics* on human agency is that "in the preservation and government of all things, God maintains this distinct existence of his creatures, causes all of them to function in accordance with their own nature, and guarantees to human beings their own personality, rationality and freedom. God never coerces anyone."[11]

The insistence on divine sovereignty being worked out noncoercively must be read against the backdrop of Bavinck's schooling at Leiden. Contrary to Scholten's account of human agency, Bavinck asserted that human agency is no illusion. The reasoning behind this assertion is also closely linked to Bavinck's rejection of Scholten's doctrine of God.

Scholten described his theological methodology—an essentially rationalistic process beginning with nature and the human being, and moving from there to God—as "reflection [on God and Scripture] grounded on observation [of the natural world]" (*bespiegeling gegrond op waarneming*).[12] In using this method, Scholten observed a natural world seemingly fixed by a closed process of cause and effect. In drawing inferences from this observation toward the doctrine of God, Scholten saw little reason that a triune God was strictly necessary to account for the world around him. As such, Scholten's theology is marked by an indifference toward the divine triunity. He deemed the Trinity an unnecessary and unprofitable doctrine, one certainly less important than the material principle of the Christian faith: absolute predestination.[13] In the

---

[11]Herman Bavinck, *Reformed Dogmatics*, vol. 2, *God and Creation*, ed. John Bolt, trans. John Vriend (Grand Rapids: Baker Academic, 2004), p. 104.
[12]Scholten, *De leer der Hervormde Kerk*, 1:lxi.
[13]Ibid., 1:18-20.

development of Scholten's mature theology, his doctrine of God became markedly less trinitarian and more monistic, a development of which Bavinck was particularly critical.[14]

Bavinck's theology represents an inversion of Scholten's methodology. Like his teacher, Bavinck believed in reflection grounded on observation. Unlike Scholten, however, Bavinck attempted to observe God's self-revelation first and, on that basis, to reflect on the nature of created reality. In short, he inverted Scholten's modus operandi of *bespiegeling gegrond op waarneming*, whereby it became "reflection on the cosmos based on observation of God as self-revealing Trinity." It seems that in Bavinck's system, a triune doctrine of God requires a noncoercive account of human agency because the reality of agency within human society reflects the (noncoercive) reality of agency within the divine society that is the Father, the Son and the Holy Spirit.[15]

As such, the origins of Bavinck's theology of sanctification-as-ethics, a theology that rests on an account of human agency quite unlike that of his former professor, are more fundamentally rooted in a renewed desire to understand human identity and agency in light of its triune Creator.

BAVINCK'S LIFE CONTEXT IN RELATION TO SANCTIFICATION

As has already been said, although Bavinck studied under the likes of Scholten and Kuenen, his origins were not in their mainline Reformed Church (*Hervormde Kerk*), and he did not join that denomination after graduation. Bavinck's approach to human nature and sanctification differed considerably from that of his professors. This difference reflects his own ecclesiastical background and ongoing commitments.

Sanctification is a major theme within Bavinck's thought. It is of such significance to Bavinck that we cannot properly understand his broad theological and ethical vision without a careful account of sanctification's place therein. Bavinck viewed sanctification as centered on the imitation of Christ, which he understood in relation to ethical norms. This, however, was not

---

[14]Bavinck, *God and Creation*, p. 43. See also Herman Bavinck, *Philosophy of Revelation* (London: Longmans, Green, 1909), p. 46.

[15]"God himself, the entire deity, is the archetype of man. . . . The triune being, God, is the archetype of man." Bavinck, *God and Creation*, pp. 554-55.

the universal view of ethics among his neo-Calvinist contemporaries. Bavinck's Amsterdam colleague Willhelm Geesink, the primary ethicist among the first generation of his neo-Calvinist contemporaries, argued that the imitation of Christ should be considered as submission to God's hidden will, rather than as an ethical norm.[16] Geesink and Bavinck approached constructing Christian ethics in the same neo-Calvinist manner: ethics, like dogmatics, should be written beginning with Scripture, then viewed in historical development through the early, medieval, Reformation and contemporary church, after which one should appraise the current position in relation to Scripture. However, Bavinck's approach to the imitation of Christ is nonetheless subtly, and not insignificantly, distinct in that he frames the entire ethical undertaking as the imitation of Christ (as opposed to Geesink's limiting of the imitation of Christ to one's submission to God's secret will).

As such Bavinck spent a great deal of time considering this theme. It is significant that he published contextually important articles on the imitation of Christ at the beginning and end of his academic career, thus highlighting that this was a constant concern during his years in Kampen and Amsterdam.[17]

Sanctification was of great importance to Bavinck for various reasons. First, his upbringing was heavily influenced by Calvinistic pietism rooted in the Dutch *Nadere Reformatie*, the Second Reformation. A central aspect of the *Nadere Reformatie* was the influence (via British-inspired Dutch Calvinists like Willem Teellinck) of practical Calvinistic piety. Common to the stories of seventeenth-century English Calvinists in the Netherlands was a perceived lack of experimental spirituality in the Dutch Reformed churches. The Anglo-American Puritan Thomas Hooker once wrote of the Dutch, "The power of godliness, for ought I can see or hear, they know not."[18] William Ames, an English divine who spent much time in the Netherlands, warned a fellow Englishman immigrating to Holland to be on his guard against "a strong head and a cold heart."[19] Keith Sprunger, a historian of

---

[16]See Wilhelm Geesink, *Gereformeerde Ethiek*, 2 vols. (Kampen: Kok, 1931). See also John Bolt, *A Theological Analysis of Herman Bavinck's Two Essays on the* Imitatio Christi (Lewiston, NY: Edwin Mellen, 2013), pp. 20-21.

[17]Herman Bavinck, "De Navolging van Christus I, II, III," *De Vrije Kerk* 11 (1885): 101-13, 203-13; 12 (1886): 321-33; Bavinck, *De Navolging van Christus en het Moderne Leven* (Kampen: Kok, 1919).

[18]Thomas Hooker, cited in Keith Sprunger, *Dutch Puritanism* (Leiden: Brill, 1982), p. 358.

[19]Thomas Goodwin, cited in Sprunger, *Dutch Puritanism*, p. 358.

British Christianity in the seventeenth-century Netherlands, remarks that "nearly every English Puritan preacher to the Netherlands became a missionary of English practical divinity."[20] The *Nadere Reformatie*, then, was in part the seventeenth-century appropriation of this English concern for greater Dutch Calvinist spiritual piety. Bavinck was raised in this tradition, with its strong aversion to "cold hearts and warm heads." Bavinck's own writings demonstrate a critical reading of the *Nadere Reformatie* tradition as being excessively *otherworldly* in pietism. Nonetheless, the issue of how the Christian's faith in Christ should affect his life was one pressed on him from an early age.

Second, sanctification came to the fore in Bavinck's thought life while studying at Leiden. There he was confronted with what he understood to be an excessively *this-worldly* approach to the Christian life. Freshers' Week, known as Green Week (*de groene week*) at Leiden, involved rambunctious behavior with which Bavinck could not agree. He withdrew from participating in this week, as he believed the activities involved—drunkenness, the encouragement of swearing and so on—were inconsistent with his faith.[21]

The clash of cultures meant that the young Bavinck was forced to consider at length the character of the Christian life. That he saw his task as being to mediate between world flight and world conformity is hinted at already within his first few weeks at Leiden. Feeling unable to participate in the student society responsible for Freshers' Week, and not wishing to withdraw from student affairs altogether, Bavinck, along with two fellow students, formed an alternative student society, the Reformed Students Society (*Societas Studiosorum Reformatorum*).[22]

That concern for an intentional approach to the Christian life in the modern world would characterize the rest of Bavinck's theological efforts. Indeed, the pursuit of Christian ethics (Bavinck would later crystallize his understanding of sanctification as an ongoing ethical process) led to his doctoral thesis in theological ethics, the composition of a major work in ethics (albeit unpublished) and, during his Amsterdam years, the constant pursuit of principled Christlikeness in various spheres of life. Among the regular prayers

---

[20]Sprunger, *Dutch Puritanism*, p. 358.
[21]Hepp, *Doctor Herman Bavinck*, p. 33.
[22]Gleason, *Herman Bavinck*, p. 56.

recorded in Bavinck's journal was that he might be "a worthy follower of Jesus" (*een waardig volgeling van Jezus*) in his diverse spheres of responsibility.[23]

The significance of ethics (and under that heading, sanctification) in Bavinck's theological efforts is such that there is a movement within Bavinck studies that asks whether to properly cast him primarily as an ethicist or as a systematic theologian. The likes of John Bolt and Dirk van Keulen currently lead the field in that regard.[24] Van Keulen has recently written that "[it] would be a biased opinion to consider Bavinck only as a Reformed dogmatician. He has presented himself as an ethicist as well."[25] More work must be done in this regard as the significance of the relationship among dogmatics, sanctification and ethics in Bavinck's work becomes more widely recognized.

SANCTIFICATION IS A LIFELONG ETHICAL PROCESS

It is important that one understands the movement from sanctification into ethics in Bavinck's thought. Without grasping that there is a lead to follow here, it will be tempting to judge Bavinck as having written a rigorous dogmatics, but having failed to provide a thorough account of our consequent human agency. This is particularly the case among Bavinck's Anglophone readership, which knows him as the writer of *Reformed Dogmatics* and *Philosophy of Revelation* but little else. To those only familiar with those works, the charge that Bavinck pays insufficient attention to human agency certainly seems plausible: after all, the section on sanctification in *Reformed Dogmatics* occupies a mere forty pages (bearing in mind that *Reformed Dogmatics* is a four-volume work within which volume four alone is almost a thousand pages in length).[26] However, when one reads this succinct handling of sanctification in view of its relationship to ethics in Bavinck's

---

[23]Bremmer, *Herman Bavinck en zijn Tijdgenoten*, 32; cf. Bolt, "The Imitation of Christ Theme in the Cultural-Ethical Ideal of Herman Bavinck," in *A Theological Analysis of Herman Bavnick's Two Essays on the* Imitatio Christi (Lewiston, NY: Edwin Mellen, 2013), p. 60.

[24]Dirk van Keulen, "Herman Bavinck's *Reformed Ethics*: Some Remarks About Unpublished Manuscripts in the Libraries of Amsterdam and Kampen," *The Bavinck Review* 1 (2010): 25-56; van Keulen, "Herman Bavinck on the Imitation of Christ," *Scottish Bulletin of Evangelical Theology* 29 (2011): 79; John Bolt, "Christ and the Law in the Ethics of Herman Bavinck," *Calvin Theological Journal* 28 (1993): 45-47; James Eglinton, "Bavinck, Dogmatics and Ethics," *Scottish Bulletin of Evangelical Theology* 29 (2011): 2-3.

[25]Van Keulen, "Herman Bavinck on the Imitation of Christ," p. 79.

[26]Herman Bavinck, *Reformed Dogmatics*, vol. 4, *Holy Spirit, Church, and New Creation*, ed. John Bolt, trans. John Vriend (Grand Rapids: Baker Academic, 2008), pp. 230-70.

thought, a whole new world of possibilities opens up. This is so because the relationship of sanctification to ethics justifies (and necessitates) a far more exhaustive separate handling of ethics than we find in his *Dogmatics*. In volume 1 of *Reformed Dogmatics*, he writes,

> Dogmatics describes the deeds of God done for, to and in human beings; ethics describes what renewed human beings now do on the basis of and in the strength of those divine deeds. In dogmatics human beings are passive; they receive and believe; in ethics they are themselves active agents. . . . Dogmatics is the system of the knowledge of God; ethics is that of the service of God. The two disciplines, far from facing each other as two independent entities, together form a single system; they are related members of a single organism.[27]

Bavinck's statement here on the "renewed" human being as true ethical agent is made clear in *Reformed Dogmatics* volume 4, where he outlines that pagan virtue is insufficient, as it can make virtues of things contrary to the divine will, and is carried out for unethical reasons.[28] The same point is central to his treatment of the Christian as ethical agent in *Gereformeerde Ethiek*.[29] Consistent with this idea is the assertion that the dogmatician, like the ethicist, must be a godly person in order to imitate Christ.[30] Sanctification is necessary for dogmatics and ethics alike.

In making such bold assertions on the uniqueness of Christian ethical action, Bavinck was positioning himself directly against the Leiden school's belief in the universality and inevitability of ethical evolution. At the core of Bavinck's account of sanctification is that only the sanctified person can be a true ethical agent, just as the sanctified person alone can be a true theologian. This insistence should also be read against the backdrop of those, like his fellow Leiden alumnus Christian Snouck Hurgronje, who rejected Christianity and instead veered toward the ethics of non-Christian religions (in Hurgronje's case, Islam).[31] The ethical element of Hurgronje's openness to

[27]Herman Bavinck, *Reformed Dogmatics*, vol. 1, *Prolegomena*, ed. John Bolt, trans. John Vriend (Grand Rapids: Baker Academic, 2003), p. 58.
[28]Bavinck, *Holy Spirit, Church, and New Creation*, pp. 256-60.
[29]Van Keulen, "Herman Bavinck's *Reformed Ethics*," p. 35.
[30]Bavinck, *Prolegomena*, p. 43.
[31]Correspondence between Bavinck and Hurgronje, from their student days in Leiden to Bavinck's death, has been published as George Harinck and Jan de Bruijn, eds., *Een Leidse Vriendschap* (Baarn: TenHave, 1999).

Islam, for example, centered on his belief that Islam provided answers to the problem of racism that he had not found in the Leiden school's presentation of Christianity. Indeed, in correspondence between Bavinck and Hurgronje this backdrop makes discussions over ethics in relation to Islam particularly interesting, bearing in mind Hurgronje's admiration for an Islamic theology of personal and societal ethical reform.[32]

In the 1895 Dutch edition of *Gereformeerde Dogmatiek*, Bavinck wastes little time in making a striking set of assertions on dogmatics in relation to ethics: in setting out their relationship, he says that they depend on each other as intellectual disciplines, and insists that only a renewed person can be dogmatician and ethical agent.[33] Here (incidentally, in the first chapter of *Reformed Dogmatics*), Bavinck argues that dogmatics *must* be followed by ethics. To understand Bavinck's ethics, one must begin (rather than end) with *Reformed Dogmatics*, and use his handling of sanctification-as-ethics under the heading of dogmatics, to lead into a far more exhaustive exploration of human agency. The Bavinck of *Reformed Dogmatics* is not the whole Bavinck. To grasp the whole Bavinck, one must understand that his identification of sanctification-as-ethics means that sanctification is the linking concept between the writing of dogmatics and of ethics.

SANCTIFICATION UNDERSTOOD DIALECTICALLY

It is also perhaps helpful to invoke the language of dialectic to highlight the sense in which Bavinck views sanctification via a series of pairings.

To explain why he relies on such a system in order to account for sanctification, one must remember the dogmatic methodology typical of the early neo-Calvinist movement. Neo-Calvinist dogmatic theology is constructed by beginning with Scripture's account of the topic at hand, following which the appropriation of said Scripture in the postapostolic church is examined.

---

[32]Ibid., pp. 127-30.

[33]Herman Bavinck, *Gereformeerde Dogmatiek*, Eerste Deel (Kampen: J.H. Bos, 1895), p. 13. "De dogmatiek beschrijft de daden Gods voor en aan en in den mensch, de ethiek beschrijft kracht van die daden Gods. In de dogmatiek is de mensch passief, ontvangt en gelooft; in de ethiek treedt hij zelf handelend op . . . De dogmatiek ontwikkelt wat God is en doet voor den mensch en doet hem God kennen als zijn Schepper, Verlosser, Heiligmaker; de ethiek zet uiteen wat de mensch nu is en doet voor God, hoe de mensch geheel en al, met verstand en wil en alle krachten, zich Gode wijdt uit dankbaarheid en liefde. De dogmatiek is het systeem der kennisse Gods, de ethiek dat van den diest Gods."

After this, the account of postapostolic Christianity's development into medieval Christianity wrestles with whether the doctrine in question still existed in a form faithful to Scripture. Following this, the progression generally moves to the Reformation's response to medieval Catholicism, after which neo-Calvinist dogmatics traces more recent trends. The end of the process is always to return to Scripture.

In that light, Bavinck's account of sanctification begins by acknowledging the two assertions made by Scripture concerning holiness. First, God's people are objectively declared to be holy. This is the case in the Old Testament, where Israel is declared a holy nation. It is more evident still in the New Testament, where the church is also declared holy in Christ. "Sanctification, accordingly, is in the first place a work of God, more specifically of Christ and his Spirit."[34] Second, Scripture in both Testaments asserts the covenantal obligation on the people of God to live and walk before him in holiness. The Lord requires that his people do justice, love kindness and walk humbly with him. So Bavinck's account of sanctification begins with these two assertions as the anchor points in Scripture.

Bavinck's account of the postapostolic church on sanctification is one of "no less stress on life than on doctrine."[35] He traces early struggles over the forgiveness of postbaptismal sin to the creation of penance—by which one could sacramentally atone for lesser sins—and portrays a church culture where "Christians were more intent on fleeing the world than on winning it."[36] The cult of the ascetic grew, and the category of negative virtue assumed a greater prominence. Bavinck views the development of the doctrine of sanctification as progressing along nomistic, legalistic lines, placing the accent firmly on virtues not commanded in Scripture, and neglecting the more objective aspect of holiness conferred by God.

Bavinck's progression then moves to the Reformation as attempting to correct this imbalance. He charges Lutheranism with failing to follow Luther's own insistence that the whole of the Christian life is repentance, largely through the leadership of Philipp Melanchthon (who, Bavinck claims, was far more reliant on Aristotle in the construction of detailed lists of virtues).

---

[34]Bavinck, *Holy Spirit, Church, and New Creation*, p. 235.
[35]Ibid., p. 237.
[36]Ibid., p. 238.

Calvin's pattern, rather, was to focus Christian virtue on the Decalogue. This focus on the Decalogue forms the basis of neo-Calvinist ethics in the ethical writings of both Bavinck and Wilhelm Geesink. "In his description of the Christian life, [Calvin] does not lose himself in a wide-ranging exposition of all sorts of virtues and duties but conceives all of life as a unity controlled by one universal rule. Calvin derives this from Rom. 12.1, where the apostle indicates that it is the duty of believers to offer their bodies as living sacrifices, holy and pleasing to God."[37] Bavinck identifies what we might call a dialectic in Calvin's approach to ethics, in Calvin's insistence on both negative (self-denial) and positive virtues. He read Calvin as someone who upheld the Pauline principle that sanctification involves a putting off *and* a putting on.

Justification and sanctification. In *Reformed Dogmatics* Bavinck writes,

> Justification and sanctification . . . while distinct from each other, are not for a moment separated. . . . In order to be completely freed from sin, we must be freed from guilt and cleansed of its stains. And that is what happens in justification and sanctification. Hence the two are equally necessary and are proclaimed in Scripture with equal emphasis. Logically justification comes first in this connection, for it is an evangelical kind of justification. . . . It is a juridical act, completed in an instant. But sanctification is ethical: it is continued throughout the whole of life and, gradually makes the righteousness of Christ our personal ethical possession. . . . *In justification Christ is granted to us juridically, in sanctification, ethically*; by the former we become the righteousness of God in him; by the latter he himself comes to dwell in us by his Spirit and renews us after his image.[38]

This handling of sanctification is an attempt to bring it in line with the related approach to the justified person as *simul iustus et peccator*. The central conviction at hand is that this formulation only partially answers questions of how a Christian can be both justified and sinful. *Simul iustus et peccator* asserts that the Christian is definitively justified—that person's legal identity is changed, guilt is removed and the person is declared just forevermore—but it creates the consequent question of how the justified person can nonetheless be a sinner.

In answering this question, Bavinck positions himself against both antinomianism and perfectionism—positions he attacks in both *Reformed Dog-*

---

[37]Bavinck, *Holy Spirit, Church, and New Creation*, p. 244.
[38]Ibid., p. 249 (emphasis added).

matics and the unpublished *Reformed Ethics* text.[39] Bavinck's schema is rather that we are *objectively justified*, and then exist between *objective* and *subjective sanctification*, following which we are *objectively glorified*. A key difference between justification and sanctification, according to Bavinck, is that the former has only an objective status, whereas the latter can be considered objectively and subjectively. Justification concerns a state of forgiveness declared by God concerning the sinner. Sanctification, unlike justification, concerns the sense in which the renewed person is objectively declared holy (by God) and yet only experiences this holiness subjectively. Sanctification, as such, concerns dual realities—one known and declared by God, the other incrementally discovered by the Christian.

Bavinck explores this initial dialectic between objective and subjective sanctification through two other pairs.

A gift and a task/reward. In describing sanctification in the categories of both *gift* and *task pursued for reward*, Bavinck wishes to account for the sense in which sanctification is a declarative act and work of God given in grace, *and* the sense in which the human agent must also (in the power of that grace) assume responsibility for his or her own actions.[40]

Bavinck is instinctively wary of lawlessness, not because his commitment to *sola gratia* wavered, but rather because in addition to its insistence that salvation is by grace alone, Scripture also firmly asserts that how Christians live matters a great deal. "Since God enables [Christians] both to will and to work . . . believers must work out their own salvation with fear and trembling. They must keep their entire spirit, soul and body blameless in sanctification until the day of the Lord Jesus Christ."[41]

How does Bavinck express these thoughts without turning the requirement to "keep one's being blameless in sanctification until the Last Day" into a synergistic nomism? He views the pairing of gift and task as central in exhorting believers to live in holiness without replacing the gospel with mere moralism. The exhortation to sanctify one's self stands as a consequence of the prior (objective) gift of grace. Furthermore, the goal of this

---

[39]Herman Bavinck, *Gereformeerde Ethiek* (in Bavinck Archives, box 13/32; number 186), §20; cf. van Keulen, "Herman Bavinck's *Reformed Ethics*," p. 38.
[40]Bavinck, *Holy Spirit, Church, and New Creation*, pp. 232-37.
[41]Ibid., p. 235.

sanctifying action is future reward. "Everyone is rewarded according to his works. Godliness holds promise for this life and also for the life to come. The thought of future glory spurs them on to patience and perseverance. For God rewards those who seek him. He distributes a just penalty for all transgression and disobedience, but also rewards generosity, confidence of faith, self-denial and the labour of his servants."[42]

The distinction between Bavinck's model of sanctification-as-task and moralism is seen in various aspects of his theology of holiness. Bavinck's insistence that only the person who has already been renewed can act as a true ethical agent is significant in that regard: the ethical agent has been a prior recipient of grace. It asserts that true ethical action as carried out by the believer is acceptable before God because it is not carried out on the pretence of self-salvation. Rather, it is carried out as the response to grace, in the power of that grace, in order to receive the "special reward" that is Christ himself. "All the benefits that believers enjoy or will obtain are gifts of the grace of God."[43]

That love for God is the motivation in true ethical action also gives the covenantal ethical imperative presented by Bavinck a nonmoralistic character: "With many compelling reasons believers are urged to live this holy kind of life. They are obligated to this because God has first loved them, has had compassion on them, and has shown his love to them in Christ."[44]

Passive and active. The final aspect of this dialectic is that between sanctification as active and passive. This appears to be an explanation of the gift-task dialectic: the gift of objective, conferred holiness is passively received; the obligation to take up the task of sanctifying oneself subjectively (in pursuing a reward) is done actively. Bavinck is aware that "many authors have seen a conflict between this all-encompassing activity of God in grace and the self-agency of people maintained alongside of it."[45] In this light Bavinck attacks *both* moralists *and* antinomians in their denial of this dialectic. In attempting to uphold the dialectic, however, he regards the Reformed as historically more successful than the Lutherans simply because they more wholeheartedly followed Scripture in asserting both aspects contained therein.[46]

---

[42]Ibid., p. 236.
[43]Ibid.
[44]Ibid.
[45]Ibid., p. 254.
[46]Ibid., p. 255.

Once again, Bavinck's desire to exhort Christians to active holiness without confusing the gospel for moralism is evident in his definition of active sanctification. He grants *passive* sanctification the priority; it is the basis for subsequent *active* sanctification. In that light, Bavinck equates active sanctification with the "continued repentance" mentioned in the Heidelberg Catechism. (His belief in the Reformed understanding of sanctification is echoed in his invocation, at various points, of the Heidelberg Catechism on this topic.)[47] His portrayal of passive sanctification accents the putting to death of the old man, which corresponds to active sanctification's putting on of Christ.

A distinction should be drawn between Bavinck's handling of sanctification and justification as active and passive. He also writes of justification as both passive and active. However, the distinct nature of justification means that, for Bavinck, the passive-active dialectic in justification does not lend itself logically to the same objective and subjective statuses that one finds with sanctification. Passive justification concerns God's declarative act that this sinner has been justified. Active justification concerns the justified person's new awareness and possession of his justification: "How could a benefit of Christ be to our advantage if it did not enter into our possession? How could a prison inmate benefit from his acquittal if he was not informed of it and the prison doors were not opened for him? And what advantage would there be for us in a justification in the eternal decree, in the resurrection of Christ, and in the proclamation of the gospel, if God did not personally impart it to us in the internal call by faith?"[48] Active justification, then, deals with one's acceptance of justification by faith alone as an objective act, and not in any sense a subjective work. It does not concern ongoing human agency in the sense that active sanctification does.

CONSEQUENCES FOR BAVINCK AND CONTEMPORARY DISCUSSIONS ON SANCTIFICATION AND ETHICS

The relationship of sanctification to ethics in Bavinck's thought is not without consequences for his own intellectual trajectory, or for our characterization of him as a Christian thinker.

---

[47]For example, ibid., pp. 253, 256.
[48]Ibid., p. 220.

The effect of Bavinck's close pairing of dogmatics and ethics via the concept of sanctification-as-ethics is suggested in the text of *Reformed Dogmatics* and obvious when one considers his writing commitments during his studies at Leiden and professorships in Kampen and Amsterdam. In *Reformed Dogmatics* Bavinck makes plain that dogmatics and ethics are organically linked.[49] Although dogmatics precedes ethics, it remains incomplete until it expresses itself in ethics. In this sense, the fullness of Bavinck's account of Christian agency should be acknowledged. While objective, passively acquired elements of Christian experience (justification and glorification) are adequately handled under the heading of dogmatics (as actions attributed solely to divine action), the active elements of Christian experience (in this case the struggle *against* sin and *for* holiness) are rooted in dogmatics but belong more fully within ethics.[50]

Accordingly, Bavinck's failure to publish *Reformed Ethics* ought to be viewed in relation to his actual publications—the early and late articles on the imitation of Christ being particularly important examples—which nonetheless demonstrate a consistent output within the field of ethics.[51] Van Keulen has demonstrated that Bavinck seems to have written the *Gereformeerde Ethiek* manuscript at the same time as, rather than after, *Gereformeerde Dogmatiek*.[52] The presence of different extant ethics manuscripts either written by Bavinck or compiled by his ethics students during his Kampen years highlights that his time in Kampen aimed at both dogmatics and ethics.[53] The production of *Reformed Ethics* was no afterthought. It was an essential companion activity while writing *Reformed Dogmatics*. According to his own ideal, the true dogmatician cannot express dogmatics in its entirety without engaging in ethics. As such it is unfortunate that Bavinck never finished his own ethics manuscript.

---

[49]Bavinck, *Prolegomena*, p. 58.

[50]For example, hamartiology (the doctrine of sin), like the doctrine of sanctification, is introduced in *Reformed Dogmatics* but handled more comprehensively in Bavinck's unpublished papers on ethics. See van Keulen, "Herman Bavinck's *Reformed Ethics*," p. 36.

[51]Bavinck, "De Navolging van Christus I, II, III"; Bavinck, *De Navolging van Christus en het Moderne Leven*.

[52]Van Keulen, "Herman Bavinck's *Reformed Ethics*," pp. 28-29.

[53]Reinder Jan van der Veen, *Gereformeerde Ethiek. Acroam. van: Prof. Dr. H. Bavinck* (originally 327 pages in two volumes, the first of which has been lost); Cornelis Lindeboom, *Gereformeerde Ethiek—Dictaat van Prof. Bavinck*; see van Keulen, "Herman Bavinck's *Reformed Ethics*," p. 29.

It seems most likely that *Gereformeerde Ethiek* never saw the light of day because Bavinck had yet to settle on its final form when he moved to the Vrije Universiteit. In comparing Bavinck's own early manuscript to the later ethics manuscripts compiled by Kampen students from his ethics classes, there is an evident desire to restructure the work. When he arrived at the Vrije Universiteit, Wilhelm Geesink was already busy preparing a neo-Calvinist *Reformed Ethics*.[54] As such it made no sense for Bavinck to continue with his own *Reformed Ethics* manuscript. In the same vein, Kuyper gave up his own project to write a neo-Calvinist Reformed dogmatics when he learned that Bavinck was already writing one.

However, the failure to publish *Reformed Ethics* should not been interpreted as Bavinck's giving up on his ethical quest. If anything, Geesink's work freed Bavinck to engage in the practice, rather than theory, of neo-Calvinist ethics, as is seen in his involvement with Kuyper's anti-Revolutionary Party.

However, without access to Bavinck's *Reformed Ethics*, it appears that his readership—familiar with his thought largely through *Reformed Dogmatics*—only sees him in part. Thankfully, his Anglophone readership is becoming increasingly aware of the issues concerning his identification as a dogmatician and ethicist. Examination of the texts in question points toward a dual identity rather than an either/or choice: just as dogmatics and ethics belong together generally, so do Bavinck's dogmatics and ethics. Without the linking concept of sanctification between these great headings in Christian thought, however, the significance of their relationship would be lost.

---

[54]Geesink, *Gereformeerde Ethiek*. While there are minor differences between Bavinck and Geesink as ethicists, their approaches are substantially the same as neo-Calvinist ethicists.

PART THREE

Theological and Pastoral Meditations on Sanctification

9

GOSPEL HOLINESS

Some Dogmatic Reflections

Ivor J. Davidson

"Holiness" may not appear a gospel matter. In a fair bit of Christian thinking, the term conjures up images of heavyweight moral demand, uncompromising otherworldliness or a seriousness of discipleship that seems more like austerity than joy. Isn't sanctity basically the repudiation of self and the world, the challenging business of denying ourselves, taking up the cross and—very gradually indeed—becoming better than we presently are? If the doctrine of sanctification represents an account of what Christians are supposed to say—and do—about such things, it sounds suspiciously like bad news rather than good. "Spirituality," especially of an eclectic, individual sort, suits the consumerist instincts of late-modern culture; sanctity does not. At best, holiness seems concerned with the hard graft of costly obedience, the lifelong discipline through which justified but recalcitrant sinners are, by pathos as much as pleasure, made fit for fellowship with a holy God. At worst, it's about the cultivation of habits so transcendent of ordinary Christian experience that they belong on another spiritual plane—the dispositions of a spiritual elite. The options are tough: either "a sair fecht to the end"[1] or a tantalizing ideal from which, in our everyday reality, we're inclined to turn away: saintliness of *that* sort is surely a special vocation. As such, we secretly hope, it's maybe an optional extra for faith.

---

[1] A description attributed to the pastoral advice of a notable Scottish churchman, Alexander Whyte (1836–1921); for those whose induction in Scots may be incomplete: "sore fight."

At other levels, things seem a little more complicated. There is an ongoing flood of popular literature on holiness, and a pretty healthy market for lives of the saints and reissues of classic texts on saintliness. There is notable contemporary interest in spiritual retreat, pilgrimage and meditation. Admiration for at least some exemplars of self-denial is common. Many Christians continue to feel a pull toward more committed spiritual practice and yearn for its benefits. They recognize the evidences of true devotion when they see them and long to find a special formula for such a state, beyond the hurlyburly of the spiritual journeys they know. Yet whatever holiness is, whatever its virtues, the *way* to it surely isn't good news, is it? The evangel itself is clear. God immeasurably loves undeserving creatures. They are redeemed from first to last by his grace, not by any merits or attainments of their own. For all the perduring disarray of their spiritual histories, they are complete in Christ. They need no higher-tier status than their personal and corporate union with him. How can sanctification be taken seriously without compromising the splendor of this declaration? Our task is to give that question some thought.

There are, not least for Protestant minds, plenty of challenges. The history of the doctrine of sanctification is strewn with evidences of theology's enduring capacity to treat holiness as something other than the gospel. All of them persist in contemporary forms. There is the subtle (or not-so-subtle) danger of a quasi-Pelagian preoccupation with salvation by works. Can we articulate a theology of sanctification that does not collapse into a form of moral self-improvement, the pursuit of favor with God for special devotion? There is the danger of condemning the world to which God has committed himself. Can we think of sanctification in a way that does not celebrate flight from the material order? God has pronounced that order primordially good; in the resurrection of Jesus, he has pledged its ultimate redemption from evil's effects. There is the danger of a privatized spirituality. Can reflection on sanctification avoid obsession with individual experience, personal milestones, the acquisition of gifts or achievements as private spiritual capital? Can it talk adequately about the gospel's vocation to life together, the declaration of a new social order in the church, the summons to a *people*, not just isolated selves, to bear witness to the world?[2]

---

[2]On such challenges, see David Fergusson, "Reclaiming the Doctrine of Sanctification," *Interpretation* 53 (1999): 380-90.

Where sanctification is seen as a higher-tier reality in Christian experience, distinct from the commencement of the Christian life, there are, of course, additional pressures. Holiness has often been said to be a matter of supplementary spiritual breakthrough, or baptism with the Spirit, understood as something distinct from the gift given in Christian initiation. On this reckoning, sanctification is the hallmark of a deeper spiritual life, a more advanced form of consecration. It means one thing to have our sins forgiven, another to embark on a road toward overcoming them every day; one thing to be justified, another to live a life of true obedience; one thing to know Jesus as Savior, another to submit fully to him as Lord. The moral and spiritual possibilities of the Christian life depend on making a successful transition from one level or stage of spiritual seriousness to another.

As any student of such a theology quickly learns, there are many differences within the genre. The most potent example, the Wesleyan vision of "perfect love" or "entire sanctification" (which in John Wesley's case coexisted with a notable modesty in regard to his own state), stands at a considerable remove from many later versions of second-blessing or Higher Life teaching found in revivalist and holiness movements, Pentecostal and charismatic theologies, or the beliefs of Keswick. Many things vary within these traditions—the nature of Spirit baptism; the role of spiritual crisis; the stability or otherwise of the higher life; the possibility of "resting" in faith; the dynamics of spiritual progress; the status of spiritual techniques; the place of gifts and signs; the degree to which indwelling sin may be overcome by the seriously consecrated. A lot of these theologies have been anything but joyless or misanthropic in intent, and rightly concerned to focus on the dramatic, real-life transformation available to broken creatures in fellowship with a wonder-working God. Their accounts have also, at their wisest, sought to distance themselves from misunderstandings of "sinless perfection," making clear that classical versions of perfectionist teaching have not always been fairly represented by their opponents. Some versions of holiness theology may claim deeper roots than their critics (or their devotees) suppose.[3]

Still, if sanctification is to be posited as a second dimension of faith's experience, can such a view be presented without infringing on the sufficiency

---

[3]For a recent creative attempt to render the tradition in broad dogmatic focus, see T. A. Noble, *Holy Trinity: Holy People: The Theology of Christian Perfecting* (Eugene, OR: Cascade, 2013).

of Christ? The challenge is a serious one. The force of the apostolic testimony is unambiguous. Christ has been set forth, all the fullness of the Godhead dwelling in him bodily. His work has been accomplished, without qualification. Its consequences are objective, not provisional. As a completed state of affairs, "You have been filled in him" (Col 2:10). Whatever is to be said about Christian progress, or growth in grace, a positional reorientation has occurred: in Christ Jesus, "the saints" have *already been* sanctified (1 Cor 1:2; 6:11)—no less than they have already been washed and justified. To "us who are being saved" (1 Cor 1:18) a specific assurance is given: dreadful as a great deal of your behavior remains, change though you must in the alignment of your lives with the situation established for you—already, now, "all are yours" (1 Cor 3:21-22; cf. 1 Cor 1:4-9).[4] Can a theology of sanctification as higher-tier experience offer adequate hope for the struggling, for those who find little if any breakthrough in practice? In the stark realities of the world as we know it, can such a message avoid fostering guilt about victory unattained, neurosis over failure yet again? If holiness theologies have often ended up qualifying the ambitiousness of their claims, hedging their exhortations to the Spirit-filled life with a fair few caveats about the persistent challenges of indwelling sin, they have done so with good reason, and with pastoral as well as biblical concerns in mind. Sanctity tied to a quest for the Spirit's anointing as key to a deeper serenity may become, in psychological terms at least, sanctity as success in devotion. Where every lapse is evidence of inadequate breakthrough, the aggregate, at worst, is spiritual hopelessness. In this, no less than in a perspective that—triumphant or cynical—discounts altogether the imperatives of grace, the good news suffers eclipse.

Western theology has of course spent not a little energy attempting to navigate all these perils, and it would be otiose to rehearse that history here.[5] For my money, the Reformed tradition has, at its best, done a rather

---

[4]For a sustained defense of the priority of positional or definitive rather than progressive sanctification in New Testament perspective, see David Peterson, *Possessed by God: A New Testament Theology of Sanctification and Holiness* (Downers Grove, IL: InterVarsity Press, 2001).

[5]A range of perspectives can be sampled in surveys such as Donald L. Alexander, ed., *Christian Spirituality: Five Views of Sanctification* (Downers Grove, IL: InterVarsity Press, 1989); Melvin E. Dieter et al., *Five Views on Sanctification* (Grand Rapids: Zondervan, 1987); see also, e.g., Gregory A. Boyd and Paul R. Eddy, *Across the Spectrum: Understanding Issues in Evangelical Theology*, 2nd ed. (Grand Rapids: Baker Academic, 2009), pp. 161-82.

remarkable job of articulating sanctification as a central and delightful[6] aspect of Christian piety, one that is not to be reduced to dogged moralism, darkly introspective piety or cheerless scrutiny for evidences of faith. There have been dire exceptions to that achievement, not least where the theology of sanctification has been overshadowed by a brooding predestinarianism, or by a conception of atonement so abstract and impersonal that we are advised to doubt whether the gospel itself is for all. Yet even these distortions, pernicious as they have proved, have been far less in evidence than some have alleged, and Reformed theology has often shown a striking capacity to paint soteriology's details in richly positive colors, especially when it has depicted the biblical coalescence of justification and sanctification around the central locus of participation in Christ. In the process, its images of sanctity have also evinced a capacity to hold together the finished work of Christ and the work of the Holy Spirit. There has been due emphasis on the essential role of the Spirit in the entirety of Christian experience, and resistance to the proposal that his activity should be seen as a supplement that funds a process of growth in grace subsequent to the immediate dynamics of Christian conversion: au contraire, the Spirit is vitally involved from the start.

In the spirit of that Reformed perspective, I assume that the theology of sanctification will inevitably go astray if it begins anywhere other than with the comprehensiveness of the gospel's announcement as we encounter it from the first: in Christ by the Spirit. If sanctification seems an oppressive theme, always existing in some degree of tension with the message of justification, forever threatening to cramp our Christian freedom, spoil our present joy and challenge our future hope—if it is a matter only of plodding ascesis, a perpetual struggle for spiritual brownie points, a technology of ascent whose benefits continually elude our grasp—it may well be that we have commenced our thinking in the wrong place: with human saintliness rather than with the God who makes saints, and with our own ideas about spiritual eminence rather than with sanctity as defined in God's prevenient movement toward us. Sanctification is indeed a "gospel mystery."[7] If we

---

[6]Contrary no doubt to the standard caricatures of dour Calvinism or joyless Puritanism.

[7]The designation of a classic text: Walter Marshall, *The Gospel Mystery of Sanctification* (1692; repr., Grand Rapids: Reformation Heritage Books, 2013).

would think about the doctrine aright, it is of fundamental importance that we view it in its true setting—as an essential aspect of the wonder of God's mighty outreach to creatures. We learn what holiness is in God's gift of himself to us.

I shall offer three basic things: (1) a sketch of some of the necessary features of a dogmatic account of holiness as gospel truth;[8] (2) some reflections on the holiness of Jesus Christ, the One whose name is that gospel's content; (3) some brief comments on the implications of such an account for the practice of Christian holiness. The overarching contention is that the theology of sanctification cannot be understood unless it is approached from the right end: with God, God's nature and God's action, rather than with believers, their duties and their hopes.

To tackle things thus is to resist a temptation that has infected discussion of sanctification far too often: the temptation to suppose that when we refer to creaturely holiness we know in advance what we are talking about. To assume that holiness consists straightforwardly in elevated forms of moral conduct or a vaguely defined set of spiritual graces, transparent to our everyday understanding of religious commitment, is to assume too much—or to listen too little to theology's proper authority. The holiness with which we are in fact concerned is, by contrast, radically particular, and sets its own terms. It refuses to be correlated with any generic or conventional notions, and stands far apart from the domestications of ethical and religious idealism. Its specificity commands our attention. It delivers us from the enduring illusion that sanctification is a less than liberating matter, capable of coordination with the message of justification only by means of some fancy theological footwork—an achievement that most of us have remained too clumsy to effect to any sustained applause.

The method is simply stated, though perpetually costly to learn: *submission to God's rule as he exercises it in his work of revelation.*

---

[8]The language of "gospel/evangelical holiness," particularly as contrasted with legalism, works righteousness or (mere) virtue, has Puritan roots, receiving notable exposition at the hands of John Owen in particular. The idiom was widely applied from the eighteenth century onward. On Owen, see Kelly M. Kapic, "Evangelical Holiness: Assumptions in John Owen's Theology of Christian Spirituality," in *Life in the Spirit: Spiritual Formation in Theological Perspective*, ed. Jeffrey P. Greenman and George Kalantzis (Downers Grove, IL: IVP Academic, 2010), pp. 97-114.

THE DOGMATICS OF HOLINESS

We begin with the bedrock of all properly Christian confession: the Christian doctrine of God. "I am the LORD your God. . . . I am holy. . . . I am the LORD. . . . I am holy" (Lev 11:44-45; see also Lev 19:2). Contrary to our instincts, we have no right to speak of holiness except as it is defined for us in the self-announcement of the One who is holy like no other (Ex 15:11). God's holiness is first and foremost his incomparable majesty, his unique identity as the One he is and not another. It is not to be viewed as a maximal instantiation of something found elsewhere. It is, like all God's perfections, an aspect of his absolute differentness from all else, his self-maintaining identity and utter distinctiveness. God's otherness cannot be correlated with religious or anthropological phenomenologies of "the holy,"[9] or transmuted into abstract notions of divinity as sacred ground of being, or characterized reliably as transcendent source or guarantor of morality, purity, truth or goodness as we know them. His holiness is not an exemplification, even an ultimate one, of that which might have any conceptual shape independently of who he is, sui generis in his own being. To acknowledge him as holy is to confess—with awe and wonder—his unqualified singularity, not to ascribe something available to us otherwise. God is not "holiness" par excellence: he is "the Holy One," incomparable to any other (Is 40:25). He names himself with unfettered exclusivity, invoking his own holiness as he swears by himself (Amos 4:2; cf. Amos 6:8). Hannah's prayer puts it in lapidary form.

> There is none holy like the LORD:
> for there is none besides you. (1 Sam 2:2)[10]

Vitally, however, the context in which God's declaration of his holiness occurs is his introduction of himself *to us*. He is the One who announces himself to be holy in his acts toward creatures. God reiterates his essential identity in the economy of his works as Creator, Redeemer and Perfecter. He does so in majestic freedom, but also—such is his nature—in authenticity, making known to creatures who he truly is. His holiness is not acquired or enhanced in the establishment of contingent reality, or in his communi-

---

[9]The classic is of course Rudolf Otto, *The Idea of the Holy* (Oxford: Oxford University Press, 1923).
[10]On the centrality of a positive dogmatic account of divine holiness, see in particular John Webster, *Holiness* (London: SCM, 2003), pp. 31-52. For some of the core investments, see Barth, *CD* II/1, pp. 358-68.

cation with it, as if God needs to create in order to mark himself off, or to secure his otherness in contestation with putative rivals. Wholly *a se* and beyond augmentation in his plenitude, he is complete in himself regardless of any world. He creates in sovereign authority, in consultation with none but himself, and to no ontological enlargement of his intrinsic majesty.

But nor is God's holiness in any sense threatened by his free determination to move *ad extra*, as though his singularity somehow stands in jeopardy if there is something other to himself. God becomes neither more nor less holy when he creates, or when he acts within creation to maintain its integrity, holding it in being and effecting his purposes for it, rendering its very elements good and holy inasmuch as they are his (see 1 Tim 4:4-5). Created objects, places and beings are holy only in relationship to him, and thus in a strictly derivative sense. "The *author* of our sanctification, who only is so, is asserted to be 'God.' He is the eternal spring and only fountain of all holiness; there is nothing of it in any creature but what is directly and immediately from him."[11] Yet God wills to *bestow* holiness, and he does it as he alone is able to do, making known, and in that—highly particular—sense "sharing" with others his own holiness; just so, he enacts the unqualified uniqueness, the absolute yet manifold simplicity[12] of his being.

God's primordial purposes to bless are, assuredly, resisted by human creatures, who—in inexplicable preference for self-destruction—repudiate the nature and ends given to them by their maker, his will that they should be the image of his glory in the world. In contempt of their holy Creator, they make wreckage of themselves and their environment, alienating themselves from him and incurring his essential judgment on their wickedness. But what stands between them and ultimate destruction is also, in fact, God's holiness, for his "jealousy" for his honor is, it turns out, his resolute will to realize his own purposes come what may, and not—*per impossibile*—to be thwarted by creaturely defiance. Setting himself to judge and overcome all that is opposed to his holiness, God will yet ensure the creature's good.

The holiness of God involves his implacable hostility toward evil, but it also involves, as an aspect of that, his determined annihilation of evil's ef-

---

[11]John Owen, *Works*, vol. 3, *The Holy Spirit* (repr., Edinburgh: Banner of Truth, 1965), pp. 367-68.
[12]To invoke a currently controversial but (to my mind) enduringly worthwhile gloss on the same theme.

fects. The negative force of his holiness is but instrumental of its primarily positive orientation. God's holiness is not the faceless terror of a relentlessly exacting celestial magistrate. It is the nature of the One whose firm and unfathomably loving desire it is to bless his creatures in spite of themselves. He is placed in no quandary by their folly, and needs to come up with no contingency measure to address their plight. Far prior to their self-ruinous choices lies the potency of his generous purposes, which are no more prevented or thrown off course by creaturely rebellion than they are dependent on some notional anticipation of creaturely merit. He will not allow their wickedness to trump his will; the wickedness itself is consumed by the intensity of his commitment. In this connection we note that while God's holiness *includes* his moral purity, it is not *exhausted* by it. His holiness, once again, is more than distance from contamination; it is his sheer otherness from everything else—and his otherness has purposive, not simply privative (or prohibitive) force. Though "of purer eyes than to look upon evil" (Hab 1:13 my translation), God does not remain afar off, or act only in catastrophic judgment: precisely *because* he is holy, not *in spite of* it, he moves to overcome the distance between himself and the estranged, remedying their incapacity to stand in his presence, purifying them, making them, just as he has purposed, his own—a creaturely correspondent to his own holiness.

If we would learn what holiness is, it is to covenantal history that we are directed. The Holy One reveals his holiness in acts of mercy to very unholy subjects: the patriarchs and Israel. It is as he establishes fellowship with these naturally unholy ones that he is seen for who he is. He summons unlikely people, sets them apart, purifies them, makes them his treasured possession. The ethical entailments of that appointment are substantial and public-facing: they are to testify before the nations as to his character (Ex 19:5-6). "Be holy, for I am holy," Israel is commanded (Lev 11:44; 19:2; cf. 20:7); their conduct is to declare it. It is not as if their Lord depends on their witness to render his holiness visible, for his name is already excellent in all the earth, and his glory need not wait in hope of being bodied forth by compliant creaturely agents. It is rather that he calls them to show they belong to him and none other. Yet even there the obligation is framed in a context of grace, for he is himself the primary agent of their sanctification—"the LORD, who makes you holy" (Lev 20:8 NIV; see also Lev 21:8).

Their obligations are derivative of, and ostensive toward, his fundamental commitment to make this people his own. He *calls* them to holiness, but the initiative from the first is his: in establishing relations with them, he *renders* them holy.

In themselves, these subjects are wholly unworthy of God's lavish love. The Holy One's commitment is inspired by nothing native to them (Deut 7:6-8), and of themselves they fail dismally to live up to their holy status as his. Israel's sinfulness necessitates cultic rituals to represent her continuing dependence on divine forgiveness as prerequisite for divine intimacy. Her sinfulness in turn necessitates prophetic critique of the reduction of holiness to mere techniques of ritual observance, the due performance of repetitive practices that afford symbolic expression of cleansing from the various actions and states that constitute impurity. In the end, it is steadfast love, not sacrifice, that the Lord desires (Hos 6:6), and the defilements of debased ethical religion call out for his righteous judgment. By no means, in their experience, is he always on the side of his people's values, schemes or causes as they perceive them. But there is an enduring wonder nonetheless: judge them though he does, the Holy One remains present in their midst (Hos 11:9; cf. Is 12:6)—and in that there is hope even in contexts of dereliction (Ps 22:3). For the exiled from divine favor, there can yet be consolation in the context of judgment; their God remains committed to them even as he excoriates their conduct and executes his righteous condemnation on their violations of his terms. The Holy One is, and will be, their Redeemer (Is 41:14; 43:3; 48:17; 49:7; 54:5; cf. Is 59:20; 60:16; 63:16).

God's holiness involves his fidelity in spite of his people's waywardness. Though a wounded lover, he cannot let them go (Hos 11:8-9). It is an aspect of his nature *as* the Holy One that he does not carry out his fierce anger on them with terminal effects. The sovereign and holy covenant-maker is, no less from his side, the holy covenant-sustainer, even for those who by rights ought to forfeit everything. In this, he is, the history declares, unlike any potentate the world knows; his holiness finds expression precisely in "the difference between his attitude and ours."[13] His essential jealousy for himself

---

[13]Wolfhart Pannenberg, *Systematic Theology* (Edinburgh: T & T Clark, 1991), 1:399. Pannenberg's strongly Hegelian account of divine holiness as synonymous with the infinite is, however, problematic.

and his people is restorative of their welfare; his holiness includes the staggering lengths to which his compassion for his own will go.

At the center of this mercy stands Israel's Jesus. In him, we find the ultimate in God's preparedness to render unholy creatures holy to himself. God's "holy servant" (Acts 4:27, 30), Jesus is the true Israelite, faithful as his people have not been. He is himself the Holy One, personally present among us, proximate as never before (Acts 2:22-32; 13:34-37 [Ps 16:8-11]; see also Mk 1:24 par.; Lk 1:35; Jn 6:69; Acts 3:14; 1 Jn 2:20; Rev 3:7). Identified completely with those he comes to serve (Mk 10:45), he obeys on their behalf, doing for them what they can never succeed in doing for themselves. As the Holy One not only in the midst of us but *enfleshed* as one of us, he renders the unholy holy in his person and work alike; his personal identity and his saving action are finally inseparable. The divine Word, God's only Son, he takes flesh and tabernacles among us; made like his human "brothers" in every way (Heb 2:17), within these same conditions he yet proves faithful, complete in his obedience as human (Heb 2:17-18; 3:2-6). "Without sin" (Heb 4:15), "holy, blameless, unstained, separated from sinners" (Heb 7:26 RSV), he is able to present himself "without blemish" to God (Heb 9:14). He is the sanctifier of sinners (Heb 2:11); acting on their behalf and standing in their place, he effects their consecration once and for all through the sacrifice of his body (Heb 10:10, 14). Raised from the dead, he is "vindicated" in the Spirit (1 Tim 3:16), his achievement confirmed. In not allowing his Holy One to see decay, designating him "Son of God in power according to the Spirit of holiness by his resurrection from the dead" (Rom 1:4), God has declared who he really is, and what he has secured once and for all: the sanctification of sinners, the concrete abolition of their sin as impediment to their fellowship with God (Heb 9:26). In his bodily ascension, the forever incarnate sanctifier takes their humanity[14] with him into heaven, there to appear for them in God's presence (Heb 4:14; 8:1; 9:24).

The beneficiaries of this achievement include all human types and conditions. Gentiles become fellow heirs with Israel (Eph 3:6); one-time aliens

---

[14]"We do not doubt but that the selfsame body, which was born of the virgin, was crucified, dead and buried, and which did rise again, did ascend into the heavens, for the accomplishment of all things; where, in our names, and for our comfort, he has received all power in heaven and earth": *The Scots Confession of 1560*, ed. G. D. Henderson, trans. James Bulloch (Edinburgh: St Andrews Press, 2007), p. 11.

from God's commonwealth become fellow citizens and members of the household of God (Eph 2:19). Ordinary human differences, of race and class and gender (Gal 3:28), are embraced within the consecration that the mediator effects. Those blessed by his action are not a faceless multitude, transferred en bloc by a nominal transaction, without reference to their human particularities or their location in history. There is, first, nothing nominal about what he does, as if his enactment of the divine salvific purpose were merely a shadow of a matter settled already by the plan it fulfills. Insofar as he has, as a divine-human subject, lived a genuine human history, the mediator's obedience within that history is of ontologically constitutive effect, securing there and nowhere else a reality that is not otherwise. There is also, second, a unique density to his relationship with us as human. Insofar as he is one with all humans, yet particular, his obedience in history is capable of representing all while relating definitively to each particular. The consecration he effects, accordingly, is personal, not generic; it renders humanity holy not as an abstract category, but in the specificity of a work wrought for particular human subjects—the eternally loved, historically situated recipients of God's electing purpose, now made holy as they are, where they are. In consequence, the human characteristics of the consecrated are not dissolved or set aside entirely; they simply exercise no restraint on the reach of his consecrating action. Those features may persist; they are no longer ultimate in the classification of our humanity.

In the plethora of their human kinds, the status of all the consecrated in Christ is definite. They are not simply *on the way* to relationship with the holy God, or told of their *potential* to experience that privilege in due course, contingent on further moral progress; they are the elect, already marked out as his, *made* holy (1 Cor 6:11). This has occurred "in the name of the Lord Jesus Christ," the name that expresses the totality of his enacted identity as mediator. In reconciling them to God and doing away with their sin, he has, as a settled action, consecrated them for the end for which they were destined all along: to be God's. Where he is, their humanity is, and will be, also.

The appropriation of this reality involves a third divine movement. It is as these subjects are incorporated into union with this Christ, as those who have died with him and been raised with him to newness of life (Rom 6:1-23; Col 2:6–3:17), that the holiness established *for* them, externally, is realized *in* them, personally.[15] Belonging to Christ means being bonded to him, engrafted into his person by the work of his Spirit. In consequence of that, his benefits, the achievements of his obedience *extra nos*, become present *in nobis*—and again *actually* so, not merely in potentiality or as a fictional imputation. Christ himself is personally present within us; we belong to him; to be united to him in his person, in the holiness of his person, is to know the blessings of his consecrated obedience as ours. In his exalted state, though bodily absent from us he has continuing proximity to us by his Spirit, for the right hand of God, where he sits, "is not confined to heaven, but fills the whole world."[16]

All this is wrought by the Spirit who is Holy, such that having Christ in us is synonymous with having his Spirit within us (Rom 8:9-11). There is no blurring of Christ's identity with ours in "substantialist" terms; still, so close is the union the Spirit effects that we really do come to possess Christ and the fruits of his personal obedience for us, such that "we can find in our nature that holiness of which we are in want."[17] In this, the Spirit's activity is crucial. We are accordingly said to have been sanctified by the Spirit (1 Cor 6:11) as well as in the name of the Lord Jesus Christ. We are chosen for salvation "through the sanctification of the Spirit" (2 Thess 2:13 my translation; cf. 1 Pet 1:2). There is, again, nothing merely symbolic here, as though the Spirit's action were only to signal to us that one day we shall be holy; the action is descriptive of what we now *are*.

Nowhere is the intimacy of the Holy Spirit's role in uniting us with the holy Christ more powerfully expressed than in the work of adoption. Israel as God's chosen covenant partner is God's son (Ex 4:22-23; Hos 11:1); in the light of

---

[15]My reading of Paul is (unashamedly) indebted to Calvin's momentous treatment. The recent literature is extensive: e.g., Michael S. Horton, *Covenant and Salvation: Union with Christ* (Louisville, KY: Westminster John Knox, 2007); Mark A. Garcia, *Life in Christ: Union with Christ and Twofold Grace in Calvin's Theology* (Milton Keynes: Paternoster, 2008); J. Todd Billings, *Calvin, Participation, and the Gift: The Activity of Believers in Union with Christ* (Oxford: Oxford University Press, 2007); Billings, *Union with Christ: Reframing Theology and Ministry for the Church* (Grand Rapids: Baker Academic, 2011); Constantine Campbell, *Paul and Union with Christ: An Exegetical and Theological Study* (Grand Rapids: Zondervan, 2012); Grant Macaskill, *Union with Christ in the New Testament* (Oxford: Oxford University Press, 2013), esp. part 2.

[16]John Calvin, *The Epistles of Paul the Apostle to the Galatians, Ephesians, Philippians and Colossians*, tr. T. H. L. Parker (Edinburgh: Oliver & Boyd, 1965), p. 346 (Col 3.1).

[17]John Calvin, *The Epistle of Paul the Apostle to the Hebrews, and the First and Second Epistles of St Peter*, tr. William B. Johnston (Edinburgh: Oliver & Boyd, 1963), p. 26 (Heb 2.11).

Christ, the filial character of God's electing purpose is taken to truly astounding lengths. By the action of the Spirit—whose "first title," as Calvin famously has it,[18] is the Spirit of adoption—an entire world of sinners is taken up as sons and daughters of the One whom Christ, the unique, eternal Son, calls Father. "*Many* sons" are now brought to glory (Heb 2:10). They share with *the* Son the astonishing privileges of his filial relation. Along with *him* they say *Abba*; along with *him*, they are joint heirs of an inheritance that is nothing less than God himself (Rom 8:15-17; cf. Gal 3:26–4:6). The Son himself knows no loss in this—"his heritage does not become narrow if many are possessors";[19] the infinite abundance that is his Father's presence and delight in him is shared with a family none can number, the children whom the Father has given him, his adopted brothers and sisters (Heb 2:10-13; see also Jn 17:6, 9).[20]

The final realization of that destiny for them is yet to be (1 Jn 3:1-2), but no higher status is conceivable than that which has already been granted to them in the here and now. In *this* world, and such as they are, they are not simply would-be children, who may one day enter the Father's house: right now, they have actual belonging, and actual privileges; indicatives not subjunctives describe their current status. "Of one [stock]" (*ex henos*) with the incarnate Son (Heb 2:11), their position is, already, the maximal expression of what being "set apart" for God could ever mean; already "raised up with [Christ] and seated . . . with him in the heavenly places" (Eph 2:6; cf. Col 3:1), they are, at a fundamental level, as sanctified as they can ever be.

This is, in outline form, something of what Scripture (read with admittedly Reformed lenses) has to say about the nature of God's holiness, and what God does to make creatures holy. It is, unambiguously, a soteriological story. A dogmatic representation of its plot line must be trinitarian from first

---

[18]John Calvin, *Institutes of the Christian Religion*, ed. John T. McNeill, trans. Ford Lewis Battles, 2 vols. (Philadelphia: Westminster Press, 1960), 1:450 (3.1.3).

[19]Augustine, *Tractates on the Gospel of John*, in *A Select Library of Nicene and Post-Nicene Fathers of the Christian Church*, ed. Philip Schaff, series 1, vol. 7, repr. (Grand Rapids: Eerdmans, 1994), p. 17 (2.13).

[20]See, e.g., Trevor Burke, *Adopted into God's Family: Exploring a Pauline Metaphor* (Downers Grove, IL: InterVarsity Press, 2006); Ivor J. Davidson, "Salvation's Destiny: Heirs of God," in *God of Salvation: Soteriology in Theological Perspective*, ed. Ivor J. Davidson and Murray A. Rae (Burlington, VT: Ashgate, 2011), pp. 155-75. For an ambitious assessment of the integration of covenant language with themes of filial and social identity in biblical theology, see Scott Hahn, *Kinship by Covenant: A Canonical Approach to the Fulfillment of God's Saving Promises* (New Haven, CT: Yale University Press, 2009).

to last. Contrary to some widespread preferences in modern theology, the scriptural testimony also requires that trinitarian dogmatics locate the essential roots of the narrative as far back as we can go, in the metaphysics of God *in se*. "God not only acts as the Holy One, but . . . as He acts He is, from everlasting to everlasting."[21] Not only is the sweep of God's reconciling action the history of his being within the sphere of creaturely temporality; the economy of his works derives from his eternally immanent holiness. Behind the covenantal history stands the God who is, in his innermost essence, the Holy Father, the Holy Son and the Holy Spirit.

As Father, God elects and purposes from all eternity to separate and sanctify these creatures as his own, in sheer mercy determining them in Christ to be "holy and blameless in his sight" (Eph 1:4 NIV). Without that electing determination, there is no holiness for creatures. There is no anticipation on God's part of their prospective holiness as ground of their election; tout court, the logic runs the other way around: God's electing will is the sole basis of their evincing the holiness "on which the eye of God may look."[22] This also means that, from the creature's perspective, the Father's election is the assurance that holiness for the creature *is*—and will remain— a reality, whatever existential doubts we may feel, and whatever evidences to the contrary there may be in our fractured moral histories. Our consecrated status does not rest on our commitment or potential to become better some day. Wholly a matter of grace, it is a present fact whose future is also assured; it is anchored in all the teleological security of the divine decree.

As Son, God enters into the conditions of the creaturely estate to deliver those whom the Father wills for fellowship with himself, securing their transference from the kingdom of darkness into the light of his presence. By coming to the aid of the estranged, taking on himself the burden of their sin and destroying its consequences once for all, he secures their reconciliation. He heals and sanctifies their condition from the inside, and takes their now decisively holy humanity with him to the Father's side, ensuring their final presentation also as holy, blameless and without reproach in God's sight

---

[21]Barth, *CD* II/1, p. 368.

[22]John Chrysostom, *Homilies on Ephesians*, in *A Select Library of Nicene and Post-Nicene Fathers of the Christian Church*, ed. Philip Schaff, series 1, vol. 13, repr. (Grand Rapids: Eerdmans, 1994), p. 51 (1.4).

(Col 1:22). He is just what they need: "Wisdom from God—righteousness, *sanctification* and redemption" (1 Cor 1:30 my translation). In him, "the sanctification of all the saints is *reality*."[23]

As Spirit, God brings this work to actuality, perfecting creatures in their personal histories by uniting them to Christ, working *in* them what has been wrought *for* them by the Son in fulfillment of the Father's purpose. The Spirit does this in our *individual* histories, making a saint of *this*, and *this*, and *the next* sinner, awakening, calling and enabling him or her, as a personal subject, to realize the freedom, obedience, love and fulfillment of a status objectively appointed and objectively secured. But he also does so by gathering and consecrating a *people* for God, a communion of saints, those loved and chosen by the sanctifying Father, reconciled and brought near by the sanctifying Son. Creatures who formerly were "no people" become "a holy nation, a people for his own possession" (1 Pet 2:9); not only Israel, but also a global covenant family with her, the *communio sanctorum* "from every tribe and tongue and people and nation" (Rev 5:9 RSV), is gathered as the family of God, his adopted sons and daughters alongside his Son.

Thus does the triune God establish a people after his own holiness. They have their holiness entirely in him, as planned, secured and realized by him. What they are given is unfathomable privilege: intimacy with the holy relations of God's boundless life in himself.[24]

THE HOLINESS OF JESUS CHRIST

What is the particular shape of the holiness of God as we find it in Christ by the Spirit? The issue is, again, more challenging than we might think. Jesus Christ is the sum of the gospel; divine holiness is exegeted for us in him as nowhere else—and it is not as we know it. When we encounter divine holiness incarnate, it interrupts us. It is worth tracing this out a little, with three closely related points.[25]

---

[23]Barth, *CD* IV/2, p. 515 (emphasis added).

[24]If this is what holiness is all about, any theology that seeks to drive a wedge between God's holiness and his *love* is of course profoundly deficient.

[25]On what follows, see further Ivor J. Davidson, "Pondering the Sinlessness of Jesus Christ: Moral Christologies and the Witness of Scripture," *International Journal of Systematic Theology* 4 (2008): 372-98. For the general context, see also Kent E. Brower, *Holiness in the Gospels* (Kansas City: Beacon Hill Press, 2005).

First, the sinlessness of Christ—theology's negative designation of his positive, lifelong obedience—is not depicted in the Gospels as an abstract moral innocence, or an unqualified representation of every human virtue. As Scripture tells it, Jesus behaves in ways that often seem outrageous to his contemporaries. To many of them, he is a flouter of torah, a libertarian, demon-possessed, a blasphemer.[26] The friend of tax collectors and sinners, he is accused of being a glutton and a drunkard,[27] a deceiver of the people. His teaching provokes dispute: is he good or not (see Jn 7:11-13)? He poses the question himself: "Why do you call me good?" (Mk 10:18; Lk 18:19; cf. Mt 19:17). In the eyes of many, he is a blatant transgressor: such is his challenge to halakah, his overturning of popular assumptions of "clean" and "unclean," "righteous" and "sinner." Full of grace and truth, he yet gets angry, curses fig trees, speaks fiercely to and of his opponents, insists that he has come to bring not peace but a sword, pronounces woes on communities in which his message is not welcomed, stages a fierce demonstration in the courts of Israel's most sacred space.

In his holiness, Jesus is simply not an archetype of our native ideas of moral beauty.[28] His redemptive power is not reducible to the impression wrought by his "unclouded blessedness,"[29] or his serene "inner life,"[30] or such other idealized state as we may suppose ourselves able to discern in his character. There is nothing so manageable about him. His holiness confounds our efforts to align it with our own images of the good. While his righteousness is firmly attested by the Gospel writers, it belongs within an overall consecration of character that is unlike anything we know save in the miracle of our experience of it. *This* is the Holy Son of God incarnate, and

---

[26]By way of survey of (parts of) a contested field, see James D. G. Dunn, "Pharisees, Sinners, and Jesus," in *Jesus, Paul and the Law: Studies in Mark and Galatians* (Louisville, KY: Westminster John Knox, 1990), pp. 61-88; Dunn, "Jesus and Holiness: The Challenge of Purity," in *Holiness Past and Present*, ed. Stephen C. Barton (New York: T & T Clark, 2003), pp. 168-92.

[27]See Craig L. Blomberg, *Contagious Holiness: Jesus' Meals with Sinners* (Downers Grove, IL: InterVarsity Press, 2005).

[28]See Immanuel Kant: "Even the Holy One of the Gospel must first be compared with our idea of moral perfection before he is cognized as such," *Religion Within the Limits of Reason Alone*, trans. Theodore M. Greene and Hoyt H. Hudson (New York: Harper, 1960), p. 57.

[29]F. D. E. Schleiermacher, *The Christian Faith*, ed. H. R. Mackintosh and J. S. Stewart, 2nd ed. (Edinburgh: T & T Clark, 1928), pp. 361-65, 371, 382-89, 413-17, 431-38.

[30]Albrecht Ritschl, *The Christian Doctrine of Justification and Reconciliation* (Edinburgh: T & T Clark, 1900), 3:574.

his saving presence with us is, at a vital level, without reference point on our grids—an instance of nothing but itself.

The holiness of Jesus refuses to be filled up by our intuitions, or made a cipher for our values; it *judges* us. As the record attests, when the world encounters the light, left to itself it prefers darkness. It does not say, "How lovely"; it says, "Away with him!" (Jn 19:15 KJV). To the New Testament's authors, this rejection is, in hindsight, inevitable, for he is the elect, suffering servant depicted in Israel's Scripture. The one who goes about doing good (Acts 10:38), divinely accredited (Acts 2:22), is shunned as God's holy servants before him have been. In this case the outrage, and the absurdity, are greater, for he is no mere prophet, but the very author of life (Acts 3:15). The point is that holiness among us bears no heroic appeal. Recognition that this is in fact the "Son . . . , the radiance of [God's] glory and the exact expression of his being" (Heb 1:2-3 my translation) occurs only in the divine apocalypse that is the Spirit's work. Without that opening of the heart (Acts 16:14), the holiness of God in Christ remains opaque and terrifying.

Second, while Jesus' holy life is the execution of a divine mission, its mandate offers him no insulation from the worldly realities he faces. His obedience in time is the enactment of his identity as the Father's eternally consecrated Son, sent into the world (Jn 10:36), the Son who consecrates himself for the sake of others (Jn 17:19). His incarnate fidelity is no stoic resignation to a purpose he does not share; it is the outworking of a common determination to take a specific earthly path.[31] That commitment does not, however, render the temporal history less than dense. The holy life of Jesus is a place of profound moral struggle, and his atoning action, the destruction of evil by holiness, is wrought in a human drama that is utterly real in time and space.[32] Flesh and blood, his course involves "loud cries and tears"; Son though he is, he learns obedience through what he suffers (Heb 5:7-10). Delight in God's will (Heb 10:5-10 [Ps 40:6-8 LXX]) involves walking by faith, being made "perfect through suffering" (Heb 2:10). Holy identity is enacted in the conditions of a broken world. As the proper human, the true image

---

[31]Theology ought not to overstate a distinction between Christ's active and passive obedience.

[32]The most arresting modern attempts to express some of these dynamics doubtless remain those of P. T. Forsyth; for a recent sympathetic study, see Jason Goroncy, *Hallowed Be Thy Name: The Sanctification of All in the Soteriology of P. T. Forsyth* (New York: Bloomsbury T & T Clark, 2013), esp. chap. 3.

of God (2 Cor 4:4; cf. Col 1:15), he does not do what sinners do. But *as* the obedient One, his reverent submission brings him no exemption from the end to which his path is destined; the God who is able to save him from death does not do so (Heb 5:7).

Third, insofar as the holiness of Jesus is climactically expressed in the judgment of the cross, there is, here especially, a "dislocation and relocation" of holiness.[33] It is as the one who "knew no sin" (2 Cor 5:21; cf. 1 Pet 2:22; 1 Jn 3:5) that he is made sin, the means by which sinners might become the righteousness of God in him, the Righteous One (Acts 7:52; 22:14; 1 Pet 3:18; 1 Jn 2:1; 3:7). The accursed death of Christ (Gal 3:13) is an outrage; he is "cut off" from the land of the living (Is 53:8), and it is by means of his dead body "outside" the gate—the epitome of all that is defiled—that holiness is secured for us (Heb 13:11-12). Divine holiness is presented to us in a violent death and a silent tomb.[34]

Taken together, these three features suggest a remarkable picture. Holiness in our midst, lived with properly human shape, does not glow in the dark, or assume stained-glass form, or walk through the world untroubled, or appear in the exercise of straightforward control over personal suffering, or escape the anguish of the innocent's "Why?" The one whose relationship with the Father remains consistently unbroken, whose life is never controlled by sin as ours by nature are (see Rom 6:15-23), he demonstrates his freedom in no simple transcendence of worldly pressures. He is deeply disturbed and troubled in spirit by the tragedies of his human circle (Jn 11:33, 38). He weeps (Jn 11:35). In Gethsemane, overwhelmed with grief (Mk 14:33-34 par.), he pleads for deliverance—if possible—from the dawning horror of his final hours. His holiness is an earthly, material, relational,[35] emotional, bleeding reality. Divine Son that he is, he himself at every point relies on the Spirit of holiness to live and die as he does (see Lk 4:1, 14, 16-21; Acts 10:38; Heb 9:14). Such is the Holy One in our midst.

---

[33]Stephen C. Barton, "Dislocating and Relocating Holiness: A New Testament Study," in *Holiness Past and Present*, pp. 193-213.

[34]For one attempt to emphasize the cross as starting point for responsible talk of divine holiness, see E. David Willis, *Notes on the Holiness of God* (Grand Rapids: Eerdmans, 2002), esp. chap. 1; the theology of the "holy day" of the grave is pondered movingly (though with mixed theological results, I believe) by the late Alan E. Lewis in *Between Cross and Resurrection: A Theology of Holy Saturday* (Grand Rapids: Eerdmans, 2001). See also Hans Urs von Balthasar, *Mysterium Paschale: The Mystery of Easter* (Edinburgh: T & T Clark, 1990), chaps. 1, 3-4.

[35]Though frightened and let down: "Could you not watch one hour?" (Mk 14:37 par.).

THE PRACTICE OF CHRISTIAN HOLINESS

Imitatio Christi has an indubitable biblical basis (e.g., Jn 13:1-17; Rom 15:1-7; Phil 2:1-11; Heb 12:1-3; 1 Pet 2:18-25): Jesus Christ is the *hypogrammos* ("pattern") we are to follow (1 Pet 2:21). If such counsel is taken simply as a general appeal to do our best to heed his teaching and copy his behavior, the consequences will be disastrous. We will almost certainly compromise the uniqueness of Christ's person, implying that he is better than the rest of us only by degree, envisaging his holiness as but a giant-sized version of moral and religious virtues as we might discern—and practice—them ourselves. If we restrict his achievement to the evocative—an inspiration to our endeavor rather than the decisive putting away of our sin—we will also suggest that his actions, strictly speaking, are locked away in the past, such that "he waits as though with tied arms for us to act,"[36] bereft himself of living potency otherwise, reliant upon his followers to make his presence known to the world in their personal ethics or ecclesial practices.[37] As far as the theology of sanctification is concerned, what we have in all this is, quite simply, the wrong center of gravity altogether. The determinative effects of who *he* is and what *he* does are supplanted by *our* responsibility, *our* action in response to his example: *he* is but the occasion for *our* projects. When *that* is what "imitation" is all about, "the Gospel . . . recede[s] into a moralistic haze."[38]

The gospel's declaration that we are made holy in Christ by the Spirit is decisive. We are not left to claw our way after divine holiness by our moral efforts, or to effect some representation of its qualities by an aspirational spirituality. A new creation in Christ (2 Cor 5:17), our existence is redefined in him; we are set up to live as those for whom he is Lord, in the moral commonwealth over which he presides.[39] Our due recognition of that does not consist in a desperate effort to copy him in a bid to *become* holy, but in acknowledging, by the Spirit's power, the reality of the relation in which we have been placed: we are already holy in him. This does not mean, of course, that holiness belongs to us in the sense that we possess it in and of ourselves,

---

[36]Barth, *CD* IV/2, p. 516.

[37]There is no shortage of possible illustrations of such mistakes in contemporary Christian ethics or ecclesiology.

[38]G. C. Berkouwer, *Faith and Sanctification* (Grand Rapids: Eerdmans, 1952), p. 138.

[39]On this see further John Webster, "'Where Christ Is': Christology and Ethics," in *Christology and Ethics*, ed. F. LeRon Shults and Brent Waters (Grand Rapids: Eerdmans, 2010), pp. 32-55, at 36-37.

a sort of capital. Ours only in Christ by the Spirit, it is a gift of "God's generosity," "grasped and possessed" solely in faith.[40] But the *duplex gratia* that we receive by partaking of Christ includes sanctification no less decisively than justification, and as such we also receive, in his consecration of us, a summons to action: the cultivation of holy character, or, as Calvin has it, "blamelessness and purity of life."[41] We are *chosen* "for obedience" (1 Pet 1:2): *called* by the Holy One, we are, as covenant children, to *be* holy in all our conduct (1 Pet 1:15), and thus to show that we are indeed his. Properly envisioned, *imitatio* is not crudely exemplarist soteriology in action; it is correspondence, by grace, to the reality into which by grace we have been brought.

Such correspondence is essentially a pattern of repentance and faith. Obedience in covenant ethics embraces many things, of course—spiritual, moral, political, social, sexual, material—but pervasively it is about *cruciformity*.[42] The gospel declares that we have been crucified with Christ and raised to life with him. In the eschatological process that is the Spirit's regeneration of us, we respond to that declaration in repentance and faith, confessing that in the dying and rising of the Holy One we have all the holiness we shall ever need. United to him, we continue to lay aside all that has already been decisively taken away, abolished, in him, and we "put on," in practical ways (Col 3:8-14; Eph 4:22-24), the reality of life with God, seeking "the things that are above, where Christ is, seated at the right hand of God" (Col 3:1). This means the ongoing repudiation of all that has occurred in the removal of our old self from the realm of falsehood, idolatry and resistance to God's will, and the joyful enactment of the new possibilities opened up on this side of the Savior's triumph.

In continuing repentance of the old and believing prosecution of the new, the pattern of mortification and vivification that is life under the baptismal

---

[40]Calvin, *Institutes* 3.11.1.

[41]Ibid.

[42]Many of the major moves in Pauline ethics especially are rehearsed by Michael J. Gorman, *Cruciformity: Paul's Narrative Spirituality of the Cross* (Grand Rapids: Eerdmans, 2001); Gorman, "'You Shall Be Cruciform for I Am Cruciform': Paul's Trinitarian Reconstruction of Holiness," in *Holiness and Ecclesiology in the New Testament*, ed. Kent E. Brower and Andy Johnson (Grand Rapids: Eerdmans, 2007), pp. 148-66; Gorman, *Inhabiting the Cruciform God: Kenosis, Justification, and Theosis in Paul's Narrative Soteriology* (Grand Rapids: Eerdmans, 2009). However, Gorman's deployment of lightly defined concepts of *theosis* and *kenosis* in support of his account of participation in the *identity* or *essence* of God invites some serious questions.

sign, I give testimony that everything I have is through participation in Christ and his achievement: "I . . . yet not I . . . : Christ . . . lives in me" (Gal 2:20 my translation; cf. 1 Cor 15:10); my life is "hidden with Christ in God" (Col 3:3). Contrary to the lie of sin, this status is in no way oppressive to my dignity, or a violation of my freedom; it is, rather, the very basis of my true liberty, and the realization of my proper status as a creature. "Disturbed sinners," shaken out of our sleep by Christ,[43] we are liberated from the delusions of self-actualization to exist instead for the end for which we were made. Costly as it is, cruciformity is, in fact, life for the dead. The consecrating rubric under which all Christian existence is set—"you are not your own" (1 Cor 6:19)—is a declaration not of infringement but of emancipation.

What all this means is that the action of human "working out" of holiness is improperly conceived unless it is viewed in the context of the overarching reality of divine prevenience: "God is at work in you, both to will and to work according to his good purpose" (Phil 2:13 my translation). Our enactment of holiness, including all our failures, violations and delinquencies, is indeed ours, and there is no option of moral equivocation in regard to our responsibilities. But our ability to evidence holiness is at every moment set in motion by divine purpose, sustained by divine energy and directed toward an end whose basis lies far back in the divine electing will: the desire that the family likeness should be borne by all who are the adopted brothers and sisters of the Son (Rom 8:29). If we are "being transformed," it is because "the Lord who is the Spirit" is involved (2 Cor 3:18). If the sanctified are summoned to show their sanctification, and thus to be transparent witnesses to the God who is holy, they will do this as those who are freed and enabled by the Spirit of Christ, their leader (Rom 8:14). He it is who takes what is Christ's, including his holiness, and declares it to them (Jn 16:14-15), who intercedes for the saints in their weakness (Rom 8:26-27) and enables them to approach the Father with confidence rather than fear (Rom 8:15-16). If it does not yet appear what it will ultimately mean for these holy children to manifest God's holiness as God intends (Rom 8:23-25; 1 Jn 3:2), the guarantee and pledge that they will yet do so is the presence of the Spirit active within them—*now* (Rom 8:16-17; 2 Cor 1:22; Eph 1:13-14).

---

[43]Barth, *CD* IV/2, pp. 524-25.

Sanctity is indeed a matter of promise, and thus of hope, but it is a promise whose down payment has been made.

We return to the holiness of Jesus. The Spirit who unites us to him and works out his pattern and likeness within us is the Spirit by whom he himself lived his own holiness in the flesh. Bearer of our humanity still, our pioneer and forerunner on our path through a world filled with challenges (Heb 12:1-3), this Jesus is able, we find, to represent and succor us on our way (Heb 2:18; 4:15-16; cf. 1 Jn 2:1). Our one-time fellow sufferer, whose memories of his own struggles are (we might say) ever fresh, he is not ashamed of us in our vulnerability (Heb 2:11). In the holiness of his person, cataclysmic as it is, faith finds all its ultimate resources. We are, and will be, holy in and with him—to the praise of God's own glory (Eph 1:3, 6, 12, 14). This wonder, not our efforts, is sanctification's chief concern. If that's not good news, what is?

FAITH, HOPE AND LOVE

A Theological Meditation on Suffering and Sanctification

Kelly M. Kapic

On June 9, 2008, my wife, and the mother of my two young children, was diagnosed with cancer. I watched her courageously and gracefully go through this diagnosis and the surgeries and treatments that were to follow. Even as I watched her, I myself was unprepared for the weight of that watching—for the weight of walking beside a suffering one. After having finally been declared cancer free for a time, in May 2010 my wife developed severe polyneuropathy, characterized by debilitating pain and fatigue, a condition that has not eased through the years, remaining a daily, even hourly presence in her and our lives. As a result of the condition, and while most people would never know when they see her, this most active and able woman has often been bedridden or severely restricted by her pain and limited mobility. Through these years we have wrestled in various ways with suffering, grief and loss. We've had to ask ourselves what hope, faith and love mean in the daily struggle. I mention this, not because I aim to write an autobiographical essay here, but to admit up front that this subject of suffering and sanctification is—unfortunately—not hypothetical to us. And, I would imagine, it is not hypothetical to you. Consequently, the reflections below do, in some way, reflect our own family's wrestling through the ravages and emotional toll of suffering.

INTRODUCTION

One of the most powerful temptations Christians face as they go through suffering is, to borrow a phrase from John Owen, to have "hard thoughts" of God.[1] Christians, perhaps even more than those without faith in a personal and loving God, can feel not just alone but also abandoned. It is one thing for sufferers to cry out to the great Unknown, echoing the unsettling words of Stephen Crane:[2]

> A man said to the universe:
> "Sir, I exist!"
> "However," replied the universe,
> "The fact has not created in me
> A sense of obligation."

Yet for the saint who confesses the personal God of Abraham, Isaac, Jacob and Mary, such moments of despair can bring the fear of divine indifference, rejection or judgment. How can believers tossed and blown by the storms of life *not* have hard thoughts about this sovereign Lord?

Writing in the wake of the Vietnam war, Dorothee Soelle, in her powerful but unnerving book *Suffering*, shows deep frustration with the orthodox Christian tradition at just this point. With special hostility reserved for the likes of John Calvin, she observes that Christian theologians have often used suffering to promote a kind of "theological sadism" and "masochistic approach."[3] While much of her attention focuses on the suffering that directly results from unjust human action, she also addresses the more general experiences of suffering, including sickness and disease. She describes a most unpleasant picture of common historic approaches: "Suffering is there to break our pride, demonstrate our powerlessness, exploit our dependency. Affliction has the intention of bringing us back to a God who only becomes great when he makes us small."[4] This conclusion grows out of Soelle's tendency to pit divine potency against divine love, believing that the two as classically understood are incompatible. She interprets classical orthodoxy

---

[1]*The Works of John Owen*, ed. William H. Goold (London: Banner of Truth Trust, 1965), e.g., 6:570; 2:34-35; 7:21; 11:390-91, 581.
[2]Stephen Crane, "A Man Said to the Universe," in *War Is Kind and Other Poems* (1899), poem 21.
[3]Dorothee Soelle [sometimes Sölle], *Suffering* (Philadelphia: Fortress Press, 1975), esp. pp. 1-32.
[4]Ibid., p. 19.

to portray God as a brutal Lord who appears to delight in torturing his saints in order to make them holy: this, she believes, is a theologically veiled way of making people insignificant and trivial. Even Jürgen Moltmann's offering of *The Crucified God* provides her little comfort or promise, though some of her moves later in the work clearly have a Moltmannian spirit to them.[5] Soelle offers provocative and honest reflections about the mysteries and disturbing tendencies that surround suffering, even—or especially—for the Christian.

While I am not interested here in debating the adequacy of Soelle's many historical or even theological claims, I believe her volume provides both helpful insights and notable failures, offering us a launching pad for our study. Drawing on the likes of Simone Weil, Soelle rightly reminds us that suffering, or "affliction," has three dimensions that cannot be forgotten: physical, psychological and social.[6] She emphasizes the importance of solidarity, the danger of isolation and the crippling effects of despair for those going through pain. Yet even amid her insights there are, I believe, deep problems that undermine key issues for Christians who try to place their suffering within the matrix of sanctification.[7] While she is understandably suspicious of attempts to talk about suffering that use the imagery of Christian growth, I think her hesitations on this point undervalue theologically informed guidance that can be drawn from earlier conceptions of spirituality. For example, as we will see throughout much of the later part of this essay, I believe Martin Luther offers a better example to guide our reflec-

---

[5]Ibid., pp. 26-27. Soelle will speak of Christ, and even his cross and resurrection, but this is not understood in any substitutionary way, nor does it appear to reveal God's redemptive historical economy; instead, Christ and his cross appear to mainly point out our need to actively engage this world, aiming to bring liberation to and for others. Although I agree with her call for Christians to be more mindful of their roles as defenders of the victim and advocates for justice, nevertheless I find her vision insufficient, especially in cases of physical suffering in which there is no clear human villain.

[6]For a recent printing of the essay, see Simone Weil, "The Love of God and Affliction," in *Waiting For God*, trans. Emma Craufurd (New York: Harper Perennial, 2009), pp. 67-82. This essay and other of Weil's works are engaged with by Soelle, *Suffering*, pp. 13-16, and passim.

[7]Too often, for example, I worry that she reduces her discussion to mere anthropology, and thus doesn't adequately account for the underlying doubts, concerns and struggles that the Christian can have, not just with fellow humans, but with God himself. This may even be seen in her involvement in the *Politisches Nachtgebet* ("political night-prayers") she organized, which "did not leave much room for actual prayer in the classical sense," focusing more on the dissemination of information and times of meditation that were then meant primarily to lead to action. See Andrea Bieler, "The Language of Prayer Between Truth Telling and Mysticism," in *The Theology of Dorothee Soelle*, ed. Sarah Katherine Pinnock (Harrisburg, PA: Trinity Press International, 2003), p. 55.

tions on such suffering. To put it in an overly simplistic way, I fear that Soelle too often reduces the challenge of faith to human activism, upholds human sympathy in a way that shortchanges eschatological hope and substitutes the profundities of divine absence for the promises of divine presence.

My aim here is to see if we can adopt some of the honest concerns scholars like Soelle have raised while not losing sight of classic orthodox instincts. To keep things more manageable, I will narrow our discussion a bit with two assumptions. First, I have in mind here Christians who suffer, and not the more general—and profoundly legitimate—questions about human suffering. Second, when speaking about suffering I will normally assume the *suffering associated with serious illness or physical pain.*[8] What does it look like for the Christian, the saint, to go through the valley of such suffering? All who suffer can hopefully relate to the reflections below, but too many questions arise if we do not carefully confine our discussion in some ways.

I want to organize our meditation on suffering and sanctification around three theological words—faith, hope and love—as Paul uses them in 1 Corinthians 13:13: "So now faith, hope, and love abide, these three; but the greatest of these is love." This, he observed earlier, is a "still more excellent way" than the path of contention and self-promotion that the Corinthian church was pursuing (1 Cor 12:31). We are to live as those who are strengthened in faith, encouraged by hope and governed by love. This triplet of theological virtues then connects to the three Christian images of cross, resurrection and feast. These words and images are vital, not simply in telling the Christian story, but for anyone trying to live within that story. By living within this story, our fellow saints strengthen their weakened sisters and brothers by drawing us to and reminding us of the word, presence and action of the triune God, becoming avenues of God's grace and mercy. Living within the embrace of God's people thus becomes the environment of sanctification for those who suffer. In this context we can examine suffering holistically, with concern for body and soul, mind and will, doubt and promise, frustration and love.

---

[8]For the surprising look at the "driving force" that questions about healing and suffering play across Christian traditions, see Amanda Porterfield, *Healing in the History of Christianity* (New York: Oxford University Press, 2005).

FAITH

I believe; help my unbelief!

MARK 9:24

Søren Kierkegaard, in his provocative work *Fear and Trembling*, retells the story of Abraham responding to God's command to sacrifice his son Isaac. Side-stepping his questions about a possible "teleological suspension of the ethical" here, I am interested in his emphasis on faith for the follower of Yahweh. Faith, he concludes, is not meant merely to acknowledge God's existence, but faith must be the very quality and substance of one's life before Yahweh.

In his epilogue to that story, Kierkegaard repeatedly claims that "faith is the highest passion in a person." Such faith is not something from which we can ever graduate, even if we are sustained and situated in a covenant context. "No generation," he observes, "begins at any other point than where the previous one did."[9] His observation is, in a sense, as obvious as it is difficult to honor. The point is that while one can grow up in proximity to the Christian religion, hearing its stories and promises, faith is an unavoidably experiential virtue. It is not something one can skip over, as it makes constant demands on the religious person.

Concerned that there were plenty in Denmark who imagined they had progressed beyond the gospel, Kierkegaard reminds his readers that "no one goes further" than faith. Kierkegaard frames the Christian life as the activity of faith, even in its passivity: "The person who has come to faith (whether he is extraordinarily gifted or plain and simple does not matter) does not come to a standstill in faith."[10] He compares faith to love, which cannot be spoken of in static terms, since it constantly moves on us and touches us in our entirety. The person of faith, like the person in love, "does not go further, does not go on to something else," for to move on to something else beyond faith (or love) would be to move on to an "explanation" rather than the reality, the passion, the truth.[11] Faith, like love, is the bond between God and us, serving as a conduit between the two. Even as one never graduates from

---

[9]Søren Kierkegaard, *Fear and Trembling; Repetition,* ed. Howard Vincent Hong and Edna Hatlestad Hong (Princeton, NJ: Princeton University Press, 1983), pp. 121-22.

[10]Ibid., p. 122.

[11]Ibid., p. 123.

faith, at the same time, we are called actively to exercise such faith: the goal is not to move beyond faith, but *to live by faith.*

This takes us back to the Reformation and Martin Luther, who not only served as an inspiration for Kierkegaard but will also serve as our main interlocutor for the rest of this essay.[12] In addition to expounding the doctrine of justification by faith alone, the German Reformer also expounded on faith as the manner of existence for the Christian. Despite the Luther-bashing that has become more popular in recent decades, Luther had an admirable sense of the complexities of the human experience. Luther's use of the language of *sanctification* and *sanctified* usually highlights the definitive rather than progressive nature of sanctification. The justified are the sanctified.[13] Consequently, God's elect are not only justified by faith alone, but also sanctified. He never set aside or downplayed the call for and significance of faith for the Christian, since sanctification grows out of faith and is always seen as a work of God's grace. This is what Kierkegaard, in his own way, was getting at centuries later, because it is so easily forgotten.

Luther's emphasis on faith is important for our discussion because it shaped his view of the Christian's struggle with sickness.[14] With the loss of health, a person—whether in the sixteenth century or the third millennium—commonly loses a sense of peace and identity; physical difficulties are often accompanied by spiritual trials, even though tracing out

---

[12]*Fear and Trembling* comes right out of the "Pauline and Lutheran tradition to which Kierkegaard belonged." Ronald M. Green, "'Developing' *Fear and Trembling*," in *The Cambridge Companion to Kierkegaard*, ed. Alastair Hannay and Gordon D. Marino (Cambridge: Cambridge University Press, 1998), p. 278. For more on Kierkegaard and Luther see, e.g., Craig Hinkson, "Luther and Kierkegaard: Theologians of the Cross," *International Journal of Systematic Theology* 3, no. 1 (2001): 27-45. Kierkegaard tended to push the demands of this faith on the individual, often because of his personality and context, while Luther was surprisingly aware of his need for others to sustain his faith, especially during seasons of weakness and suffering.

[13]Oswald Bayer notes that for Luther, "justification by faith alone meant that everything was said and done; living by faith is already the new life. When, nevertheless, Luther speaks about 'sanctification' he simply talks about justification. Justification and sanctification are not for him two separate acts that we can distinguish, as though sanctification follows after justification, and has to do so. In talking about sanctification Luther stresses the institutional side of the event of justification." Oswald Bayer, *Living by Faith: Justification and Sanctification* (Grand Rapids: Eerdmans, 2003), p. 59.

[14]In a survey of the two-volume collection of *Luther's Correspondence and Other Contemporary Letters*, ed. and trans. Preserved Smith and Charles M. Jacobs (Philadelphia: Lutheran Publication Society, 1918), it appears that with age and experience Luther's sensitivity to the plight of physical pain becomes more pronounced—he and those he knows face such trials—and dealing with the plague furthers these reflections. Unless otherwise noted, all quotations from his letters come from this edition.

the exact relationship between the two is impossible. A person's life be-comes unavoidably narrow when severely limited by debilitating pain or weakness. Amid such difficult seasons of life, Luther understood that the fog of doubt often comes rolling in, obscuring the believer's vision: ac-cordingly, the taunts of hell often grow louder during those periods. He recognized this because he lived it himself.

During his life Luther experienced various levels of physical ailment.[15] Sometimes it was so severe that he thought he was on the verge of death, frightening not only his wife and friends, but even himself.[16] As he stumbled through such events, he was not normally known for his stoicism; given that he viewed physical pain as often woven together with spiritual challenge, he approached such moments not with indifference, but more like a sailor fighting a vicious storm that would inevitably leave damage and pain through its thrashings. Amid such storms he believed all hands were needed on deck to survive the turbulence.[17]

For example, in 1527 he wrote to Melanchthon explaining how for a full week he had been terribly ill and "in death and hell." Through these mo-ments of weakness and pain he describes his vulnerability: "I almost lost Christ in the waves and blasts of despair and blasphemy against God, but God was moved by the prayers of saints and began to take pity on me and rescued my soul from the lowest hell."[18] Luther knew that, in times of physical and emotional distress, saints often struggle to believe and are af-flicted with confused images of God and his work in the world. During such seasons, the Christian leans heavily on the faith and prayers of other saints, for by them one is sustained, or even "rescued."

Writing to Nicholas Hausmann on a different occasion, Luther describes

---

[15]In a biography of Luther's wife it is said that possibly her "biggest challenge was as a nurse, doctor, and counselor to her husband," who "suffered from many illnesses and seemed to reck-lessly disregard symptoms" on many occasions. "He had serious bouts of depression, attacks of dizziness, constipation, pyosis in his leg, and kidney stones." Rudolf K. Markwald and Marilynn Morris Markwald, *Katharina von Bora: A Reformation Life* (St. Louis: Concordia, 2002), p. 124.

[16]E.g., Letters, 765, pp. 403-7. For more on his dealing with death as faced by others and himself, see Neil R. Leroux, *Martin Luther as Comforter: Writings on Death* (Leiden: Brill, 2007).

[17]See, e.g., how he often relied on his "pastor" for care and comfort, especially during times of illness. Martin J. Lohrmann, "Bugenhagen's Pastoral Care of Martin Luther," *Lutheran Quarterly* n.s. 24, no. 2 (2010): 125-36.

[18]Letter 768, p. 409. Elsewhere he writes, "Blessed be my Christ, even amid despair, death and blasphemy!" Letter 786, p. 428.

how he stands in the midst of great suffering even as the plague seems to be ending in his area: at least three times the affliction had hit his household, with even his son Hans greatly malnourished and ill, appearing for a time to be on the verge of death.[19] Here it is not Luther who is sick, but those he loves, and so again he admits that in this context, while it is "Christ's will," he has still been struggling with "restlessness and faintheartedness." Consequently he implores Hausmann for prayers that "my faith fail not."[20] Luther never doubted the significance of faith, but he likewise also never forgot how fragile it could become in instances of duress. What was really at stake in such moments of weakness was not merely his physical condition but also his belief in God's goodness and provision. While Luther's life was fraught with various battles, including struggles against the pope and other power structures, he always seemed to have a sense that the underlying battle was one of faith. Or as David C. Steinmetz concludes, "The central problem for Luther remains the problem of God. The mercy and compassion of God are always set against the background of God's hiddenness."[21] This tension often grew during times of physical weakness, when uncertainties and temptations fostered uncomfortable questions: Is God really loving? Could he welcome a sinner like Luther into his holy presence? Would Luther's heart worship this God or merely fear him?

Luther lived, as Heiko Oberman memorably says, between God and the devil, and so he serves as a useful model of the Christian struggle.[22] When he suffered from serious sickness, the threefold taunt of sin, death and the devil was always nearby. Original sin brought judgment and brokenness into this world, including illness. The ache of disease often awakens an awareness of one's sin, thus increasing even the believer's susceptibility to imagine divine judgment. Those living with such pain are often made more aware of the darkness of death, a darkness that allows the devil to move about like a lion, seeking to devour the vulnerable. At stake during these times of illness

---

[19]For a fascinating response in which he outlines who should remain and who might leave during an outbreak of the plague, see Martin Luther, "Whether One May Flee from a Deadly Plague," in *Luther's Works*, vol. 43, *Devotional Writings II*, ed. Gustav K. Wiencke (Philadelphia: Fortress, 1968), pp. 119-38.

[20]Letter, 779, p. 420. He appears to be referencing Lk 22:32.

[21]David C. Steinmetz, *Luther in Context* (Grand Rapids: Baker, 1995), p. 31.

[22]Heiko A. Oberman, *Luther: Man Between God and the Devil* (New Haven, CT: Yale University Press, 1989).

is the saint's ability to trust in God's gracious reign and rule. What is needed is light, the light of faith.[23]

Illness was unquestionably tangled up with spiritual trial in Luther's mind. And, as the editors of the classic collection of Luther's correspondence put it, his afflictions were often accompanied with "spiritual depression."[24] Once Justus Joan wrote as a firsthand witness of a time when Luther was suddenly overcome with grave physical pains, after having gone through a "grave spiritual trial" earlier in the morning.[25] That evening Luther's body gave out, starting with ringing in his ear but then quickly spreading so that his entire flesh seized up until he appeared frighteningly faint. Luther's response was not only to beg Justus to splash him quickly with cool water, but also to fervently pray. His prayers in this instance, as we have them recorded by Justus, are a mixture of his reciting the Lord's Prayer and various psalms. Luther was mainly just physically weak, and so his friends brought physical relief, but just as important to his mind was their encouragement and comfort. They reminded him of his hope, which we will talk more about below. Turning to everyone in the room one by one, Luther requested, "Pray for me, please."[26] Thinking he was about to die, Luther alternated between giving what appear to be final encouragements to Katie, his wife, and fits of prayer. But Luther did not die, and when the physical pains subsided and he was more stable the next day, he reported that he had just been to "school," and that "his spiritual trial of yesterday was twice as great as this bodily illness which came on in the evening."[27] In retrospect, however, the spiritual and the physical appear interwoven in a way that was repeated throughout his life. While it may be debated whether spiritual trials provoke physical vulnerability, or how bodily weakness may open one up to

---

[23]At one point Luther seems to conclude that wrestling through suffering, persecution and the endurance of evil really is the "Christian life," and to be free from them seems to entail being on the far side of glory. Letter 217, p. 275.

[24]Letter 768, p. 409 n. 3. See also Letter 779, p. 420, where he tells Nicholas Hausmann of his continued trial, which appears to be a reference to his abiding illness.

[25]Letter 765, p. 404. Luther does not seem here to directly link the spiritual trial with the later physical struggle, but in many ways the narrative begs for such connections.

[26]Letter 765, p. 406. Justus Jonas wrote a letter to Bugenhagen, the city church pastor, the day after Luther's episode, recording what he had said and heard because he did not want Luther's words, which were spoken "in his pain to be lost to us, for they were full of the most ardent feeling." Letter 764, pp. 403-4.

[27]Letter, 765, p. 407.

spiritual challenges, it does seem that these two often go together for us as psychosomatic beings.

Writing to Gerard Wilskap at Herford in 1528, Luther notes that while he has suffered illness from his youth, he is now facing things at their most severe. His note describes his precarious situation: "So far Christ has triumphed, but He holds me by a very slender thread," and so Luther desperately requests their prayers: "I have saved others, myself I cannot save."[28] Such moments require the prayers of other saints rather than self-referential prayer. And what Luther wants to be "saved" from is not merely death but more importantly from blasphemy, doubt and distrust of his loving God. Asking others to petition God on his behalf, he recognizes the paradox that such prayers are offered for "dead men who live, as captives who are free, as sufferers who are safe."[29] God employs his people's prayers to help the saints genuinely feel alive, free and safe, even as they at times are tempted to believe they are dead, enslaved and insecure. Luther's letters serve as powerful examples of someone who recognizes not only the centrality of faith but also our dependence on others through their prayers and presence to provide a hedge around us during our weakness.[30]

God freely employs the faith of others, which expresses itself through prayer, as a means to sustain and uphold the fragile faith of the suffering Christian. Faith is not simply the means through which a person becomes a Christian, but is the essential manner of the Christian life. During times of challenge, including illness, which can breed vulnerability, the wounded believer often depends on other saints to sustain him or her through seasons of suffering. While Luther and others from the Reformation are often accused of brash individualism in their conceptions of faith, these examples of Luther's sickness remind us that he never imagined faith as a purely individual activity. Yes, the individual was called to believe, but that faith can in fact only be lived within an organic connection to the locally constituted church.

One of the regular ways the body of Christ maintains its health, even as parts of the body are attacked with disease, is for the other parts to carry

---

[28]Letter, 786, p. 428.

[29]Letter, 768, p. 409.

[30]Oberman observes Luther's dependence on the prayers of others, especially for his health; so strong was this dependence that when he fell ill he wouldn't hesitate to blame others for apparently failing to pray for him. Oberman, *Luther*, p. 311.

some extra weight. If a person's ankle is broken they instinctively place more weight on the strong leg. This is not because they despise the weak leg, but because it can only return to full health if its burden is born by the other limb. Similarly, Christians bear one another's burdens (see Gal 6:1-5).

Such a relational setting allows, even requires, a more holistic response to suffering, not only by attending to the legitimate physical, social and psychological concerns of the wounded saint, but also by offering the distressed pilgrim the faith, prayers and acts of mercy of the surrounding body of Christ (see 2 Cor 1:4-7). When we are distressed and find it easy to doubt God's grace and provision, we find shelter and sustenance under their canopy of faith. Together as the body of Christ the worries about divine apathy, judgment or abandonment can honestly be faced and answered. Alone the flame of faith diminishes, but in true community the fire of faith illumines the night.

HOPE

Why are you cast down, O my soul,

and why are you in turmoil within me?

Hope in God; for I shall again praise him,

My salvation and my God.

PSALM 42:5-6

Christian faith affirms not simply the affirmation of God's existence but also the far more difficult call to trust in God's holy kindness and tender provision. John Calvin described faith as "a firm and certain knowledge of God's benevolence toward us, founded upon the truth of the freely given promise in Christ, both revealed to our minds and sealed upon our hearts through the Holy Spirit."[31] Maintaining a "firm and certain knowledge" can sound easy when things are going well, but the pain, misery, injustice, despair and hypocrisy in the world assaults confidence in any good and gracious God, not just for the non-Christian, but also for the saint. Prolonged physical suffering easily induces despair and fatigue,

---

[31]John Calvin, *Institutes of the Christian Religion*, trans. Lewis Ford Battles, ed. John T. McNeill, Library of Christian Classics (Philadelphia: Westminster Press, 1960), 3.2.7.

for both the sick and the caregivers. Hope, which nourishes faith, thus plays a pivotal role in sanctification.

Seasons of physical distress challenge Christian hope, so the suffering saint leans hard on other believers for spiritual sustenance. Fellow pilgrims not only rescue us in our struggling faith but also strengthen us by embodying gospel promises. Notice that Calvin's definition of faith doesn't ground confidence in the Lord's benevolence by making empirical observations about the way the world works (which in fact is full of injustice and pain); instead, his certainty is "founded upon" the realities of the Son and Spirit. And the promises of Christ and the power of his Spirit are normally linked to the people of God.

Under the previous heading of "faith," we noted that the saints *speak to God for us* when we struggle to believe and speak alone. Here we note that saints are called to *speak to us for God* when we seem unable to hear him on our own. Their prayers sustain our faith; their proclamation reignites our hope. Hope is not achieved through the power of positive thinking, but in the promises of Word and Sacrament. Of course, one can read the Scriptures while alone, and it is the individual who must swallow the bread and wine, but the corporate life of the church strengthens the soul by reminding us that we are not alone but in a body. Here both particularity and community meet.

The Holy Spirit mysteriously draws us into communion with God in the proclamation of the Word, speaking into our fragile condition. For example, the Psalms often display a movement from anxiety to hope.[32] Beginning occasionally with questions or a sense of impossibility, the Psalms often urge the singer or reader to invoke the power of remembrance and anticipation. Remember who this God is, the Creator Lord who has been faithful through the ages. Remember the stories of his deliverance, his constant care, his steadfast love. Such remembrances rekindle hope by assuring the sufferer that Yahweh neither leaves nor forsakes. Comfort is offered to those who suffer, whether their pain comes as a result of national exile or physical weakness. Offering generation after generation a hymnbook to shape their memory of God's trustworthy concern, the corporately sung and recited psalms have served to renew the hope of his people without denying the

---

[32]See Claus Westermann, *Praise and Lament in the Psalms* (Atlanta: John Knox Press, 1981). See also Walter Brueggemann, *The Psalms and the Life of Faith* (Minneapolis: Fortress, 1995).

struggle of living in a fallen world. These songs affirm the pain and per-
plexity of life, but they also call us to trust God even during these agonizing
seasons. Significantly, the Psalms do not attempt to explain suffering or what
mysterious purposes God may have for our pain. Instead, they display the
character of Yahweh as trustworthy, brimming with compassion for his
people. In this movement from despair to hope, the wounded saint is not
belittled, as some like Soelle fear, but rather reminded of our Redeemer's
fatherly concern that somehow still mysteriously moves in and through his
compromised creation, which so longs for shalom.

Returning to Luther for a moment, we observe that in his "Preface to the
Psalms" he writes lovingly of their value, as compared to the popular books
of his day on the legends of the saints. Noticing that these volumes depict the
glorified lives of the saints, Luther observes that such stories never had the
saints speak, for their "tongues were tied."[33] For Luther, human speech is a
vital aspect of what separates us from the animals. In this way the Psalms
resonate with us, because "every man on every occasion" can easily find
words in the Psalms that speak to his struggle. Here we can find words to
speak when we become speechless. Or, put differently, the community can
speak or sing these sacred words when it does not know what to say. Luther
observes that when people try to imitate the romanticized lives of the saints,
rather than echo the realistic words of the Psalms, then we often find the
"beginnings of sects and factions," so that they tend to "lead and even drag
one away from the fellowship of the saints."[34] The beauty of the Psalms is that
they openly move between the glories of hope to the depths of despair: they
neither belittle pain nor trivialize promises. In the Psalms, the church is "depicted in living colours," able to encourage the saint, comfort the afflicted and
humble the proud.[35] It makes sense, then, that upon hearing of his father's
death, after much weeping and anguish, Luther turned to his Psalter.[36]

Not only do the Psalms give us voice with which to pray to God, but in
them we also hear God's voice to his people. This is the Creator we can trust
with the details of creation, including the lives of his people (e.g., Ps 8; 93; 104;

---

[33]Luther, "Preface to the Psalms," in *Martin Luther: Selections from his Writings*, ed. John Dillen-
berger (New York: Doubleday, 1962), p. 39.
[34]Ibid., p. 40.
[35]Ibid., pp. 40-41.
[36]Oberman, *Luther*, p. 311.

148); he is the Shepherd who cares for his sheep even as they walk through the valley of darkness (e.g., Ps 23; 28; 80); the Lord who governs with wisdom and love (e.g., Ps 5; 25; 36; 86; 89; 136); the God of his people who will not forget them in their time of need (Ps 94); and the one who is worthy to be praised even amid our trials (Ps 95). By retelling the stories of God's acts of deliverance and concern, the Psalms renew the hope of God's people.

Similarly, the epistle to the Hebrews functions like an extended sermon given to a struggling congregation.[37] Soaked in the testimony of the Old Testament, it contains one of the most extended discussions of faith found in the Bible, and describes faith as nurtured in hope. Hebrews 11 walks us slowly through the history of God's people, moving from Abraham to the intertestamental period. While the chapter certainly serves to provide great examples of personal faith, their faith must always be understood first in light of God's faithfulness. Hebrews 10:23 anticipates this point: "Let us hold fast the confession of our hope without wavering, for he who promised is faithful." The saints' examples of faith provide the means by which God's faithfulness is revealed. Rehearsing key stories in chapter 11, the author calls the congregation to put their hope in the God who has been trustworthy through the ages. Whether one thinks of Noah, Sarah, Jacob or the "women [who] received back their dead by resurrection" (Heb 11:35), their faith was upheld by the steadfastness of divine character and promises. Again, like the Psalms, it does not portray hope as achieved through denial or escape, but through looking to the eschatological promises of God. Often amid great distress, including examples of physical weakness and facing immediate death, these saints kept their hope in Yahweh despite their circumstances. "Hope" is used throughout Hebrews, concludes William Lane, as a "vivid reminder that the entire Christian life is christologically and eschatologically stamped."[38] All of these stories were meant to point to the promised Messiah who has come, who as the sympathetic high priest suffered on behalf of his people, the forerunner who has secured our future even amid the apparent insecurity of our present (Heb 6:20), for he now rests at the

---

[37]William L. Lane, *Hebrews 1–8*, Word Biblical Commentary 47a (Dallas: Word, 1991), pp. liii-lxii.
[38]William L. Lane, *Hebrews 9–13*, Word Biblical Commentary 47b (Dallas: Word, 1991), p. 288. Here Lane is drawing from numerous folks, but quoting a bit from O. Michel, "Zur Auslegung des Hebräerbriefes," *Novum Testamentum* 6 (1963): 189-91, 347.

right hand of God (Heb 10:12). Through the Word proclaimed the people of God were to find their hope in the crucified, risen and ascended Christ.

Biblical hope, then, grows out of a confidence in God's redemptive actions and trustworthy presence. But such hope can become hard to muster when we are physically or mentally vulnerable, and so again we depend on others to bring this proclamation, to sing these songs. Thus our fellow saints speak to us for God. They remind us that God never forgets his people, for this is the God and Father of Jesus Christ who offers an eschatological foretaste when he heals the sick and provides for the needy. Even though those whom Jesus healed of their sickness would eventually face death, and those whom he fed would again feel hunger pains, they were given a foretaste of the full restoration of shalom. Their microstories were meant to point to the macrodrama. Because Jesus Christ is the hope of the gospel, God's people serve one another in their times of suffering by offering each other the good news of Christ crucified and risen. Only in Christ do the Psalms and the rest of the Scriptures take on their full power of hope. In our weakness we may find it impossible to proclaim this hope ourselves, but when it is offered to us in the liturgy or by fellow pilgrims, when we hear, "Christ is risen," we are able to reply, "He is risen indeed!"

LOVE

I will rejoice and be glad in your steadfast love,

because you have seen my affliction;

you have known the distress of my soul. . . .

Be strong, and let your heart take courage,

All you who wait for the LORD!

PSALM 31:7, 24

To the sufferer, the body of Christ offers faith and graciously supplies needed gospel hope. Yet by the remark in 1 Corinthians 13 that of these three—faith, hope and love—the greatest of these is love, Paul shapes our understanding of them and how they affect each other.

Even great gifts can be upended and used for ill. Faith without love can turn abusive, belittling the struggling saint by substituting impersonal axioms for heartfelt prayers. Likewise, hope void of love can devolve into insensitive forms of activism and arrogance, replacing empathetic grace with cheap platitudes or an impersonal vision of what must be done. So if faith and hope are to mean anything to us in our suffering, they must come to us in the context of love; or, to put it another way, faith and hope are only properly applied with love: a love accomplished and given through the person and work of Christ. Nicholas Wolterstorff, grieving over the death of his son, illustrates some of these connections.

> Suffering is a mystery as deep as any in our existence. It is not of course a mystery whose reality some doubt. Suffering keeps its face hid from each while making itself known to all. . . . We are one in suffering. Some are wealthy, some bright; some athletic, some admired. But we all suffer. For we all prize and love; and in this present existence of ours, prizing and loving yield suffering. Love in our world is suffering love. . . . This, said Jesus, is the command of the Holy One: "You shall love your neighbor as yourself." In commanding us to love, God invites us to suffer.[39]

We experience divine love most concretely in our suffering as we receive and give it to others. In his economy, God expresses his love and extends his comfort through the agency of his people. This is not merely a sociological observation but also a theological reality.

One aspect of our secure union in Christ is our secure union with one another. The church, as the body of Christ, recognizes "no division in the body, but that the members may have the same care for one another. If one member suffers, all suffer together, if one member is honored, all rejoice together" (1 Cor 12:25-26). We, under the normal means of grace, receive and extend the love of Christ through our union with the saints. Such love is governed by grace and truth even as the arms of forgiveness and mercy uphold it. Such love is received by faith, bolstered by hope and protected through self-giving. When faith and hope are detached from love, they are drained of their power and efficacy. When they grow out of love, they are like food for the hungry and medicine for the sick. Thus we need faith, hope and love, but without love we lose all three.

Luther helps us here as well. He appears to assume that the relationship between suffering and sanctification is best seen within the context of the

---

[39]Nicholas Wolterstorff, *Lament for a Son* (Grand Rapids: Eerdmans, 1987), p. 89.

community, even in its imperfect expressions of love. Eric W. Gritsch explains that when unpacking his view of communion of the saints as his definition of the church, Luther emphasized the role of the Holy Spirit in calling the saints together in fellowship.

> Accordingly, the church consists of people who are incorporated into Christ and each other like the ingredients of a cake: none is for himself, but instead each is blended with the others in the fellowship of love. Luther himself depended on the "consolation of the brethren" (*consolatio fratrum*) whenever he suffered inner turmoil and temptation—especially in the year 1527, when he was plagued by illness, the loss of friends, and various other forms of *Anfechtung*. Communion meant true communication to Luther, through word and sacrament, in the giving of oneself to Christ and to one's neighbor. Just as Christ emptied himself for the world on the cross (Phil. 2:5–11), so the Christian is to empty himself to his neighbor in love.[40]

Luther of all people was not naive about the turbulence of living among sinful saints, and so perfectionist portraits of the church did not seduce him. Yet he never let cynicism crowd out his theological instinct that the healing power of communion with God is found in the prayers, words and love of the saints. For as the body of Christ, the saints are connected to one another and to their head, so that Luther can confidently conclude, "When we feel pain, when we suffer, when we die, let us turn to this, firmly believing and certain that it is not we alone, but Christ and the church who are in pain and suffering and dying with us."[41] Within the matrix of love Luther holds together the church and the Savior through a robust view of union with Christ.

And yet, vital as our fellow pilgrims are as a means to our sanctification amid suffering, we ultimately look not to them but *with them* to the revelation of God in Christ. For faith, hope and love all must ultimately point to and come from the triune God and not merely from the community of the saints. Therefore, we need to conclude our reflections by returning to key christological images.

---

[40]Erich W. Gritsch, "Introduction to Church and Ministry," in Martin Luther, *Luther's Works*, vol. 39, *Church and Ministry I*, ed. Eric W. Gritsch (Philadelphia: Fortress Press), p. xiv.

[41]Quoted from Luther's "Fourteen Consolations," in Jane E. Strohl, "Luther's Fourteen Consolations," in *The Pastoral Luther: Essays on Martin Luther's Practical Theology*, ed. Timothy J. Wengert (Grand Rapids: Eerdmans, 2009), p. 320; see 310-24. Cf. Robert A. Kelly, "The Suffering Church: A Study of Luther's *theologia crucis*," *Concordia Theological Quarterly* 50, no. 1 (1986): 3-17.

KEY IMAGES AND WORDS

Blessed be the God and Father of our Lord Jesus Christ, the Father of mercies and God of all comfort, who comforts us in all our affliction, so that we may be able to comfort those who are in any affliction, with the comfort with which we ourselves are comforted by God. For as we share abundantly in Christ's sufferings, so through Christ we share abundantly in comfort too.

2 CORINTHIANS 1:3-5

Saints who suffer need the ministry of God's people. We depend on one another for faith as the medium of life in God, the forward momentum and motivation that grows out of hope, and love as the very substance of life in the gospel. But to understand and use these dynamics of the Christian life correctly we must see their nature and origin in Christ and in our union with him.

The suffering Christian needs a steady diet of three christological images: cross, resurrection and feast.[42] These provide the theological wellspring for our faith, hope and love. Gaining and deepening a christological understanding of these truths provides the appropriate basis to understand suffering and sanctification.

First, we think of the cross. Those who suffer often wonder if God understands, or whether he is a distant deity unconcerned with the bleak world of physical pain. Yet looking to the cross reminds the sufferer of this strange God who has come near, entered our sin and pain, and offered himself on our behalf.[43] While Good Friday points to more than the physical suffering of Christ, it should never point to less than that. The cross reveals the sympathetic high priest, the one who has faced all manner of temptations and yet remained faithful, even unto death. He knows what it is like to feel

---

[42]While I did not originally remember Richard Hays's use of three focal images (community, cross and new creation) in his important volume, I believe we are on the same page in terms of arguing for the value of such images to guide the life of the church. See Richard B. Hays, *The Moral Vision of the New Testament: Community, Cross, New Creation; A Contemporary Introduction to New Testament Ethics* (San Francisco: HarperSanFrancisco, 1996), pp. 193-205.

[43]Discussing Luther's theology of the cross, and misapplications of that idea, Timothy J. Wengert is right to argue that such a theology "has good news—news mind you, not solutions. It is the good news that, in the Crucified One, God has simply willed to force the curse to be a blessing, that the Crucified has, thus, borne our very suffering, that this suffering cannot destroy God's choice about us but, rather, points to God's preference to save the weak, broken, and to resurrect the dead." See "'Peace, Peace . . . Cross, Cross': Reflections on How Martin Luther Relates the Theology of the Cross to Suffering," *Theology Today* 59 (2002): 203.

shocking physical pain and dereliction, crying out, "Eloi, Eloi, lema sabach-thani?" And yet, even in this cry we hear the first words of Psalm 22, which opens up the event of the cross for us; the psalm concludes with the expec-tation that "he has done it" (Ps 22:31; cf. Jn 19:30).[44] Hanging on the cross, Jesus trusted the Father and found a steadfast hope in the promises of his Father. Now we cry out—but as those who have received the Spirit of Christ, we cry out, "Abba Father." Fellow saints are called to remind us of our abiding in Christ, but they do so without trying to substitute our connection with them for our connection with Christ. In this way our faith, as received and offered to one another, must always be cross-shaped.

Second, we think of Christ's resurrection, which points us to our own eventual resurrection. Eschatological realities do not give us a way to escape this world, but they do give us a kingdom perspective. The substance and meaning of our lives are not confined to our present circumstances, as we discover in the Gospels with the in-breaking of the kingdom of God; we live in the now and not yet, between the coming of the kingdom and the full real-ization of that kingdom. United to Christ, Christians live as those who have not only died with him but also risen with him (Rom 6:8; Col 2:12; 3:1-4). Even as the head of our body now lives in the heavens, we can have a sure and steady confidence that we will never be separated from him. Mindful of Christ's resurrection, we look not only backward to his rising but also forward to the completion of his eschatological intrusion, where the pains of this world dis-solve in the fulfilled promises of shalom: the blind see, the lame walk, the poor experience liberation, tears are wiped away and the grave is overcome. Christ the prophet has come to offer good news. While we often depend on other saints to remind us of the promises of hope, we can never forget that the strength they bring depends on the resurrection of Christ. Apart from that promise actualized, all the other promises become futile, and it is better to eat and drink away our misery (see 1 Cor 15:14-17, 32). But in Christ, the crucified and risen prophet, we claim the secure promises of eschatological hope: he who began a good work in us will carry it on to completion (Phil 1:6).

Third, we think of the feast. Christ is not simply the priest who offers the once-for-all sacrifice, or the prophet who proclaims the good news to the

---

[44]For more on this argument, see Kelly M. Kapic, "Psalm 22: Forsakenness and the God who Sings," in *Theological Commentary*, ed. R. Michael Allen (London: T & T Clark, 2012), pp. 41-56.

needy, but also the king who has the authority and desire to call together the great feast. Kingly and priestly images merge here. Anticipating the great wedding banquet, we celebrate the Eucharist by believing that because God is for us in Christ, no one can ultimately destroy us. Through eating and drinking the Eucharist, and by knowing what it truly entails, we gain strength to endure our suffering by feasting on the life-giving body and blood of Christ. Suffering can be like a famine: a famine of comfort and peace, a famine of joy and health, a famine of community and self-worth. To this famine Christ offers the feast of himself.[45] Faith and hope meet in the Eucharist, here the past and the future collide, here we taste and see that the Lord is truly benevolent, and here we gain a taste of eternal communion with God.

CONCLUSION

When having "hard thoughts" about God, Christians can better understand their lives within the matrix of sanctification that calls them to faith, hope and love, which is grounded in God himself and extended to us through others. Others speak to God for us by their faith and prayers, when we cannot ourselves speak. And these saints speak to us for God, when we by ourselves find hope elusive. Faith and hope become powerful and healing when they come to us through genuine love. Christians themselves give and receive love, but it is always ultimately a response to and an extension of God's love. In the crucified and risen Messiah we encounter the love of God, who on the cross and through the resurrection acts as the prophet, priest and king. He is the one who not only sympathizes with us in our weakness but also has secured our redemption and wholeness, and thus can declare it accomplished with final certainty. Christ has died; Christ is risen; Christ will come again. Only in him can we appropriately see our suffering and the suffering of others through the lens of sanctification. May it be so. Amen.

---

[45]While reading a draft of my essay, Tabitha, my wife, wrote this sentence and the one before it in the margins. She has it exactly right, recognizing both the realities of the famine and the promises of the feast.

11

SONSHIP, IDENTITY AND TRANSFORMATION

Julie Canlis

It is necessary to fix in our minds this doctrine of Paul, that
no man is a Christian who has not learned,
by the teaching of the Holy Spirit,
to call God his Father.[1]

JOHN CALVIN

Many Reformed Christians have been watching the recent explosion of material in Calvin studies on "union with Christ" with eager (and perhaps horrified?) fascination. What was once a consoling doctrine has fast become the lightning rod for a much larger, more entrenched debate. One of my recent excursions to the blogosphere more closely resembled a fall down Alice's rabbit hole than a research-gathering outing in the park. I discovered terms that I never knew existed, terms that, to put it delicately, were not terms of endearment. There were the Unionists, the Owenites, the Gaffinites, the Tiptonites, the FVers, the Hypers, the NPPs (new perspective on Paul), the equally derogatory NPCs (new perspective on Calvin)—all of which made a considerable impact on whether you accepted the IAOC (imputed active obedience

---

[1]John Calvin, *Commentary on Galatians* 4:6. All references to Calvin's commentaries are from the Calvin Translation Society edition (Edinburgh, 1843–1855), reprinted by Baker, 1979.

of Christ) and, for that matter, which seminary you followed (WTS, WSC, RTS) or which denomination you sided with (RCA, CREC, PCA, PCUSA, EPC, OPC). I had not only fallen down Alice's rabbit hole, but I had also drunk the poison in the bottle. Or perhaps I had confused my metaphors—could it be that I had worked my way straight into Calvin's own labyrinth?

In this chapter, I want to look at union with Christ briefly (no point going back down the rabbit hole), for the purpose of moving into a more creative discussion regarding union with Christ and sonship. Despite the flurry of words over "union with Christ" and the disputed order of justification and sanctification, Calvin at least is clear about one crucial point: both happen in Christ and reflect the person of Christ—the shape of his life and identity. In the midst of the vehement debates of his own day (to which he did not hesitate to contribute!), Calvin retained the humility that should accompany the fact that we are not speaking of theological concepts but of theological *persons*. He never lost his wonder over the graciousness and reality of union: "It is a remarkable sentiment, that believers live out of themselves, that is, they live in Christ; which can only be accomplished by holding real and actual communication with him."[2]

Thankfully, a resurgence of study on Calvin's theology of union with Christ is underway; let us begin with a brief overview to orient all that will come below.[3] The Reformers' main contention with the medieval Catholic Church was that it made our justification—our being "right with God"—dependent on the quality of our sanctification. After a long life of various spiritual practices and mortifications, one died with the *hope*—not assurance—of justification. The first-generation Reformers reversed all this: righteousness is not what we achieve, but is that which God shares with us from his personal treasury. Justification is a free gift. Calvin, though, as a

---

[2]Calvin, *Commentary on Galatians* 2:20.

[3]For more on Calvin's doctrine of union with Christ, see Julie Canlis, *Calvin's Ladder: A Spiritual Theology of Ascent and Ascension* (Grand Rapids: Eerdmans, 2010); J. Todd Billings, *Union with Christ: Reframing Theology and Ministry for the Church* (Grand Rapids: Baker Academic, 2011); Marcus Johnson, *One with Christ: An Evangelical Theology of Salvation* (Wheaton, IL: Crossway, 2013); Robert Letham, *Union with Christ: In Scripture, History, and Theology* (Phillipsburg, NJ: P & R, 2011); and Michael Horton, *Covenant and Salvation: Union with Christ* (Louisville, KY: Westminster John Knox, 2007). For an example of the recent debate on "union with Christ," see the exchange between Marcus Johnson and Thomas Wenger in *Journal of the Evangelical Theological Society* 50, no. 2 (2007); and 51, no. 3 (2008), and again between William Evans and J. V. Fesko in *Westminster Theological Journal* 72 (2010).

second-generation Reformer, is able to give a far more nuanced account of this than those who had cleared the ground before him.

For Calvin, justification and sanctification are different sides of the same coin, the same singular grace (not graces) offered in Jesus Christ. We are not so much given righteousness, or sanctification, but we are given Christ himself. This is what Calvin calls the "mystical union" (3.11.1),[4] effected in and only through the Spirit. As Calvin says, "justification rests solely on our being *partakers of Christ*; for in possessing him, we possess all his riches with him" (3.11.23).[5] This both encompasses and goes beyond a change in legal status; it is a change in where we look for the truth about ourselves.[6] One could say that it is a change from being self-circumscribed to having a joint identity: to being *en Christo*. "Do you, then, wish to obtain righteousness in Christ? You must first possess Christ; but you cannot possess him without becoming a partaker of his sanctification; for he cannot be divided into pieces" (3.16.1). Justification and sanctification are different aspects of a single reality.[7] And what is this reality? Jesus Christ himself.[8]

It is when union with Christ ceases to be a personal reality that Calvin scholarship begins its steep descent down the rabbit hole. When there is an obsessive focus on the benefits of Christ, to the abstraction of his person, union then descends into an impersonal mechanism of salvation.[9] When

---

[4]All references to Calvin's *Institutes of the Christian Religion* are to the 1559 edition. I am working from the two-volume Library of Christian Classics edition, ed. John T. McNeil, trans. Ford Lewis Battles (Philadelphia: Westminster Press, 1960). This passage is from the *Institutes* book 3, chapter 11, section 1, hereafter as 3.11.1.

[5]Italics mine. The role of faith is that by it we "apprehend the righteousness of Christ" (3.16.1).

[6]Yes, it is an "acquittal. . . . God acquits us not by admission of our personal innocence but by an imputation of righteousness; so that we, who are unrighteous in ourselves, are considered as righteous in Christ" (3.11.3).

[7]Calvin brings this home in his *Commentary on Mark* 2:1-12, when Jesus forgives and heals the paralytic. He spoke, remarks Calvin, and the man was forgiven *and* healed. "Christ's meaning was, that forgiveness of sins ought not to be sought from a distance: for he exhibits it to men in his own person, and as it were in his hands."

[8]This is perhaps the greatest gift that the Torrance brothers have given to Calvin scholarship: a return to Calvin's own emphasis on the person of Christ as the control for dogmatics. For an introduction to T. F. Torrance's method (while also serving as a delightful theological book), see his *The Christian Doctrine of God: One Being, Three Persons* (Edinburgh: T & T Clark, 1996). For a more pastoral and ecclesiological work, see J. B. Torrance's *Worship, Community and the Triune God of Grace* (Downers Grove, IL: InterVarsity Press, 1997).

[9]The title of this article, "Is There a Reformed Way to Get the Benefits of the Atonement to 'Those Who Have Never Heard'?" certainly reflects this dissociation (Todd R. Mangum in *Journal of the Evangelical Theological Society* 47 [2004]: 121-36).

this happens, we become guilty of doing precisely that of which Jesus accused the crowd in John 6:26, "Very truly I tell you, you are looking for me, not because you saw the signs I performed but because you ate the loaves and had your fill" (NIV). In his *Commentary on John*, Calvin offers further comment, saying, "They sought in Christ something other than Christ himself." Bonhoeffer later warned that theologies of the "benefits of Christ" have "often apostatized here."[10]

By now it should be apparent that Calvin has no category for divine gifts to humanity that are not connected to the person of Christ. There is no gift given to us that does not come directly from the person of Christ. He is their sole mediator. He has always been the way that God offers "things" to us, because God refuses to give us things in which he is not personally involved. "Such is the determination of God," writes Calvin, "not to communicate himself, or his gifts to men, otherwise than by his Son."[11] We are not offered holiness, except that it is Christ's holiness; we are not called "beloved," except that it is his belovedness; we are not offered justification, except that it is his propitiating righteousness. These are personal realities, not detachable gifts (though at times we are tempted to speak of them this way), kept personal because they are only realized *through the person of the Holy Spirit*. "We do not regard [Christ] as outside of and distant from us; rather, we hold ourselves to be united with Christ by the power of his Spirit" (3.11.10).

UNION WITH CHRIST AND ADOPTION

I am going to sidestep the rabbit hole altogether, and focus on one aspect of union with Christ that is often lost in the stale warren of competing interpretations. For Calvin—and I know it seems odd to say this—union with Christ is not an end in and of itself. It serves a deeper trinitarian structure in his theology, in which everything is moving toward our being *en Christo*, toward the glorious freedom of the children of God (Rom 8:21). "There are innumerable other ways indeed," remarks Calvin, "in which God daily testifies his fatherly love toward us, but the mark of adoption is justly preferred to them all."[12] This term *adoption* is used at times by Calvin to speak of our

---

[10]Dietrich Bonhoeffer, *Christology* (London: Collins, 1966), p. 48.
[11]Calvin, *Commentary on Colossians* 1:19.
[12]Calvin, *Commentary on John* 17:23.

election, our justification or "acceptance," our regeneration, and even our sanctification.[13] Calvin does not use it consistently as a precise category but rather as one interrelated with many theological loci, perhaps for the obvious reason that these are not concepts, nor things, but aspects of *one* personhood. I am going to be using it in the sense that Calvin sometimes uses it, where he makes explicit connection between Christ's Sonship and our becoming sons, between Christ's being called "the beloved" and our being included in this. I wonder whether this topic is often lost, because in all of our talk of "union with Christ" we forget to talk about being united to Christ's own union. But this too, Calvin says, is "for us."

If we are to take the character of our union with Christ seriously, not just as an ethereal fact, but as having an actual historical shape, then we must take the character of Christ's union to the Father seriously. Why? Because Calvin says that Jesus was not united to the Father in his thirty-three years on earth in order that this grace might not come to us. Calvin believes that central to Christ's mission was this restoration of union through his living out perfect union with the Father, which was also the fulfillment of the law.

But here we must tread with care: Calvin speaks of Christ's oneness with the Father *only from the point of view of Christ's human experience of it*. Calvin's shorthand for this is Christ's "mediatorial" office—meaning what Christ accomplished on earth so he could share it with us. Calvin tackles this in his *Commentary on John* 17: "Again, it ought to be understood, that, in every instance in which Christ declares, in this chapter, that he is *one with the Father*, he does not speak simply of his Divine essence, but that he is called *one* as regards his mediatorial office, and in so far as he is our Head."[14] Calvin is not sloppy here: he is not reasoning from the Trinity that because the Father and he are one, and we are one with Christ, then we are one with the Father. Those of us writing on union with Christ could certainly avoid much trouble were we to be as careful as Calvin to delineate between the

---

[13]This wide application of the term has caused Tim Trumper in his extensive work on adoption in Calvin to wonder whether it is a term synonymous with union—an interesting observation that needs further development. Trumper summarizes, "This suggests that either Calvin preferred to regard adoption as co-terminous with union with Christ . . . or that he subsumed it under justification and regeneration respectively." See Tim Trumper, "An Historical Study of the Doctrine of Adoption in the Calvinistic Tradition" (PhD diss., University of Edinburgh, 2001).

[14]Calvin, *Commentary on John* 17:21. Calvin calls divine-divine as *unitas* ("unity"), while he speaks of divine-human as *unio* ("union") in his *Dedication* in his *Commentary on Jeremiah*.

perichoretic union (in the Trinity), the hypostatic union (of the two natures) and our mystical union![15] Calvin has a strict method for speaking of our union with God, and bringing in the perichoretic unity among the members of the Godhead is certainly not it. As a matter of fact, Calvin never uses the term *perichoresis*.[16] Not that it can't be applied to Calvin's trinitarian theology, and it can be very helpful at times, but strictly speaking Calvin does not use it. However, Calvin's careful delineation did not keep him, as it seems to do for some scholars, from making the obvious—but "dangerous"—positive affirmations as well! For example, "as Christ is one with the Father, so we are one with Him."[17] Calvin is not here being "messy" but rather stating that *in Christ we have God as well*. Sometimes our careful hedging can keep this in the background, rather than the gospel foreground.

Our adoptive sonship is dependent not on Christ's preexistent sonship but is a new relationship between God and humanity forged in the trenches of Jesus' human existence because, as human, that is where our salvation must be waged. For if Christ is going to offer us the hard-won benefits of his obedient life and death, then these benefits must be human, not divine—at least by Calvin's books. (If anything is to be learned from his debate with Osiander, then it certainly must be that.)[18] The benefits that Christ amassed for us over the course of his life were not by virtue of his superhuman divinity but by virtue of his obedient humanity, dependent—as we ever are. So does this mean that Calvin has separated Christ's divine and human nature so profoundly that he has violated the *indivise, inseperabiliter* of the Chalcedonian Creed? No. As Joseph Tylenda documented years ago, Calvin keeps these two natures fiercely apart, communicating not directly one with the other but, instead, each communicating their properties to the divine-human *person* of Christ.[19] What must be noted is that Calvin separates *in*

---

[15]My only complaint is that Calvin can be so eager to clearly delineate between these that he doesn't reflect on how they also reflect one another.

[16]See John McClean's helpful article, "Perichoresis, Theosis and Union with Christ in the Thought of John Calvin," *Reformed Theological Review* 68, no. 2 (2009): 130-41.

[17]John Calvin, *Sermon on 1 Samuel 2:27-30 (CO* 29:353).

[18]For more on the differences of opinion between Calvin and Osiander on the role of Christ's humanity, see Julie Canlis, "Calvin, Osiander, and Participation in God," *International Journal of Systematic Theology* 6 (2004): 169-84.

[19]Joseph Tylenda, "Calvin's Understanding of the Communication of Properties," *Westminster Theological Journal* 38 (1975): 54-65.

order to join in an even more profound way. This is a distinctive aspect of Reformed spirituality, that the separateness of natures is in order—not to denigrate human nature, but—to honor it. Calvin explains how our adoptive sonship is dependent on Christ's own human sonship in his *Commentary on John*: "Thus will the chain of thought be preserved, that, in order to prevent the *unity* of the Son with the Father from being fruitless and unavailing, the power of that *unity* must be diffused through the whole body of believers. Hence, too, we infer that we are *one* with the Son of God not because he conveys his substance to us, but because, by the power of his Spirit, he imparts to us his life and all the blessings which he has received from the Father."[20] Our union with the Son is made real not by an impersonal sharing in Christ's human substance but by the personalizing and creative work of the Holy Spirit. The Spirit's unique work is to take that which was worked out in the life of the Son and to "actualize" it in us, by uniting us with Christ. Moreover, the Son's unity with the Father is not for us privately, but is to be spread through the whole body of believers. Adoption is thus both a mystical blessing and one that obligates us to being part of a family. This is part of our renewed identity.

So can this adoptive sonship be called *theosis*, as many are claiming? Yes and no, depending on how you define *theosis*. If *theosis* is based on the interpenetration of the divine and human natures in Christ such that our human natures are penetrated with the divine nature of Christ, then no—not that kind of *theosis*.[21] Calvin certainly has no room for that. If it is dependent on our humanity becoming not-human, "divinized" in its participation in the new creation, then no—not that kind of *theosis* either.[22] It is at times like this that those of a Reformed ilk often breathe a collective internal sigh of relief (and perhaps self-congratulation?), grateful that they have once again escaped the pitfalls of the mingling Lutherans, divinizing

---

[20]Calvin, *Commentary on John* 17:21.

[21]See Bruce McCormack, "Union with Christ in Calvin's Theology: Grounds for a Divinisation Theory?," in *Tributes to John Calvin*, ed. David W. Hall (Phillipsburg, NJ: P & R, 2010). My gentle response to McCormack, though, is that the two natures must not be used to set up a dividing line in the person of Christ, which then is transferred to all theology! The two natures are, in some ways, then functioning as many Orthodox use the energies/essence distinction, which is an improper way to use the difference in the two natures. Rather, we must remember that the properties of both are transferred to the *person* of Christ.

[22]It can be argued that this is not the Orthodox view of *theosis* either, although the caricature persists.

ecumenists or—worse—Barthians. But unfortunately, I am going to press those of the Reformed camp much further than this. We all know by now what Calvin did not say. But what are the implications of what he did say?

1. The Holy Spirit is the only way for us to experience the heart of this love of the Father and Son.

2. The Holy Spirit does not lead us to this reality. The Holy Spirit manifests this new reality of sonship within us.

3. The Holy Spirit enables us to live out this new identity in meaningful action that bears the marks of sonship.

THE HOLY SPIRIT IS THE ONLY WAY FOR US TO EXPERIENCE THE FATHER-SON LOVE

The Spirit's work is to make God's Fatherhood concrete.[23] There is nothing more concrete than the Sonship of Jesus, so it is this to which the Spirit unites us. "We are the sons of God, because we have received the same Spirit as his only Son."[24] Jesus is our way that we know God as loving Father, but it is only *in the Spirit* that we are led into Jesus' experience of this. Calvin explains:

> But Paul means, that the Spirit of God gives us such a testimony, that when he is our guide and teacher, our spirit is made assured of the adoption of God: for our mind of its own self, without the preceding testimony of the Spirit, could not convey to us this assurance. There is also here an explanation of the former verse; for when the Spirit testifies to us, that we are the children of God, he at the same time pours into our hearts such confidence, that we venture to call God our Father. And doubtless, since the confidence of the heart alone opens our mouth, except the Spirit testifies to our heart respecting the paternal love of God, our tongues would be dumb, so that they could utter no prayers. For we must ever hold fast this principle,—that we do not rightly pray to God, unless we are surely persuaded in our hearts, that he is our Father.[25]

Calvin knows that God's love would be a shadowy promise without "the Spirit [who] is the earnest and pledge of our adoption, and gives to us a

---

[23]I see a parallel here to Calvin's doctrine of Scripture, which has as its sole testimony the "*internal* testimony of the Holy Spirit" (1.1.3).

[24]Calvin, *Commentary on Galatians* 4:6.

[25]Calvin, *Commentary on Romans* 8:16.

well-founded belief that God regards us with a father's love."[26] This love is not a message for us to believe, but a divine reality to which we are united. This is so difficult for us to believe that Calvin asserts that we cannot even believe it for ourselves: the Spirit speaks our acceptance of this love for us, because on our own it is too great for us to dare to believe. He himself gives us the word, *Abba*.

There is a tactical reason as to why it is only through the Spirit that we taste this adoption, this grounding reality of love. It is because the Son—in whom we possess our adoption—*is ascended to the Father*. Some may see in this a crude literalism. History has shown that others have read into it a devaluation of embodiment. Calvin used the reality of the ascension to preserve our humanity, and Christ's. Because Christ is absent, we have a real possibility of participating in him through the ministry of the Spirit. If our adoption is merely a benign feeling of God's love, then this is not a problem. But for Calvin, our adoption is a true participation in Christ and his Sonship, a Sonship that is part of his ongoing ministry to us at his Father's right hand. As such, we can't break off a little piece of Christ for ourselves; we must, instead, "go up" to him. Calvin's language of going "up" always signals that he takes seriously the Holy Spirit's activity to join us to Christ and all his benefits. It is his metaphor for participation in the *whole* Christ.

It is imperative to note that it is not just a divine son to whom we are united, but this is the Son *crucified and resurrected* for human sin and salvation. It is an atoning Sonship. Calvin reminds us that even though the ancients were adopted by the same covenant, they "could not audibly call on God as Father . . . since the veil kept them far from the sanctuary. But, now, when an entrance has been opened by the blood of Christ, we may glory . . . in full voice that we are the sons of God."[27] The relationship of adoption to justification is not a straightforward one because Calvin never sought to clarify it (as far as we know), but clearly the theme of "acceptance"[28] binds

---

[26]Calvin, *Commentary on Galatians* 4:6.

[27]Calvin, *Commentary on Romans* 8:15.

[28]For example, in the *Institutes* 3.11.4, Calvin writes, "For Paul certainly designates justification by the term *acceptance*, when he says to the Ephesians, 'Having predestinated us unto the adoption of children by Jesus Christ to himself, according to the good pleasure of his will, to the praise of the glory of his grace, wherein he has made us accepted in the Beloved' (Eph. 1:5, 6). His meaning is the very same as where he elsewhere says, 'being justified freely by his grace' (Rom. 3:24)."

the two together. Calvin's use of adoption powerfully expresses both the forensic and filial aspects of our reconciled relationship to God, ensuring that reconciliation has both a backward glance toward propitiation and forgiveness and a prospective glance toward a transformed identity in the Spirit. Calvin says that *both* must be remembered: "God has joined these two things together: that he will be propitious to his sons, and will also renew their hearts. Hence those who lay hold of only one member of the sentence, namely, the pardon, because God bears with them, and omit the other, are as false and sacrilegious as if they abolished half of God's covenant."[29] Reconciliation to God was offered in Christ's person, in the form of propitiation for sins *and* a new way of being with God, characterized by Christ's own Sonship. To speak of adoption as "imputed" to us, although correct in that it denotes that unmerited gift that comes from outside of ourselves, can blur this point. As Brian Gerrish remarks, "The familial imagery runs alongside the forensic imagery and finally supplants it. In the end, Christ saves us, reconciles us, justifies us as God's Son who takes us for his brothers and sisters."[30]

THE HOLY SPIRIT DOES NOT LEAD US TO THIS REALITY. THE HOLY SPIRIT MANIFESTS THIS NEW REALITY OF SONSHIP WITHIN US.

When the Spirit enables us to cry, "Abba," this is the remarkable sign that we are relating to God from the transformed reality of *adoptive sonship*. This certainty of sonship is not only cerebral but also wholly pneumatological. We are not living out of new knowledge, but out of a new relationship. For Calvin, adoption is such that we are brought, by the "Spirit of adoption,"[31] to live out of the risen Son in his relationship to the Father. It is in the triad of this new relationship that *our new identity is to be found*. It is an identity that automatically puts us "out" of ourselves, while confirming the deepest truth about ourselves. It is the antidote to Adam's self-referentiality.

This cry of Abba is active. It signals that we have been brought to the place where we—firmly ensconced in the Spirit—are actually living, acting and re-

---

[29]Calvin, *Commentary on Ezekiel* 11, lecture 30.

[30]Brian Gerrish, *Grace and Gratitude* (Minneapolis: Fortress, 1993), p. 61.

[31]"He is the 'Spirit of Adoption' because he is the witness to us of the free benevolence of God with which God the Father has embraced us in the beloved only-begotten Son to become a Father to us; and he encourages us to have trust in prayer. In fact, he supplies the very words so that we may fearlessly cry, 'Abba, Father!'" (3.1.3)

lating from our transformed identity. We have the Spirit of the Son. We act and, above all, love from this new center: "And certain it is, that no other thing is taught by Paul than that the true fountain of all love is when the faithful are convinced that they are loved by God, and that they are not slightly touched with this conviction, but have their souls thoroughly imbued with it."[32]

From this certainty of sonship (neither cerebral nor emotional, but pneumatological), we are transformed—"imbued"—to the extent that now we ourselves truly love.[33] Calvin's primary point here (against Augustine, Calvin admits) is that it is difficult for Christians to love until they themselves know that they are loved by God. This is less "emotive" for Calvin than it reads for us today, because for Calvin it is a primarily pneumatological reality.

It is the resurrection that makes this possible. In the resurrection and ascension, Jesus the Son is revealed in all his glory *still as human*. In the resurrection are all the possibilities of renewal made living and active. In union with the ascended Christ, we taste the powers of the age to come. The creative power of the Spirit was poured out on the church for precisely this purpose—to inaugurate the promises of Christ's transforming life for the church here and now, as fully human.

Here we come up against the liability and the promise of Calvin's "separation of natures" language. The liability is when we start to think that calling it "human" is a limitation rather than a promise. Calvin certainly used Christ's humanity as a ballast to keep renegade theologies of union weighted down. "When God regenerates his elect, he does not change either their flesh, or skin, or blood,"[34] Calvin wryly notes. Instead, sonship involves a truly new center of our willing and acting *within our humanity* that is nevertheless akin to that of the sonship of Christ.[35] "Ezekiel promises that a new spirit will be given to the elect, not merely that they may be able to walk in

---

[32]Calvin, *Commentary on Romans* 5:5.

[33]Calvin's account of sin and its impact on us was profoundly psychological for its time. We act out of what we believe most deeply about ourselves. So, although we have been adopted since the foundation of the world, our adoption is "here put for *actual possession*" (*Commentary on Galatians* 4:5, my emphasis) and this transforms us. "It is . . . received only when it possesses the whole soul, and finds a seat and resting place in the inmost affection of the heart" (3.6.4).

[34]Calvin, *Commentary on Ezekiel* 11:19-20, continued into lecture 30.

[35]This is certainly the point of all the modern deification language as it is applied to Calvin. "But we shall not be satisfied with having Christ, if we do not know that we possess God in him. We must therefore believe that there is such unity between the Father and Son as makes it impossible that they shall have anything separate from each other" (*Commentary on John* 17:10).

his precepts, but *that they may really walk in them*" (2.3.10).[36] This is the ministry of the Holy Spirit, that we are made into children, to will and act from this new nature. From this transformed identity flows all the imperatives of grace, which are not mere commands that we are suddenly empowered to do. No, they are signs of sonship, harbingers of our new identity. The biggest evidence of this transformation is our renewed relationship to the law: we no longer obey the law like slaves but as *sons*. Calvin writes, "Such children ought we to be, firmly trusting that our services will be approved by our most merciful Father, however small, rude, and imperfect they may be" (3.19.5). This is the Spirit's work—not just to unite us to Christ and all his benefits but also to so transform us that these properly become part of our new identities.[37]

The Holy Spirit Enables Us to Live Out This New Identity in Meaningful Action, Characterized by Sonship

First, I have been arguing that the Spirit's reconciling work is to unite us with Christ, who shares with us his own relationship as the Father's beloved Son. This love that the Spirit allows us to taste is not as the eternal Son to the Father, but as that love concretely worked out by the Son on earth, for us in our full humanity. For Calvin, this is a summary of our salvation. "Adoption . . . is not the cause merely of a partial salvation, but bestows salvation entire."[38] Second, the Spirit's work is not to passively "apply" this to us but to himself inaugurate our transformation, to bring us to the place where our new identities are taking on the pattern of Father and child. This takes place as we "possess Christ and all his benefits." Third, as we are brought to share in the Father-Son relation, we are given new agency as befits children. This new agency is never apart from Christ, or separated from him, and yet it is still our own. This is the territory of the Holy Spirit.

---

[36]Calvin further exegetes Ezek 11:19-20, saying that salvation consists of two things: "That he will be propitious to his sons, and will also renew their hearts. Hence, those who lay hold of only one member of the sentence, namely, the pardon . . . and omit the other, are as false and sacrilegious as if they abolished half of God's covenant."

[37]For this reason, Calvin says that Christians grow in righteousness and holiness because they resemble their Heavenly Father, who is righteous and holy, thus "proving themselves sons true to their nature" (3.18.1).

[38]John Calvin, "True Method of Obtaining Concord," in *Tracts and Treatises in Defense of the Reformed Faith*, ed. Henry Beveridge (Grand Rapids: Eerdmans, 1958), p. 275.

Calvin never shared our modern obsession with questions of agency,[39] as this prayer that closes his Lecture 29 on Hosea reveals.

> Grant, Almighty God, that as thou hast deigned to choose us before the foundations of the world were laid, and included us in thy free adoption when we were the children of wrath and doomed to utter ruin, and afterwards embraced us even from the womb, and hast at length favoured us with a clearer proof of thy love, in calling us by thy gospel into a union and communion with thy only-begotten Son,—O grant, that we may not be unmindful of so many and so singular benefits, but respond to thy holy calling, and labour to devote ourselves wholly to thee, and labour, not for one day, but for the whole time designed for us here, both to live and to die according to thy good pleasure, so that we may glorify thee to the end, through our Lord Jesus Christ. Amen.

Calvin obviously had no problem both in setting forth the gracious, unmerited nature of our salvation and the call to *labor* for God's glory. So why do we? The criticisms of Calvin just won't go away. Is it true that the theological starting point of Calvin's theology renders humans passive? Is it true that the finished work of Christ makes our work superfluous? If Christ's vicarious humanity is "applied" to the believer who accepts the promise of God, is there any meaningful role for the person to cultivate habits that result in holy living?

Perhaps it is the lingering Reformed fear of works righteousness that has pulled the plug from meaningful talk of action. Ironically, this has led to an unrestful "workaholism for Christ," a loss of Sabbath, a mania of unreflective activity that characterizes so many of our churches today. How is union with Christ guiding our activity in all this? As Eugene Peterson comments in his recent memoir, *The Pastor*, the unacknowledged belief of the American church is that "God takes the first step, the rest is left to us."[40] This lacks an understanding of how *our response to Christ* is also to be a participation in Christ, an expression of our adoption, a form of relation.[41]

Briefly, and in closing, I want to home in on two ethical trends (A, B) that I have observed in association with Calvin's theology of union with Christ (par-

---

[39]See the wide array of accusations of Calvin on precisely this front by the Radical Orthodox in J. Todd Billings's *Calvin, Participation, and the Gift* (Oxford: Oxford University Press, 2009), chap. 1.

[40]Eugene Peterson, *The Pastor: A Memoir* (San Francisco: HarperOne, 2011), p. 22.

[41]T. F. Torrance developed his twofold ministry of Christ in a way that is not at all incompatible with Calvin, though Torrance streamlines it in a way Calvin doesn't. I find it pastorally helpful.

ticularly christological renderings of sanctification), both of which are ethical (as well as anthropological) dead ends because neither of them take seriously enough the implications of the Spirit's role in participation in Christ (C).

UNION ETHICS AS DIVINE REPLACEMENT

In various strands of pietism (particularly associated with Wesleyan holiness and the Keswick movement), there is an emphasis on "Christ in you" as the empowerment for ethics. The key to this ethic is to acknowledge that you are nothing and to "empty yourself" in order that Christ might replace you and reign. The promise is that if you truly empty yourself, the Holy Spirit will be able to do something through you (but that "something" won't be you). In this version, there are only sinners and replaced sinners, no saints.[42]

For example, in his 2010 book, *Mystical Union*, John Crowder writes, "God didn't save you so you could do good. He saved you so you could be dead and He could work through you. He doesn't want you trying to please him. He is only pleased with Christ." And again, "God doesn't help you. God does things for you."[43] In this theology, we have the mystical union taken with deadly seriousness: God must eliminate you in order to replace you with himself. Agency is not redeemed; it is removed. Without a rigorous anthropology, the human being just disappears into Christ here. Calvin would not be happy with this—probably for the same reasons that Christ's body was not allowed to disappear in the bread and the wine.[44]

Creaturely integrity was a priority for Calvin, because of the ascended Christ. Christ's ongoing humanity is central as a benediction on our humanity—and therefore on our agency. Partaking of Christ does not trump our humanity, or overwhelm it in some Osiandrian fashion, but affirms it

---

[42]I often discover that the "spiritual disciplines movement" finds a home in these circles, as "emptying one's self" eventually yearns for some kind of pattern, some kind of form to give it discipline and shape.

[43]John Crowder, *Mystical Union* (Marylhurst, OR: Sons of Thunder Publishing, 2010), pp. 54, 88.

[44]Every discussion of agency is fraught with the identical misunderstandings of the Eucharist, because both are trying to understand how it is that the Spirit makes Christ present in the physical realm—whether it be bread or my human agency. The Lutheran (mis)understanding of the two natures reveals an inadequate understanding of the personalizing ministry of the Holy Spirit. So too do conceptions of human agency in which the believer is spoken of in ways such that they are replaced by Christ. This is very pious, but it does injustice to Christ (who is ascended) and to the Spirit, whose ministry is to enable us to participate in Christ in new and creative ways.

and undergirds it through Christ's own Spirit. This is our humanization, not our divine replacement. We are not spanners in the hands of God, getting his job done on earth. Because a human one is at the right hand of the Father, all our work becomes valuable. Because he is the crucified one, our renewed agency must always repent.

As Calvin's emphasis is always to bring us "up" to Christ (signaling our participation in his humanity), we are reminded that we are not to be replaced by Christ, but to live in *communion* with this human one. Communion implies the fellowship of the Spirit that makes room for us. His person *personalizes* us, rather than absorbs us. Communion *in the Spirit* implies relation *and* otherness, or as Calvin says, "join[ing] in one, things that are separated by distance of place, and far remote."[45] The Spirit mediates both Christ *and* our uniqueness to us. For it is when we are found in Christ that our uniqueness is guaranteed.

UNION ETHICS AS APPLIED CHRISTOLOGY

This is a more theologically savvy version of the above (and one that has a long standing in Reformed circles).[46] It claims the finished *work* of Christ as all we need—but the lag between our praxis and theology is due to the fact that we have not yet "claimed" the finished work of Christ. We are told to "become who we are"—which is a provocative way of putting things, but still puts the pressure on me (or my "faith") to make up for what is lacking between what Christ has done and who I am. This scenario is more difficult to unravel, but the consequences are equally impersonal (meaning that we don't have to deal with the person of Christ, but merely his benefits, his work applied passively to me). It seems to me that the goal is not Christ as much as it is an impersonal reality called the "victorious life in Christ" or even the "vicarious life of Christ" that I need to claim. The Spirit is involved, but only as a means for siphoning the benefits of Christ to us, like a divine aqueduct. (Be wary of these "channel" metaphors, which belie the fundamentally *personal* reality that we have entered.)

---

[45]Calvin, *Commentary on 1 Corinthians* 11:24.
[46]A helpful article summarizing this trend (locating its modern origin in biographies of Hudson Taylor) is Robert Pyne and Matthew Blackmon, "A Critique of the 'Exchanged Life,'" *Bibliotheca Sacra* 163 (2006): 131-57.

Fundamental to this ethical response is *gratitude*. Christ has done every-thing; our only job is to be grateful. Provocatively, may I suggest that "grat-itude" may not fully capture the fullness of Calvin's vision for the redeemed, even if it is one of his favorite themes? Gratitude captures the proper hu-mility and acknowledgment that *all we are is of God*, and is eloquently ex-pressive of our anthropological position as creatures with our Creator. Even so, Calvin expresses that our *gratitude is a gift of the Holy Spirit* (3.20.14, 19, 28, 41) and therefore flows naturally from our newly transformed identities. In one sense, this ethical version is correct: Christ's finished work is for me—not, however, by application, but rather by active *participation*. Ethics are not simply the application of salvation as a gift, or the dutiful response of grateful children. There is a deeper transformation required: sonship. Cal-vin's theology goes beyond the model of forgiveness/gratitude (of course we need to be grateful!) to that of new identities that flow from changed hearts.[47] Sonship provides a more organic connection between justification and the virtuous life than gratitude.

UNION ETHICS AS SONSHIP

In neither the pietist (A) nor (what I'm calling) the Reformed (B) ethical version is the Holy Spirit as a *person* who is involved with unique *persons* given sufficient attention. (Part of the problem is that the Spirit is given much attention, but it is of the wrong kind.) In the first scenario, we are Christ's instruments, his vehicles for getting his job on earth done. This is called "hilariously easy" and "instant and effortless" by Crowder.[48] But there is no communion, for the human being has been replaced. In the second scenario, the work of Christ is applied *to* us, by the Spirit. But let me high-light that it is the abstracted *work* of Christ, rather than the *person* of Christ with whom we are dealing. And if we don't have to deal with the person of Christ, then our own person is not being honored and recognized as well. Christ's personhood affirms our own unique personhood. Uniqueness must be honored, because it is the Spirit's territory.

---

[47]This is when the language of imputation can *blur* rather than clarify. Imputation is a helpful term when considering the unnecessary and unmerited gift of God, but I find that we need to use it with care when discussing the impact of this gift on us.

[48]Crowder, *Mystical Union*, p. 62.

The Spirit is the new eschatological reality in which we live. Calvin's term *sonship* is shorthand for this pneumatological sphere where Jesus calls us to a life in the Spirit like his own—full of radical trust, dependence, faith.[49] In this sphere of the Spirit, our redeemed agency is given a place. This is the self of the new creation, a pneumatological miracle in which we are living more and more deeply into our union with Christ. It is from this new reality that our ethics flows. "To sum up," writes Calvin,

> Those bound by the yoke of the law are like servants assigned certain tasks for each day by their masters. These servants think they have accomplished nothing, and dare not appear before their masters unless they have fulfilled the exact measure of their tasks. But sons, who are more generously and candidly treated by their fathers, do not hesitate to offer them incomplete and half-done and even defective works, trusting that their obedience and readiness of mind will be accepted by their fathers, even though they have not quite achieved what their fathers intended. Such children ought we to be, firmly trusting that our services will be approved by our most merciful Father, however small, rude, and imperfect these may be.[50]

The Spirit's work is not so much to do things *to* us or *with* us, but *in* us. Calvin's focus is not on "getting rid of ourselves," nor on the duties to which we are obligated as saved people, but on the freedom we have as children of God.[51] We can't simply paint ourselves with the finished work of Christ. Rather, in union with Christ by the Spirit, we—truly ourselves—are taught to live out of another such that we are honored and reconstituted. Jesus himself spoke of ethics as a way of knowing God.[52] Ethics is not so much a "grateful response" to knowing God, but a way of living and being such that

---

[49]When we fail to take Jesus' own Sonship seriously, we fail to understand that this is precisely how we live as well—by and in the Spirit. When this is misunderstood—when we attribute Christ's actions to his divinity—then we often attribute our own *in*activity to his divinity as well. In this sense, a nonpneumatological doctrine of providence has always stood as a threat to a Reformed doctrine of human agency. Similarly, the Kuyperian "Lordship of Christ over all spheres" can stand to undermine a creative engagement with the world if it is not clearly related to an awareness of the Spirit's activity *in* the world.

[50]Calvin, *Institutes* 3.19.5.

[51]Calvin does have a strong doctrine of denial of self, but it functions as a part of union with Christ and participating in him. See Julie Canlis, "Why Calvin's Theology Fostered a Spirituality of Participation Rather Than Imitation," in *Calvinism and the Making of the European Mind*, ed. Gijsbert van den Brink and Harro Höpfl (Leiden: Brill, 2014).

[52]"Anyone who chooses to do the will of God will find out whether my teaching comes from God or whether I speak on my own" (Jn 7:17).

our identity in Christ is confirmed. Outside of the Spirit's work of confirming our hearts, ethics is our most reliable epistemological access to our adoption.[53]

Adoptive ethics is *personal*, living out of our new identities that are held in union and communion *with the person* of Christ. We have, in a very real sense, become *persons* in him. We are never "given" anything that would then function apart from him. His way with us is that we cannot function without him—due, not to our sinfulness, but to the way we were created. Our *re*-creation too involves him to such a depth that our very being is now tied up with his very being. Everything we do is now supported and upheld by him, even as we actively use our talents, minds, creativity. All activity and virtue, therefore, become part of the process of *knowing God and being known by him*. All flows from sonship.

CONCLUSION

Although in my blogosphere research on union with Christ, I had taken a tumble down a rabbit hole (and had even found myself drinking the poison in the bottle labeled *DRINK ME*), I had a flash of insight. As much as I wanted to separate myself from the bloggers, from their acrimony and arrogance (aided by the anonymity that blogging affords), I realized that their problem was my own. In all their talk (and very unmystical wrangling) over union with Christ—and indeed, all throughout this very paper I've just delivered—they do not take seriously what Calvin thought union with Christ was for. From his *Commentary on John*, he writes, "Thus will the chain of thought be preserved, that, in order to prevent the *unity* of the Son with the Father from being fruitless and unavailing, the power of that *unity* must be diffused through the whole body of believers."[54] The Spirit's work is not to privatize our little franchises on "union with Christ." This, Calvin says, is fruitless. But if we are to take our union with Christ seriously, it must take the form of—not doctrinal correctness—but of unity. (If everyone has the same doctrine, being unified isn't really that hard.) Unity among one another is the fruit of our participating in Christ's union with the Father. And

---

[53]Romans 12 and the "renewing of our minds" is often assumed to be referring to our brains. But Paul gives quite explicit instructions as to how we renew our minds . . . and it is through love. It is as if ethics are a way of confirming (and shaping) our new identity.

[54]Calvin, *Commentary on John* 17:21.

so, like Alice, I found myself at the bottom of the rabbit hole even throughout much of the writing of this chapter. But next to the poison in the bottle that was labeled *DRINK ME* was also an antidote, with the command that now resonated with Scripture: *EAT ME*. There has always been an antidote to the problem of our shrinking theological selves, shrinking due to the manner in which we treat our (theological) neighbor, shrinking due to the manner in which we look to doctrine to provide the boundaries of our selves . . . or to define what we perceive to be the selves of others. *There is one loaf, and we who are many, partake of the one loaf.* This is a hard saying. Who among us can accept it?

12

SANCTIFICATION THROUGH PREACHING

How John Chrysostom Preached for Personal Transformation

Peter Moore

For many years my primary ministry in New South Wales was to shape congregations through preaching and through other word ministries in smaller groups. Now my main ministry in the New South Wales Presbyterian Church is to shape pastors leading congregations. My understanding of both preaching and mentoring is that one disciple is supported and equipped in fruitfulness through a personal encounter with another disciple. In my experience, it is the truth of God expressed in a preacher's or mentor's values—their commitments, passions and goals—that have the greatest potential impact on the one mentored.

This brings me to the topic of this essay: sanctification through preaching. John Chrysostom, or "Goldenmouth" (347–407), is reputedly one of the greatest orators in Christian history. Most of his recorded sermons (and there are over a thousand of them extant) are from his time in Antioch as a priest and assistant bishop. He went on from there to become bishop of Constantinople, and that is of course where he attracted the enmity of the emperor and empress, leading to his death.[1]

---

[1] My favorite treatment of Chrysostom's history is J. N. D. Kelly, *Golden Mouth: The Story of John Chrysostom; Ascetic, Preacher, Bishop* (Grand Rapids: Baker, 1995).

However, while these rulers disliked "Goldenmouth," his congregation adored him. He was a master of fourth-century Greek rhetoric, and he was able to provide his congregations with an intense intellectual, aesthetic and emotional experience. But for Chrysostom, these skills and experiences had but one goal: the transformation of people's lives.[2]

This essay is a study in Chrysostom's art in motivation and transformation. My central thesis follows: although at times Chrysostom has been pictured as a moralist—someone who focuses primarily on external behavior (and perhaps inspiring through carrots and sticks, rewards and punishments)— that is far from the truth. There is no doubt he is interested in people's behavior, and rewards and punishments are part of his preacher's toolkit. But our preacher is seeking something more than this, namely, a profound change in his listeners. He is satisfied with nothing less than a reorientation of life, a personal transformation that comes very much from within.

The way Chrysostom does that—and now I return to my opening illustration of a preaching or mentoring ministry—is through exposing a teacher's personhood to his congregation, and especially, exposing the heart and mindset of biblical characters like Paul, or Christ, or even God the Father, to his congregation. Chrysostom believed that it is when one person reveals herself (and particularly her "mindset"—or perhaps better, "chosen life trajectory") to another person, that second person will be changed by the experience.

Before unpacking Chrysostom's ideas, let me more clearly draw attention to how I imagine this perspective has relevance for preachers today. To do this, let me say a little more about my own ministry context. I do not think moralism is a major issue in the evangelical and Reformed church in Australia. Perhaps it is in isolated pockets, but not generally. We have a different model of word ministry. On the whole, Australian evangelicals believe not so much in transformation through engaging external behavior (moralism)

---

[2]On Chrysostom's program in preaching, and his value as a model, see, e.g., Montefalconius in his early seventeenth-century preface to the homilies on Matthew's Gospel: "If anyone in both letter and its meaning wants to be well skilled in moral teaching, let him engage with the Homilies of Chrysostom on Matthew. . . . In all the homilies, serious moral principles and most severe warnings always fill a part of the sermon. There he (Chrysostom) considers the life of the people under him and he provokes them so that they pursue virtue": Montefalconius, "Montefalconii Praefatio," in *Sanctis Patris Nostri Joannis Chrysostomi—Homilae in Matthaeum*, ed. Fridericus Field AA (Paris, 1612–1862), pp. 3-4.

but transformation through the power of ideas. Our method assumes that if you give another person a new idea, it will change everything. In contrast, Chrysostom sees that it is *truth as it practically orients a person's life choices* that is the most powerful agent of transformation.

Before undertaking the major part of this paper, let me quote Chrysostom himself, lest there be any doubt that he was intensely concerned with this goal of changing his listeners. In his ninth homily on Hebrews, Chrysostom first laments, then justifies the need for repetition in preaching ministry.

> I am afraid that this may properly be said to you also, that "when for the time you ought to be teachers," (Hebrews 5:12) you do not maintain even the rank of learners, but ever hearing the same things, and on the same subjects, you are in the same condition as if you heard no one. And if any one should question you, no one will be able to give a satisfactory answer, except a very few who may soon be counted. . . . For if our preaching were a matter of display and ambition, it would have been right to jump from one subject to another and change about continually, taking no thought for you, but only for your applauses. But since we have not devoted our zeal to this, but our labours are all for your profit, we shall not cease discoursing to you on the same subjects, till you succeed in learning them. . . . We shall not cease to say the same things, whether you be persuaded or not.[3]

Chrysostom has no interest in the erudite discourse of a dispassionate orator or scholar. Neither does he preach in order to entertain his listeners or himself. Rather, Chrysostom preaches for a change in, and the genuine benefit of, his hearers. Because this is the *only* thing that he wants, he will continue at it whether he gets it or not![4] The fundamental nature of that

---

[3]I propose to use the translations in Schaff's volumes, but with minor changes to remove archaic English, and so here: John Chrysostom, *Nicene and Post-Nicene Fathers*, series 1, vol. 14, *Homilies of St John Chrysostom on the Epistle to the Hebrews*, ed. Philip D. Schaff, trans. P. E. Pusey and Frederic Gardiner (repr., Peabody, MA: Hendrickson, 1994), pp. 408-9; Iohannes Chrysostomus, *In Epistulam Ad Hebraios*, ed. J. P. Migne, Patrologia Graeca (Paris, 1862), p. 75 (hereafter PG). In Calvin's own draft endorsement and defense of Chrysostom's preaching, he makes mention of Chrysostom's wish to "shake them out of their [his listener's] complacency (*desidiam illis suam excuteret*)." Ian Hazlett, "Calvin's Latin Preface to His Proposed French Edition of Chrysostom's Homilies: Translation and Commentary," in *Humanism and Reform*, ed. James Kirk (Oxford: Basil Blackwell, 1991), p. 149; CO 9:836.

[4]Raymond Laird comments, "His preaching was the vehicle whereby their lives could be adjusted and brought to perfection. . . . There is no doubt as to how Chrysostom viewed his vocation." Raymond Laird, *Mindset, Moral Choice and Sin in the Anthropology of John Chrysostom*, Early Christian Studies (Strathfield, Australia: St Pauls Publications, 2012), p. 18. Margaret Mitchell

change, and Chrysostom's strategies for achieving that aim, will require us to better understand how he relates his understanding of anthropology, sanctification and preaching.

In order to present how Chrysostom employs preaching for the purpose of sanctification, we will first begin by placing him in his historical context. This requires that we also learn something about classical rhetorical theory. Second, I will offer an analysis of recent scholarship on Chrysostom's preaching, focusing on his anthropology. At this point I will outline Chrysostom's method of preaching for sanctification. Finally, in the third, shorter section, I will offer some points that those in ministry might consider helpful in applying Chrysostom's perspective.

AN INTRODUCTION TO CHRYSOSTOM AND CLASSICAL RHETORICAL THEORY

We may introduce John Chrysostom's historical setting by noting that he was born in about A.D. 347 in Antioch. Antioch was a city of the Roman province of Syria, populated with 150,000 to 300,000 people, and its citizens were justified in seeing it as one of the great cities of its time.[5] Cosmopolitan in its ethnic, religious and economic diversity, its overall prosperity was directed to culture, education and entertainment.

As to John Chrysostom's early life, he was born into a relatively wealthy family, and like many young men of his day he studied rhetoric in one of the rhetorical schools of Antioch. This was probably under the direction of the official sophist for Antioch: Libanius. No doubt a comfortable career in law and administration was anticipated for him.[6] However, not long after his rhetorical training was complete, Chrysostom broke away from Libanius and the anticipated future associated with this Asian "Greek" heritage. Instead of embracing this prosperous future, he spent years in a monastic community and then in solitude. It was only when his health had deteriorated through the privations of this period that Chrys-

---

claims that "the goal of Chrysostom's epideictic rhetoric aimed at creating a new social order" (Laird cites Margaret M. Mitchell, *The Heavenly Trumpet: John Chrysostom and the Art of Pauline Interpretation* [Louisville, KY: Westminster John Knox, 2002], pp. 401-2).
[5]Kelly, *Golden Mouth*, pp. 1-3; Wendy Mayer and Pauline Allen, *John Chrysostom*, Early Church Fathers (New York: Routledge, 2000).
[6]Kelly, *Golden Mouth*, pp. 7, 14.

ostom returned to Antioch. Even then, he was reluctant to accept a preaching ministry in the church.[7]

Chrysostom's rise to prominence as an orator took place during a particularly turbulent period in his native Antioch. Only about one year after his ordination as a priest, the city was engulfed in crisis because of the unlawful destruction of statues of the emperor.[8] For the next few weeks, Chrysostom preached to a terrified city under the threatening likelihood of savage imperial retribution. However, the young preacher stood the test, the vengeance of the emperor was mitigated and in the midst of these turbulent times Chrysostom's reputation was made.[9]

In Chrysostom's preaching career as priest and assistant bishop he seems to have been widely loved. So popular was he during his eleven years of Antiochene ministry, for example, that his rise to the episcopacy and installation in 397 to the see of Constantinople could only take place through a certain subterfuge on the part of the emperor's agents. Chrysostom was lured out of Antioch and apparently only then informed that he was to be taken to the imperial capital for installation.[10] He preached in Constantinople as bishop for much of the next decade, delighting his congregation. Unfortunately his clear biblical exposition was not always tactful, and his blunt talk displeased the emperor (and more particularly the empress). Yet throughout these years Chrysostom enjoyed the support of most of his congregation. When the emperor orchestrated his exile and eventual death in 407, Chrysostom remained a popular hero. In time, the manner of his fall would be acknowledged by the emperor's own son as an injustice and sin.[11]

As to Chrysostom's standing among the ancient preachers, John Calvin considered him the "most eminent of them all" (*Chrysostomus ex omnibus potissimum*).[12] This was because of Chrysostom's commitment to present the plain meaning of Scripture to plain people.[13] Both Calvin and Martin Luther

---

[7]Ibid., pp. 34, 83.
[8]Ibid., pp. 72-82.
[9]Ibid., p. 82.
[10]Ibid., pp. 104-5.
[11]Ibid., p. 290.
[12]"Praefatio in Chrysostomi Homilias," in *CO* 9:834.
[13]Peter Moore, "Plain Talk with a Gilt Edge: An Exploration of the Relation Between 'Plain' Biblical Exposition and Persuasion in Chrysostom and Calvin," *Westminster Theological Journal* 73, no. 1 (2011): 157-72.

used Chrysostom extensively in their exegetical writings and cited him there more than any other ancient author.[14] John Wesley also was influenced by Chrysostom profoundly.[15] Yet to appreciate this respect and Chrysostom's influence, we must also understand him as a master of classical rhetorical method.

UNDERSTANDING CHRYSOSTOM'S METHOD

Over the past two centuries there have been different views held about the importance of classical rhetorical method for Chrysostom's expository preaching. These views fall generally into three major phases. In the first phase it was suggested that there was minimal evidence of Greek rhetorical forms in Chrysostom's preaching.[16] This consensus gave way to a second period of scholarship, from the 1920s to the 1980s, when Chrysostom was portrayed as a fierce critic of the sophists and rhetoric, but it was suggested that he consciously or unconsciously used the very rhetorical forms he despised, and even to tasteless excess.[17] In the current phase in Chrysostom studies, his employment and mastery of classical rhetoric has been more happily accepted.[18] Trained in classical rhetoric, Chrysostom freely used these techniques for gospel aims, never believing these methods compromised his message or created problems for the pastoral goals he had in mind.[19]

Classical rhetorical theory could be helpfully summarized under a number of headings. Given my interest in preaching that produces sanctified choices, I mention here the three levels of persuasion in ancient rhetoric.

---

[14]E.g., Peter Charles Moore, "Gold Without Dross: An Assessment of the Debt to John Chrysostom in John Calvin's Oratory" (PhD thesis, Macquarie University, Sydney, 2013), p. 47; Kenneth Hagen, *A Theology of Testament in the Young Luther* (Leiden: Brill, 1974), p. 15.

[15]S. T. Kimbrough, ed., *Orthodox and Wesleyan Spirituality* (Crestwood, NY: St Vladimir's Seminary Press, 2002), p. 168.

[16]Thomas E. Ameringer, *The Stylistic Influence of the Second Sophistic on the Panegyrical Sermons of St. John Chrysostom: A Study in Greek Rhetoric*, Patristic Studies of the Catholic University of America (Washington, DC: Catholic University of America Press, 1921), p. 10; Mitchell, *Heavenly Trumpet*, p. 10 n. 40.

[17]E.g., Ameringer, *Stylistic Influence*, p. 102; John Alexander Sawhill, *The Use of Athletic Metaphors in the Biblical Homilies of St. John Chrysostom* (Princeton, NJ: Princeton University Press, 1928), p. 110; Mary Albania Burns, *Saint John Chrysostom's Homilies on the Statues: A Study of Their Rhetorical Qualities and Form*, Patristic Studies 22 (Washington, DC: Catholic University of America Press, 1930), pp. 117, 119.

[18]E.g., Mitchell, *Heavenly Trumpet*, p. 27; Ottorino Pasquato, "Forme Della Tradizione Classica Nel De Inani Gloria Et De Educandis Liberis Di Giovanni Crisostomo," *Orientalia christiana periodica* 58 (1992): 253-64, 264.

[19]Moore, "Gold Without Dross," chap. 2.

- *docere* (to "teach")

- *delectare* (to "delight" or "please")

- *mouere* (to "move" or "affect")[20]

In classical theory, "teaching" was thought properly directed to the intellect, whereas "delighting" and "moving" were thought properly directed to the emotions.[21] Chrysostom's homilies are profoundly shaped by these three levels. As an exegetical preacher, Chrysostom constructed much of his speech as a biblical exposition, laying out the ideas he finds in Scripture as authoritative "principles." However, in the course of this he also worked skillfully to retain his listeners' attention by "delighting" them. Finally, he aimed to gain a "decision" for change through techniques that would "move" his hearers. Only when we understand how Chrysostom employs these three levels of persuasion can we fully appreciate his preaching strategy, which seeks the personal transformation of his listeners.

In the third phase of research on Chrysostom's rhetorical methods there have been a number of studies that particularly touch on our present topic.[22] These range from research into more foundational issues through to the more "superficial" aspects of Chrysostom's thought and technique. For our purposes here, I will restrict myself to a study of Chrysostom's theological anthropology. We need to grapple with his view of the structure and operations of our humanity, trying to discern what principles emerge that guide him in preaching for sanctification.

As already mentioned, many discussions of Chrysostom's preaching have portrayed him as a "moralist" who in his exhortations to godliness engages

---

[20]These are the labels employed by the Latin rhetoricians: Heinrich Lausberg, *Handbook of Literary Rhetoric: A Foundation for Literary Study*, trans. Matthew T. Bliss, Annemiek Jansen and David E. Orton, ed. David E. Orton and R. Dean Anderson (Leiden: Brill, 1998), §257 (hereafter *Lausberg*). The philosophers claimed to prefer *docere* in rhetoric, even rejecting *delectare* and *mouere*. However practitioner-teachers like Quintilian had no such difficulties: Matthew Leigh, "Quintilian on the Emotions (Institutio Oratoria 6 Preface and 1-2)," *Journal of Roman Studies* 94 (2004): 126-27. Aristotle, who yearned for a world where judgments ignored emotional appeal, nevertheless was well aware that he was not living in that world. His work *Rhetoric* identifies the engagement of emotions as critical in persuading juries: cited in Leigh, "Quintilian on the Emotions," nn. 43-45.

[21]*Lausberg* §257.

[22]The material in this section also owes something to my own paper on Chrysostom: Peter Moore, "Chrysostom's Concept of γνώμη: How '*Chosen* Life's Orientation' Undergirds Chrysostom's Strategy in Preaching," *Studia Patristica: Papers Presented at the Sixteenth International Conference on Patristic Studies Held in Oxford 2011* 67 (Leuven: Peeters, 2012), pp. 351-58.

humanity only at the level of instruction about good and evil deeds.[23] By implication, our preacher is pictured as less interested in engaging his hearers' humanity at a more profound level.[24]

Senior Australian scholar Ray Laird has decisively challenged this description of Chrysostom as "moralistic." The most important recent scholarship on Chrysostom's anthropology, and the most important work for this present essay, is Laird's 2008 study, "St John Chrysostom and the γνώμη: The Critical Faculty Accountable for Sin in His Anthropology."[25] Laird claims that for Chrysostom the γνώμη (gnōmē), which Laird translates as "mindset," is the heart and center of our humanity.[26] Laird defines γνώμη (and his English equivalent "mindset") as "the way in which the psyche is habitually inclined."[27]

At the end of chapter four, Laird explains something of the importance of γνώμη for Chrysostom: "Γνώμη, then, occupies a vital, authoritative role in the human psyche according to Chrysostom's usage of the term. It has authority over the body and its members. It has the power either to resist or to side with conscience. It has authority over desire, wish, and will, and determines free choice. The passions find in it their superior command. It is the locus of a person's attitudes. As the responsible cause of a person's actions, it determines their quality."[28] Previous depictions of Chrysostom's thought have identified προαίρεσις (proairesis) or some expression of "choice" as the critical element in this part of his theology, but Laird claims to refute this.[29]

---

[23]Thus, for example, "generally a moralist as a preacher": Robert B. Eno, "Some Patristic Views on the Relationship of Faith and Works in Justification," *Recherches augustiniennes* 19 (1984): 119. Contra Danassis, who addresses the significance for Chrysostom of the Logos acting on the human soul: Antonios Danassis, *Johannes Chrysostomos: pädagogisch-psychologische Ideen in seinem Werk* (Bonn: Bouvier Verlag Herbert Grundmann, 1971), p. 232. Klasvogt concludes that Chrysostom is exactly the opposite of a moralist: Peter Klasvogt, *Leben zur Verherrlichung Gottes: Botschaft des Johannes Chrysostomos; ein Beitrag zur Geschichte der pastoral*, ed. Ernst Dassmann and Hermann-Josef Vogt, Hereditas: Studien zur alten Kirchengeschichte (Bonn: Borengässer, 1992), p. 243.

[24]We might also picture a man like Chrysostom, steeped in the Greek world, as believing somehow in the power of ideas to change lives. The present essay attempts to challenge this.

[25]Raymond John Laird, "St John Chrysostom and the Γνώμη: The Critical Faculty Accountable for Sin in His Anthropology" (ThD thesis, Australian College of Theology, Sydney, 2008); now published as Raymond Laird, *Mindset*.

[26]Laird, *Mindset*, p. 28.

[27]Ibid.

[28]Ibid., p. 82.

[29]On the side of προαίρεσις, for example: Christopher A. Hall, "John Chrysostom," in *Reading Romans Through the Centuries: From the Early Church to Karl Barth*, ed. Jeffrey P. Greenman and Timothy Larsen (Grand Rapids: Brazos, 2005), pp. 47-48, 50; David M. Rylaarsdam, "Interpretations of Paul in the Early Church," in *Rereading Paul: Protestant and Catholic Perspec-*

"Choice" is not autonomous and absolutely free, argues Laird; for Chrysostom even "choice" is subject, at a more profound level, to the person's existing "mindset." Choices will be made in line with this existing chosen trajectory, albeit in a dynamic where future choices may have a strengthening or weakening effect on the "mindset" as it currently exists.[30]

Mindset is a relatively recent English word. The 1989 second edition of the twenty-volume *Oxford English Dictionary* identifies *mindset* as first used in 1934 and defines it as a "habit of mind formed by previous events or earlier environment which affect a person's attitude."[31] This definition attributes the origin of *mindset* to events and environment, but not explicitly to personal choice. Is that an adequate rendering of γνώμη in Chrysostom? In the thought world of Chrysostom, where Christian thinkers were doing battle with deterministic theologies of fate or fortune, this is an important question.[32]

In order to move the debate forward I shall offer my gloss to Laird's translation. I suggest that we will understand γνώμη more clearly if we interpret it as a "chosen life trajectory."[33] This gloss has two critical elements: the choice and the life trajectory.

Chrysostom was in no doubt, and those who read him should be in no doubt, that γνώμη is well capable of self-correction. Chrysostom's own ascetic experiences in his monastic period, as well as his ongoing ascetic commitments, demonstrate his belief in a human capacity for self-discipline, self-responsibility and the possibilities of self-orientation. All this, for

---

tives on Justification, ed. David E. Aune (Grand Rapids: Baker Academic, 2006), p. 160. Also note Boularand: "When often the beginning of faith and good deeds is attributed to human freedom" (*cum saepius initia fidei et bonorum operum libertati hominis attribuat*). Ephrem Boularand, "La nécessité de la grâce pour arriver a la foi d'après Saint Jean Chrysostome," *Gregorianum* 19 (1938): 515. Kenny places προαίρεσις at the head of a list of Chrysostom's terms, with γνώμη listed fourth: Anthony Kenny, "Grace and Freedom in St John Chrysostom (1958)," in *Reason and Religion: Essays in Philosophical Theology* (Oxford: Basil Blackwell, 1987), p. 109.

[30]Laird, *Mindset*, pp. 121-27.

[31]"Mindset," in *The Oxford English Dictionary*, ed. J. A. Simpson and E. S. C. Weiner (Oxford: Clarendon, 1989), 9:800.

[32]On Chrysostom's explicit rejection of pagan ideas of "nativity" (Γένεσις) and "fate" (Είμαρμένη) see, e.g., John Chrysostom, "Homily 1 on 1 Timothy," in *Nicene and Post-Nicene Fathers*, series 1, vol. 13, *Homilies on the Epistles of St Paul the Apostle to Timothy, Titus, and Philemon*, ed. Philip Schaff, trans. James Tweed (repr., Grand Rapids: Eerdmans, 1848), p. 411.

[33]Lampe translates γνώμη as having "many meanings," namely, "mind," "opinion," "view, doctrine," "will" and "decision or judgment." G. W. H. Lampe and Henry George Liddell, *A Patristic Greek Lexicon* (Oxford: Clarendon, 1961), pp. 317-18.

Chrysostom, is in synergistic cooperation with divine grace.[34] This focus on choice also resonates with recent research into Chrysostom's philosophy of education. For Chrysostom, students need to learn the habit of good choices, and developing this habit is a pastoral process.[35]

Our interpretation of γνώμη thus needs to make clear Chrysostom's commitment to a role for self-determination. His approach is partly a rejection of the pagan world's deterministic views about human potential and freedom. This determinism was partly shared by Chrysostom's teacher Libanius.[36] While I don't have time to unpack this dynamic, I think "chosen life trajectory" does more justice to the element of choice involved.

Coming now to the second critical element to my gloss, "chosen life trajectory" also makes clear the foundational quality of this choice. It sets a direction and agenda for everything else. It is not just a mindset, but a "trajectory." It is a "direction" set to life itself. In what Laird considers a hendiadys, Chrysostom even refers to ἡ γνώμη as ὁ τῆς ψυχῆς τρόπος—"the way of the soul."[37] It is in fact a life vector!

Only when one appreciates that a critical part of our humanity—γνώμη— represents a chosen life's trajectory, can one make sense of Chrysostom's theory of personal transformation. It is this faculty of γνώμη that the preacher must engage and change, and all other godly choices will come from this. Indeed, Chrysostom believes that you engage the γνώμη of one

---

[34]On Chrysostom's vision of the relation between faith and προαίρεσις as reflecting "a fundamental synergism" and "a contribution human beings make to salvation itself." See Hall, "John Chrysostom," p. 50.

[35]Danassis: "As educational resources, we can in Chrysostom distinguish the following: 1. Habituation. Chrysostom considered the force of habit to be very effective": Danassis, *Johannes Chrysostomos*, 230-31. Klasvogt observes "that in the present the much-discussed notion of 'gradation in the pastoral care' is not so new!" Klasvogt, *Leben zur Verherrlichung Gottes*, p. 124.

[36]On the relationship of John with Libanius: Jorit Wintjes, *Das Leben des Libanius*, ed. Wolfgang Altgeld et al. Historische Studien Der Universität Würzburg 2 (Rahden: Verlag Marie Leidorf, 2005), pp. 177-90. On the tendency of the Fathers to react against the "deep-seated fatalism prevalent in many aspects of Hellenistic religion," see John Anthony McGuckin, "Will," in *The Westminster Handbook to Patristic Theology* (Louisville, KY: Westminster John Knox, 2004), pp. 363-64. Note, though, Nussbaum's account of potential human freedom in three ancient "therapeutic" philosophical schools of "Hellenism." "These philosophers claim that the pursuit of logical validity, intellectual coherence, and truth delivers freedom from the tyranny of custom and convention, creating a community of beings who can take charge of their own life story and their own thought." Martha C. Nussbaum, *The Therapy of Desire: Theory and Practice in Hellenistic Ethics*, Martin Classical Lectures (Princeton, NJ: Princeton University Press, 1994), p. 5.

[37]Laird, *Mindset*, p. 28; PG 57.34.46.

person, and transform that γνώμη, by exposing it to another person's firmly held and clearly articulated γνώμη. If you like, what really matters to one person, the trajectory of one person, as it is made explicit, has a power of influence and transformation over what matters to another, their trajectory. The things we strive to pursue in life are infectious.[38]

Recognizing the power of one person's clearly articulated γνώμη for the transformation of another person's γνώμη will, in preaching for sanctification, profoundly affect our exegesis. It is not just the preacher's clearly articulated γνώμη that may operate on listeners, but even more, the exposition of the γνώμη of each biblical writer. Laird notes the importance for Chrysostom not only of wrestling with the γνώμη ("mindset") of a biblical writer but also, in order to exegete that, of searching for their διάνοια ("intention") and σκοπός ("aim"). Thus Chrysostom states in his commentary on Galatians 1,

> This then let us do; for it is not the right course to weigh the mere words, nor examine the language by itself, as many errors will be the consequence, but to attend to the intention of the writer [τῇ διανοίᾳ . . . τοῦ γράφοντος]. And unless we pursue this method in our own discourses, and examine into the mindset [or chosen life trajectory] of the speaker [τὴν γνώμην . . . τοῦ λέγοντος], we shall make many enemies, and everything will be thrown into disorder.[39]

And a little later,

> Unless we attend to this rule, we shall not be able to discriminate in these matters . . . that is, if we go about to scrutinize the bare facts, without taking into account the intention [or chosen life trajectory] of the agents [τὴν τῶν ποιούντων γνώμην]. Let us then inquire into the intention of Paul [τοῦ

---

[38] A critical transformative moment for γνώμη is conversion: Laird, *Mindset*, pp. 120-23. Arguably we could explain this as the gospel exposing a faulty γνώμη to the "life's trajectory" of God himself. To put it another way, the sacrificial love of God in the gospel overwhelms the sinner at his conversion and reorients his γνώμη. Similarly, the power of the "blood of Christ" in Chrysostom's thought comes from its demonstration of Christ's γνώμη reapplied to communicants time after time. In his discussion of this, Laird translates the phrase Τὸ τίμιον αἷμα τοῦ Χριστοῦ as "the precious blood of Christ" (ibid., p. 128). Perhaps we could render it better "the *costly* blood of Christ." The transformative power of the Lord's Supper liturgy is that it is repeated evidence of the sacrificial love of Christ. It gains its power through the display of Christ's γνώμη.

[39] Chrysostom, *Commentary on Chapter 1 of Galatians*, in *Homilies on the Epistle of St Paul the Apostle to the Galatians and Ephesians*, p. 11; PG 61.629.4. I appropriate here points from Laird's treatment of this topic: Laird, *Mindset*, pp. 119-21.

Παύλου τὴν διάνοιαν] in thus writing, let us consider his scope [αὐτοῦ τὸν σκοπόν], and general deportment towards the Apostles, that we may arrive at his present meaning [ἐκ ποίας ἐλέγετο γνώμης].[40]

Sound exegesis of Paul involves considering intention, goals and even the γνώμη of the apostle. And it seems to me that this is a general theme in Chrysostom's exegesis. He is always asking: Why did the apostle say this? Why did the Lord Jesus say this? Why did God say this? What were they trying to achieve? He consistently interprets any sentence and any paragraph in the light of the overall goals of the words, and of their author. This simply represents grammatico-historical exegesis—trying to read the text in the light of the original author's goals—and it is wonderfully done.[41] And we need to understand that it is done, not just to understand the biblical author in each case, but to present their γνώμη to the congregation. As we have already seen, Chrysostom believes it is this exposition of the biblical writer's γνώμη that will produce the transformation of each listener's γνώμη.

Add to this a second point. For Chrysostom, teaching is all about shaping the students according to the teacher's own γνώμη, passing on that γνώμη. It is about passing on your values, because that is your trajectory, which is what you give the greatest importance. In Homily 4 on 1 Thessalonians, Chrysostom explains that there is nothing else that concerns a teacher (οὐδὲν ἂν ἅψαιτο λοιπόν) than that his disciples are proceeding according to the teacher's own chosen life trajectory (κατὰ γνώμην αὐτῷ προχωρῇ).[42]

Third, Chrysostom believes that the teacher's γνώμη, their chosen life trajectory, is grasped by the students not just through passing on precepts but through the shape of the teacher's own life. In his Galatians commentary Chrysostom exegetes Paul's talk of apostolic wounds as evidence of the apostolic γνώμη: "If anyone desires . . . to thoroughly learn my sentiments [τὴν

---

[40]Chrysostom, *Commentary on Chapter 1 of Galatians*, in *Homilies on the Epistle of St Paul the Apostle to the Galatians and Ephesians*, p. 11; PG 61.629.20-25.

[41]This involves Chrysostom's taking his congregation on the same emotional journey as Paul's first listeners: a journey of alternating "harsh and gentle rhetoric." Rylaarsdam, "Interpretations of Paul in the Early Church," pp. 157-58.

[42]Chrysostom, *Homily 4 from 1 Thessalonians*, in *Homilies on the Epistles of St Paul the Apostle to the Philippians, Colossians and Thessalonians*, p. 340; PG 62.418.31. I appreciate Chrysostom's use of the spatial term προχωρέω ("to go forward, proceed, advance"), which again affirms the propriety of my favored spatial term *trajectory*.

γνώμην μου καταμαθεῖν]"—or as I would interpret it, chosen life trajectory—"let him consider my wounds [βλεπέτω τὰ τραύματα], which afford a stronger proof than these words and letters."[43] A clearly articulated and firmly held γνώμη can be so compelling that it can win over opponents and other observers who come to adopt the same γνώμη.

I suggest that all this explains Chrysostom's interest in the "intention" of the apostolic authors, the supremely loving intentions of the sacrifice of Christ, and generally his use of life portraits in preaching.[44] He believes that the γνῶμαι embodied in Christ's sacrifice, Scripture and the lives of biblical characters and saints, portrayed to his congregation, have a transformative power on their γνῶμαι and will lead not to surface change but reorientation at a profound level.

If this interpretation is correct, Chrysostom is no moralist preacher but a preacher seeking the thorough transformation of his listeners. His whole preaching strategy is calculated to achieve this. Laird identifies what he sees are Chrysostom's three key ways for this transformation to be stimulated: "The precious blood of Christ, the divine Scriptures, and almsgiving."[45] First, the "initial application of the sacrifice of Christ to the soul was to be followed by regular application through the Eucharist. This provides the major shaping factor of the γνώμη."[46] Second, "the Scriptures" have the power to transform our "deformity . . . into extraordinary beauty."[47] Third, "almsgiving is presented as one of the roads toward repentance. Here is where words become deeds, where the state of the γνώμη is observed in a very practical and obvious way."[48]

Although Laird only identifies preaching with the second of this "triumvirate" (i.e., Scripture),[49] I believe preaching implicitly relates to all three modes. It is in preaching Christ's sacrifice, coupled with participation in the

---

[43]Chrysostom, *Homilies on the Epistle of St Paul the Apostle to the Galatians and Ephesians*, p. 47; PG 61.680.30-35.

[44]Pak-Wah Lai, "John Chrysostom and the Hermeneutics of Exemplar Portraits" (PhD diss., University of Durham, 2010).

[45]Laird, *Mindset*, p. 128.

[46]Ibid., pp. 128-29.

[47]Ibid., p. 129.

[48]Ibid., p. 131. In somewhat similar vein, Klasvogt calls Chrysostom's love of almsgiving "the test case for the compassion of the *koinonia* community" (*der Testfall der Koinonia die Sorge der Gemeinde*). Klasvogt, *Leben zur Verherrlichung Gottes*, p. 244.

[49]Laird, *Mindset*, p. 129.

Eucharist (and Chrysostom also connects the two by frequently preaching on the Eucharist), that the γνώμη of Christ is understood, experienced and appropriated. It is in preaching that the γνώμαι of the scriptural authors are heard, understood and appropriated. And it is in almsgiving (which seems to be Chrysostom's favorite "preaching application" in his fourth-century context of conspicuous poverty) that preached γνώμαι are most readily acted on as reorienting personal choice. All this leads not to surface change but to transformation to godliness.[50]

Add to this that Chrysostom often speaks of his *own* purposes or goals as a teacher. He believes that as he expounds his own mindset or chosen life trajectory it too will have power to transform his hearers. Near the beginning of this essay I mentioned how costly that chosen life trajectory was for Chrysostom. He preached in Antioch and Constantinople at times of great danger of imperial rage. He survived this danger in Antioch, but later in the Eastern Roman capital his fearless preaching cost him his life. Thus Chrysostom proved to his congregation that the grand biblical truths he expounded were much more than "rhetoric," expert in the "tricks" of rhetoric though he was. For Chrysostom these principles were deeply embedded in life. On Chrysostom's own preaching theory, this enhanced his influence. If biblical truth was so shaping this giant man's life trajectory, this should in turn have transformative effect on the life trajectories of those who watched.

Let me summarize: recent scholarship has argued the possibility that Chrysostom is not a moralist, but rather a thoughtful pastor-theologian who engages his congregation's humanity at a profound level. His goal is to reshape their γνώμη, "mindset" or "chosen life trajectory," as he preaches for sanctification. His method is rooted in theological and philosophical principles, as well as being grounded in his own experience, and his own "chosen life trajectory"!

---

[50]"More significant is that the critical function for his preaching is the proclamation of the merciful, benevolent and majestic God": Klasvogt, *Leben zur Verherrlichung Gottes*, p. 98. "Lived faith is not primarily the fulfillment of norms, but personal response to the God who loves man. The people's response can therefore be nothing other than personal: love the one who loves. The renewed 'yes' to God and his offer of salvation—always in the 'now'—is somehow already the sum of faith. It gives Chrysostom certainty, and the courage to constantly challenge the listener to his next possible step and to assure him: 'You can do it!' Just because God allows it" (ibid., p. 243; see also pp. 53-54).

APPLICATIONS

This essay is designed as an introduction to Chrysostom's preaching theory and does not attempt to offer a comprehensive case for the accuracy of this analysis of "Goldenmouth." For that I simply point you to other studies.[51] However, I do want to conclude with some "applications" for contemporary practice.

Can we learn from Chrysostom? His synergistic soteriology. Without question, Chrysostom's soteriology is synergistic. He sees a role for human choice in cooperation with God, for the production of justifying faith. For a monergist such as myself, does this render Chrysostom's preaching method so liable to suspicion that it should not even be appropriated critically? My conclusion is that, read critically, there is great value in Chrysostom's insights into persuasion and into preaching for sanctification.

We can learn here something from Calvin's generosity toward Goldenmouth. In about 1538–1540 Calvin was working on a plan to publish Chrysostom for the benefit of the French Calvinist pastors. At the very least he commenced work on a preface to his proposed volume, explaining his decision to promote Chrysostom as an example worth following.[52]

In his introduction to Chrysostom, Calvin makes specific mention of the problems with Chrysostom's doctrine in "being unrestrained in asserting human free will" (*in praedicando hominis libero arbitrio . . . immodicus*). But then Calvin goes on rather generously to defend him as having a sound theology, but that he "modified his own opinion in such a way as to avoid being at too great a variance with public opinion."[53] A little later he speaks of Chrysostom's pastoral concern to repudiate "some individuals who used to prattle about 'fate'" (*erant et nonnulli qui de fato garriebant*).[54] Finally, Calvin remarks, "Such a formulation is not particularly consistent with the Holy Spirit's manner of speaking. But this is just what I indicated initially: that [this] trusty minister of Christ did deviate somewhat from the right way, although he had the best of intentions. Yet just as lapses of this kind in such a great man are easily excused, so it is

---

[51]Laird, *Mindset*; Moore, "Gold Without Dross."
[52]On the timing of this project, see Hazlett, "Calvin's Latin Preface"; Moore, "Gold Without Dross."
[53]Hazlett, "Calvin's Latin Preface," p. 148.
[54]Ibid., pp. 146, 149; CO 9:835, 836.

important that a devout reader is reminded not to be diverted from the plain truth by [Chrysostom's] authority."[55] Whether or not you agree with Calvin that Chrysostom's doctrinal "fudging" is easily excused, and that he can be read with profit (albeit with discernment), there is a second reason why we can learn from him.

Transformation/sanctification is an interpersonal experience. Chrysostom's preaching theory resonates with my own experience of transformation being an interpersonal experience. It is not so much "ideas" that transform as truth. In this way "truth" could be understood as ideas embodied in real persons, given expression by persons and applied in their lives. Here we move from the philosophical to the relational, from the abstract to the concrete. In my own life, it has been the teachers and pastors who have revealed their personhood to me, and particularly their earnest life direction (their γνώμη), who have provoked me to lasting change. Of course that is not a scholarly reflection: it is entirely anecdotal, but it nevertheless is my authentic experience.

Passion is infectious! A leader who is going somewhere, offering a coherent and consistent personal life direction, and who puts that γνώμη on display in an authentic life accessible to his or her followers, has great power to influence others to follow. This is true of us because it is also true of God. I think that is what the gospel itself is and what it produces! God came into the world to give effect to and embody his goals for the world: his chosen life trajectory. The church today is the fruit of the power of that γνώμη of God.

My experience of mentoring and leading congregational change. Given the power of such passion, what might occur when a leadership team embodies different γνώμαι? In my work with leaders in Australia, I use the language of "core values." Core values are "the things that really matter to me"; they are the direction-setting commitments I hold. Any satisfactory team will thrive only when those values are held in common, because they set the direction for the team. Conflict and confusion come about when core values are not shared; one team, one "chosen team trajectory," one team γνώμη, one set of values. Chrysostom's example as a

---

[55]Hazlett, "Calvin's Latin Preface," pp. 149-50.

congregational leader in Antioch and Constantinople sixteen hundred years ago suggests that he made it his goal to impart those values to his congregation: he put on show his own γνώμη, which in turn resonated with the γνώμη of God. In our days, with more relational leadership structures, we can still unite a team through such preaching, but we also may employ other means.[56]

Preaching γνώμη. If we accept Chrysostom's model, or learn anything from it, we will be constantly engaging, in our preaching, with the γνώμη of a Bible text, of a biblical character and of God. Not only will this drive our exposition of the Bible, but we also need to personally have a chosen life trajectory driven by the gospel, and to reveal that to others. The gospel as embodied in our lives will have transformative power for others. We know that it is "the power of God for salvation to everyone who believes" (Rom 1:16), but will we accept that it is conveyed not just through words or ideas but also in lives as a lived principle, a driving commitment, a chosen life trajectory? Chrysostom did!

If all this is so, then openness and authenticity are two key skills of a Bible teacher and church leader, not just scholarly rigor and ideological conformity. Rigor and conformity are wonderful, but they must be embodied in an accessible and authentic life.

CONCLUSION

This essay has offered a study of the method that John Chrysostom uses for the sanctification of his listeners through preaching. Enjoying some of the fruits of recent research on Chrysostom's anthropology, I have challenged the common view that Chrysostom operates as a moralistic preacher, primarily engaging behavior. Chrysostom's modus operandi is to facilitate a personal encounter between the teacher (especially the biblical authors) on the one hand and congregation on the other. As the congregation encounters God and his servants in preaching, and particularly their "goals," their "chosen life trajectory" will often infect others. The congregation will be changed; this is a normal means by which God accomplishes his sanctifying work in congregations.

---

[56]For example: small congregational teaching groups, leadership retreats and other ministry team meetings where a common set of values or team γνώμη can be engaged.

Sixteen hundred years after Chrysostom, what can we learn from this? In the Western tradition we place great importance on ideas, and even in theological education (where we ought to know better), we seem to think that ideas in themselves will transform our students. Using the categories of classical rhetoric, we may say that we believe in the first level of persuasion (teaching).[57] I want to suggest that we might consider the method of John Chrysostom and believe in the third level (moving) as well. Personal transformation, in the Chrysostomic modus operandi, takes place not through the power of abstract truths but by an intensely affective encounter with truth embodied in persons. In particular, that truth involves our "chosen life trajectory." It is not mere ideas that we need to convey to our hearers. It is *values* that will transform them: our revelation of the things that we and God himself strives for—the things that really matter to us.

---

[57]Perhaps we also believe in the second level (pleasing), and another essay could explore that.

SUBJECT AND NAME INDEX

SCRIPTURE INDEX

Finding the Textbook You Need

The IVP Academic Textbook Selector
is an online tool for instantly finding the IVP books
suitable for over 250 courses across 24 disciplines.

ivpacademic.com